Microsoft®
Word
Version 2002 Microsoft® Office XP Application

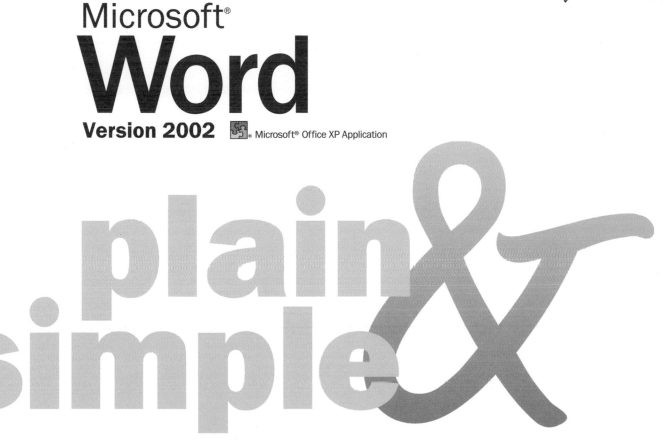

plain &
simple

Your fast-answers, no-jargon
guide to Access 2002!

Jerry Joyce and Marianne Moon

PUBLISHED BY
Microsoft Press
A Division of Microsoft Corporation
One Microsoft Way
Redmond, Washington 98052-6399

Library of Congress Cataloging-in-Publication Data
Joyce, Jerry, 1950-
  Microsoft Word Version 2002 Plain & Simple / Jerry Joyce, Marianne Moon.
      p. cm.
    Includes index.
    ISBN 0-7356-1450-4
    1. Microsoft Word.   2. Word Processing.   I. Moon, Marianne.   II. Title.

  Z52.5.M52 J73   2001
  652.5'5369--dc21   2001044401

Printed and bound in the United States of America.

1 2 3 4 5 6 7 8 9   QWT   6 5 4 3 2

Distributed in Canada by Penguin Books Canada Limited.

A CIP catalogue record for this book is available from the British Library.

Microsoft Press books are available through booksellers and distributors worldwide. For further information about international editions, contact your local Microsoft Corporation office or contact Microsoft Press International directly at fax (425) 936-7329. Visit our Web site at www.microsoft.com/mspress. Send comments to *mspinput@microsoft.com*.

Acquisitions Editor: Kong Cheung
Project Editor: Kristen Weatherby
Manuscript Editor: Marianne Moon
Technical Editor: Jerry Joyce
Body Part No. X08-24305

Contents

4 Writing a Letter — 45

5 Working with E-Mail and Faxes — 63

6) Creating a Long Document — 73

7) Creating a Technical Document — 95

11 Working with Others   157

12 Alternative Ways to Add Content — 181

13 Reviewing Your Document — 203

Acknowledgments

This book is the result of the combined efforts of a team of people whose work we trust and admire and whose friendship we value highly. Kristin Ziesemer, our talented typographer, did the work of two people and did it superbly. She not only refined and produced the interior graphics but also laid out the complex design, wrestling heroically with problems ranging from limited space to logical numerical arrangement of numbered steps. We think she does beautiful work. Our dear friend Alice Copp Smith has helped us improve every book we've written. Alice does so much more than proofread and copyedit: her gentle and witty chiding on countless yellow sticky notes makes us groan but always teaches us to write better. And we are fortunate indeed to be able to work with indexer *par excellence* Jan Wright, whose index reveals in microcosm the soul of the book. We thank this dedicated and hardworking trio for their exceptional work and their unwavering good humor in the face of grueling deadlines.

At Microsoft Press we thank Kong Cheung for asking us to write this book, and Kristen Weatherby for her valuable insight and helpful suggestions. Thanks also to Jim Kramer, Gregory Beckelhymer, Kevin Coomes, and Candace Jorgensen, all of whom provided assistance and advice along the way.

On the home front, as always, Roberta Moon-Krause, Rick Krause, and Zuzu Abeni Krause provided love, laughter, and inspiration.

As ex-New Yorkers, with New York City always in our hearts, we dedicate this book to the victims of the September 11th 2001 tragedy and to their families. A portion of the authors' proceeds from the sales of this book will be donated to Mercy Corps for its Comfort for Kids and scholarship programs that benefit the children whose parents never came home.

1 About This Book

If you want to get the most from your computer and your software with the least amount of time and effort—and who doesn't?—this book is for you. You'll find *Microsoft Word Version 2002 Plain & Simple* to be a straightforward, easy-to-read reference tool. With the premise that your computer should work for you, not you for it, this book's purpose is to help you get your work done quickly and efficiently so that you can get away from the computer and live your life.

No Computerese!

Let's face it—when there's a task you don't know how to do but you need to get it done in a hurry, or when you're stuck in the middle of a task and can't figure out what to do next, there's nothing more frustrating than having to read page after page of technical background material. You want the information you need—nothing more, nothing less— and you want it now! *And* it should be easy to find and understand.

That's what this book is all about. It's written in plain English— no technical jargon and no computerese. No single task in the book takes more than two pages. Just look the task up in the index or the table of contents, turn to the page, and there's the information you need, laid out in an illustrated step-by-step format. You don't get bogged down by the whys and wherefores: just follow the steps and get your work done with a minimum of hassle. Occasionally you might have to turn to another page if the procedure you're working on is accompanied by a *See Also*. That's because there's a lot of overlap among tasks, and we didn't want to keep repeating ourselves. We've scattered some useful *Tips* here and there, pointed out some features that are new in this version of Word, and thrown in a *Try This* or a *Caution* once in a while. By and large, however, we've tried to remain true to the heart and soul of the book, which is that the information you need should be available to you at a glance.

Useful Tasks...

Whether you use Microsoft Word 2002 for work, school, personal correspondence, or some of each, we've tried to pack this book with procedures for everything we could think of that you might want to do, from the simplest tasks to some of the more esoteric ones.

...And the Easiest Way to Do Them

Another thing we've tried to do in this book is to find and document the easiest way to accomplish a task. Word often provides a multitude of methods to achieve a single end result—and that can be daunting or delightful, depending on the way you like to work. If you tend to stick with one favorite and familiar approach, we think the methods described in this book are the way to go. If you like trying out alternative techniques, go ahead! The intuitiveness of Word invites exploration, and you're likely to discover ways of doing things that you think are easier or that you like better than ours. If you do, that's great! It's exactly what the developers of Word had in mind when they provided so many alternatives.

A Quick Overview

First, we're assuming that Word is already installed on your computer as a part of Microsoft Office 2002. If it isn't, the Windows Installer makes installation so simple that you won't need our help anyway. So, unlike many computer books, this one doesn't start with installation instructions and a list of system requirements. If Word is installed on its own without the other Office 2002 programs, you can still use everything in this book except the instructions for those tasks that incorporate material from other Office components.

Next, you don't have to read this book in any particular order. It's designed so that you can jump in, get the information you need, and then close the book and keep it near your computer until the next time you need it. But that doesn't mean we scattered the information about with wild abandon. The tasks you want to accomplish are arranged in two levels. The overall type of task you're looking for is under a main section title such as "Writing a Letter" or "Desktop Publishing." Then, in each of those sections, the smaller tasks within the main task are arranged in a loose progression from the simplest to the more complex.

Section 2 covers the basic tasks you can use to produce professional-looking documents: starting, saving, reopening, and closing a Word document; entering, editing, formatting, copying, and moving text; learning how to use Word's spelling- and grammar-checking tools; printing your documents; and getting some help if you need it.

Section 3 takes you beyond the basics and focuses on customizing your documents, using templates, styles, and wizards to create letters, memos, and other types of frequently used documents. You'll see how simple it is to create your own styles: custom-formatting text, paragraphs, or an entire document; using ready-made templates or creating your own templates to produce documents with consistent design elements; and setting up your pages for two-sided or bound documents.

Sections 4 and 5 are about communicating, by either so-called "snail mail," e-mail, or fax. Even though so much of today's business and personal correspondence is conducted via e-mail, most of us still need to communicate on paper as well. Using the power of Word, you can do a lot more than create business letters—you can design your own letterhead stationery, add a watermark behind your text, and print crisply professional envelopes. You'll also learn how to use Word's mail merge feature to create mass mailings. For speed and convenience, though, we all know that it's hard to beat e-mail! We'll show you how to use Word to format your e-mail messages, how to send attachments with your e-mail, how to add an automatic signature to your messages, and so on. And you'll learn how to send faxes from your computer rather than from a separate fax machine.

Sections 6, 7, and 8 walk you through the creation of long documents and technical documents. These interrelated sections of the book examine elements that are common to such seemingly dissimilar documents as company reports, collections of short stories, scientific papers, and your Great American Novel. Just a few of the topics we cover here are numbering pages and creating running heads; working with a document's outline; copying and inserting information from various sources; creating a table of contents, a table of figures, or an index; inserting symbols and characters that don't exist on your keyboard; creating footnotes and endnotes; inserting diagrams, charts, and captions; and creating and formatting tables and lists.

Sections 9 and 10 are interrelated too—both focus on using your own creativity to spice up your documents with pictures, drawings, and so on. You'll learn how to insert a picture into a document, add a border to the picture, or wrap text around it. And you'll feel your creative juices flowing as you use simple techniques to create artistic borders, drop caps, captions, pull quotes, and margin notes; to combine text and graphics; to flow text into columns or around objects; and to transform ordinary text into eye-popping art with WordArt.

Section 11 is about working on line and reaching beyond your computer to collaborate with your coworkers: creating and formatting online documents; creating your own Web pages or Web sites; using hyperlinks to access other documents or Web pages; sharing templates; and sharing documents by circulating them on line for comments or reviews from your colleagues.

Section 12 focuses on some ways to automate everyday tasks and introduces you to some different ways to do your work. In the first part of this section, you'll learn how to set Word's AutoText and AutoCorrect features so that they do your bidding; how to use *smart tags* to add links to supplemental information related to the content of your work; how to make fields work for you; and how to translate foreign-language text. The second half of this section deals with alternative ways of working: dictating text that Word will type for you; using voice commands to control Word; scanning text and turning it into a Word document; converting a fax into a Word document; using the On-Screen Keyboard and your mouse to enter text; and using the new Handwriting feature to create "handwritten" text.

Section 13 is about reviewing your documents: using Word's proofreading tools and dictionaries to check your spelling and grammar and improve your hyphenation and word usage (even if you're working in more than one language), standardizing your formatting, and reviewing and perfecting your page layout.

Section 14 lets you take control of Word by customizing almost everything: add or remove components, change the way the windows work, make your system more secure, create your own commands, customize menus, add tools to toolbars, and so on. If you think these tasks sound complex, rest assured that they're not; Word makes them all so easy that you'll sail right through them.

What's New in Word 2002?

When we started using this much-changed version of Word, we said, *"Why didn't they think of this before?"* And we think you'll agree that the design and scope of the new features in Word simplify and speed up your work and greatly expand what you can do.

The first conspicuously new feature you'll encounter when you start Word will probably be a *task pane*. A task pane is a section of the Word window that appears and offers you a choice of actions or tasks specific to the work you're doing—for example, you can choose to create a new document, apply a style to the text, or search for a document on your computer. It takes no time at all to get comfortable using the task panes, and you'll find them to be great time-savers—no hunting through menus and dialog boxes to find the option or check box you need.

In addition to the automatic changes Word executes as you're working—formatting text as you type, using AutoCorrect features to fix common typing errors, and so on—Word now provides *Actions buttons* that, like task panes, let you control such automatic actions "on the fly." There are three main types of Actions buttons: a Paste Options Actions button that lets you choose how you want pasted text to be inserted, an AutoFormat Actions button that lets you control automatic formatting changes, and a Smart Tag Actions button that links you to associated information or that performs other actions associated with the smart tag. So what *is* a smart tag? When Word searches your document and finds specific information—an address, the name of a contact, or a stock symbol, for example—Word attaches a smart tag to that information. You use the smart tag by clicking the Actions button for the tag and choosing an action—instantly getting a map and directions to an address, quickly finding a contact's e-mail address, or checking the current price quote of a stock. It's easy to adapt to new features when they're this intuitive!

Working with pictures, drawings, and other graphics is easier than ever. You can modify the resolution of a picture—using a high resolution for a picture you're putting into a printed document or a lower resolution for a picture you'll be posting on a Web site, for example. You can compress a picture to shrink its file size so that you can send it out in an e-mail message. A nice new feature is Word's *Drawing Canvas,* on which you can do all your graphics work—adding pictures, charts, and drawings; changing your composition by moving items around; grouping items to keep them together; and scaling or formatting the pictures as needed. You'll also find two new types of styles in Word: *table styles* and *list styles.* With these, you can quickly apply consistent—and, if you want, customized—formatting to the tables and lists in your document. You'll find other features that have been improved too: do a little experimenting and see how easy it is to create an artistic watermark to appear behind some text, or try playing around with a variety of ready-made diagrams.

This version of Word, along with some tools from Office, gives you a variety of new and interesting ways to put text into your documents. Provided your computer is powerful enough, Word can convert your spoken words into written text, your handwriting into standard text, your printed documents into electronic text, your received faxes into standard Word documents, and your text from one language into another.

Word provides other new features that greatly enhance collaboration on a document. When you review or edit a document, you can view the document at every stage—as it was before your edits, showing your own and your colleagues' edits, and how it will look after the edits have been incorporated. With *SharePoint Team Services* installed on your network or supplied by an Internet provider, collaboration is further improved. For example, more than one person can work on a document at the same time, and you and your coworkers can discuss a document by adding comments to a newsgroup-like structure that's connected directly to the document.

And there are more enhancements to Word. You can save documents and templates to a personal storage area on the Internet so that you can access them from any computer. You can increase the security of your documents by eliminating personal information from them and, if high security is necessary, by encrypting those documents. You can save any Web pages you've created in Word in a variety of different ways, depending on how you want to use them.

But one old feature in Word is new again. In early versions of Word, all your open Word documents were contained in a single window; in later versions of Word, each document had its own window. While the argument among Word aficionados has been raging as to which way is better, Word 2002 has quietly come up with a solution—you can simply decide for yourself whether you want to work in a single window or in multiple windows.

A Final Word (or Two)

We had three goals in writing this book:

- Whatever you want to do, we want the book to help you get it done.

- We want the book to help you discover how to do things you *didn't* know you wanted to do.

- And, finally, if we've achieved the first two goals, we'll be well on the way to the third, which is for our book to help you *enjoy* using Word. We think that's the best gift we could give you to thank you for buying our book.

We hope you'll have as much fun using *Microsoft Word Version 2002 Plain & Simple* as we've had writing it. The best way to learn is by *doing,* and that's how we hope you'll use this book.

2 The Basics

NEW FEATURE

NEW FEATURE

You can use Microsoft Word 2002 as a word processor or as a multifaceted *idea* processor. Word was designed to be either or both, and you can choose how you want to use its multitude of tools and features. You can stick with the basics or you can jump right in and go exploring—opening menus and drop-down lists, clicking buttons, selecting check boxes, turning options on and off to see what happens, and so on. You'll learn a lot about Word and the way it works by simply trying to accomplish a task.

This section covers many of the basic skills you'll use every day—creating documents, editing and formatting text, printing documents, and getting help if you need it. If you're not familiar with Word, step through these first few tasks and see how easily you can produce professional-looking documents. Once you realize how intuitive Word is, you'll find it easy and rewarding to explore and try things out—in other words, to learn by doing.

If you try one of the more advanced tasks and you get stuck in some way, you'll find the answers to most of your questions in other sections of this book, or in Word's Help system. Even if you never try any advanced tasks and never read the rest of this book, you'll have learned the basics, and Word as a "smart typewriter" will make your life that much easier.

But Word really shines as an idea processor. Try it. (And read this book!)

What's Where in Word?

Microsoft Word has many faces and can be customized in countless ways. The pictures on these two pages show many of the common features you'll see when you're working with Word, and they also introduce just a few of the customizations you can use. We've identified many of the screen elements for you, but it's a good idea to explore Word's interface while

you're looking at these two pages. For example, open each of the menus and familiarize yourself with the names of the commands. If you're not sure what the buttons on the toolbars are used for, point to one of them. In a moment or two, you'll see a *ScreenTip* that tells you the button's name and usually gives you a pretty good idea of the tool's function.

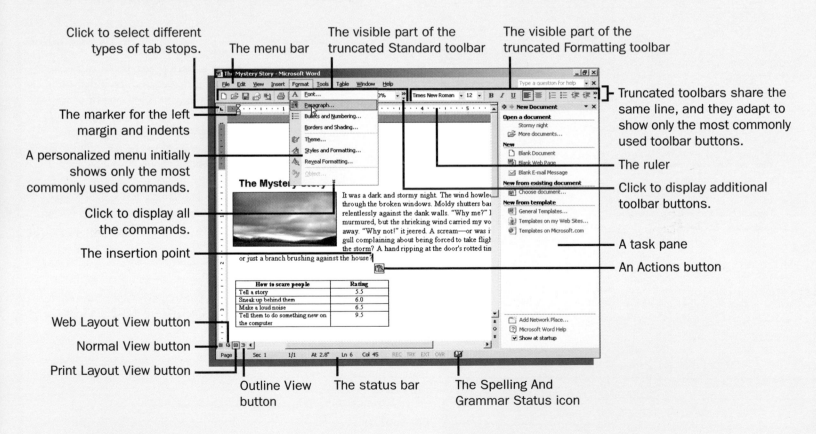

Click to select different types of tab stops.

The menu bar

The visible part of the truncated Standard toolbar

The visible part of the truncated Formatting toolbar

The marker for the left margin and indents

A personalized menu initially shows only the most commonly used commands.

Click to display all the commands.

The insertion point

Web Layout View button

Normal View button

Print Layout View button

Outline View button

The status bar

The Spelling And Grammar Status icon

Truncated toolbars share the same line, and they adapt to show only the most commonly used toolbar buttons.

The ruler

Click to display additional toolbar buttons.

A task pane

An Actions button

The picture below shows the Word interface with a few changes. But as you use Word and experiment with its multitude of options, you'll realize that the customizations shown here illustrate only some of the *many* ways you can view Word's interface. You can see more toolbars, including a *floating* toolbar, and many toolbar buttons that were hidden, in the picture on this page. You'll find all you ever wanted to know about toolbars in "Using Word's Toolbars" on page 22.

Shows or hides formatting marks.

The Ask A Question box

The Zoom box

A ScreenTip

A floating toolbar

The Standard and Formatting toolbars are now on separate lines.

A paragraph mark

A space mark

The Reviewing toolbar docked at the side of the window

Text wrapped around a picture

A scroll bar

A reviewer's comment

A table

The Browser

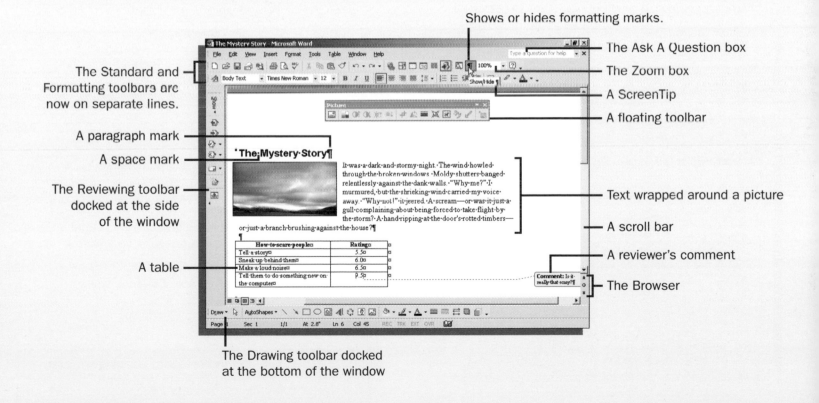

The Drawing toolbar docked at the bottom of the window

Creating a New Document

You can start Word in several different ways, depending on how it was installed, but the tried-and-true method is to choose Microsoft Word from the Windows Start menu. When Word starts, it automatically opens a new blank document for you. If you've been experimenting and Word is already running, you can open a new blank document with a click of a button.

Start Word, and Enter Some Text

1 If Word is already running and you've entered some text, click the New Blank Document button on the Standard toolbar to create a new blank document.

2 If Word isn't running, start it from the Programs submenu of the Windows Start menu. Click the Close button to close the New Document task pane.

3 To show paragraph marks and other formatting marks such as spaces and tabs, click the Show/Hide ¶ button. Click the button again if you want to hide the marks.

4 Type your text. When you reach the end of a line, continue typing. Word automatically moves, or *wraps,* your words onto the next line.

5 Press Enter to start a new paragraph. Continue typing to complete your paragraph.

> **TIP:** The New Document task pane, like all task panes, can be set so that it won't be displayed automatically. If you start Word and there's no task pane, just start working on your document.

> **TIP:** The green squiggles in the document shown here tell you that Word thinks these items are sentence fragments. You can ignore the squiggles, tell Word to ignore them, or customize the grammar rules to accept this type of sentence.

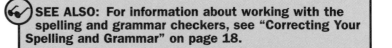

> **SEE ALSO:** For information about working with the spelling and grammar checkers, see "Correcting Your Spelling and Grammar" on page 18.

Save the Document

1 Click the Save button on the Standard toolbar.

! TIP: After you've named your document, click the Save button or press the key combination Ctrl+S periodically as you work. Word will save the document and all your changes under that document's name, and the Save As dialog box won't keep popping up. It's so quick and easy that you can do it every few minutes, and you'll never have to worry about losing your work if the computer is accidentally shut off or if there's a power failure.

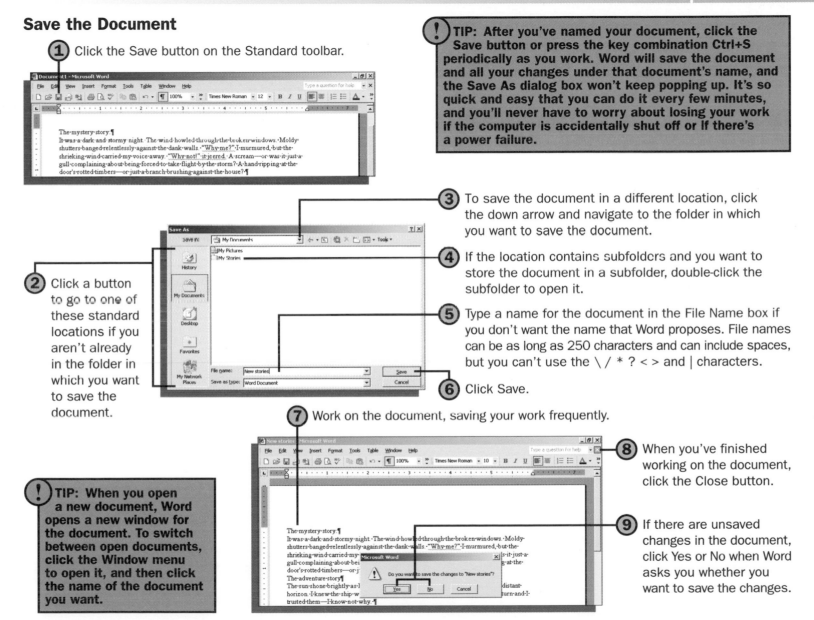

3 To save the document in a different location, click the down arrow and navigate to the folder in which you want to save the document.

4 If the location contains subfolders and you want to store the document in a subfolder, double-click the subfolder to open it.

2 Click a button to go to one of these standard locations if you aren't already in the folder in which you want to save the document.

5 Type a name for the document in the File Name box if you don't want the name that Word proposes. File names can be as long as 250 characters and can include spaces, but you can't use the \ / * ? < > and | characters.

6 Click Save.

7 Work on the document, saving your work frequently.

8 When you've finished working on the document, click the Close button.

! TIP: When you open a new document, Word opens a new window for the document. To switch between open documents, click the Window menu to open it, and then click the name of the document you want.

9 If there are unsaved changes in the document, click Yes or No when Word asks you whether you want to save the changes.

Working with an Existing Document

Unless you always create short documents—letters, memos, and so on—you'll often need to continue working on a document that you started but didn't complete in an earlier session. You simply open the saved document, add more text, and then save and close the document again.

Open a Document

The Open button

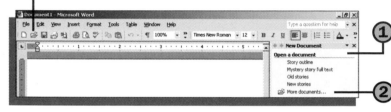

SEE ALSO: For information about selecting, deleting, replacing, and moving text, see "Editing Text" on page 12.

TIP: If the task pane isn't open, and if the document you want to open is one you used recently, it might be listed at the bottom of the File menu. If so, click the document's name to open it.

(1) Start Word if it isn't already running. If the New Document task pane is displayed and the document you want to open is listed, click it to open it, and then skip to step 5.

(2) If the document isn't listed, click More Documents. If the task pane isn't displayed, click the Open button on the Standard toolbar.

(4) Double-click the document to open it.

(3) Use the buttons or the Look In box to locate the document you want.

TIP: To open a document as a copy or as a read-only file, click the document to select it, click the down arrow next to the Open button on the Standard toolbar, and click an option in the list that appears. Read-only lets you open the document but doesn't allow you to save it to the same folder using the same file name.

(7) Close the document.

(6) Click the Save button periodically to save the document and again when you've finished working on the document.

The sun shone brightly as I squinted across the water, looking for a sail on the distant horizon. I knew the ship would come, sooner or later. They had promised to return and I trusted them—I know not why.

(5) Add new text or edit the existing text.

Finding a Document ⊕ NEW FEATURE

If you need to work on an existing document but you don't know its name or where it's stored, you can ask Word to search for the document, based on any text in the document or any of the document's properties (date, author, and so on). By default, Word wants to use an Office feature called Fast Searching. Fast Searching is built into Microsoft Windows XP and Windows 2000 (where it's called the Indexing Service), but earlier operating systems use Office's Support For Fast Searching. If Fast Searching isn't already installed on your computer, Word will prompt you to install it. If you don't install it, you can continue searching, but the search will take much longer and you won't be able to take advantage of the more powerful tools of advanced searches.

Search for a Document

(1) Click the Search button on the Standard toolbar.

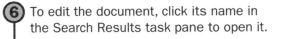

(2) In the Basic Search task pane, type some text that you know is in the document.

(3) If you have some idea where the document might be located (or if you know where it definitely *isn't* located), click the Search In down arrow, and select the check boxes for the locations you want to search, or clear those you don't want to search.

(5) Click Search.

(4) Click the Results Should Be down arrow, and clear all the check boxes except the Word Files check box.

> **! TIP:** If Fast Searching is installed but isn't enabled, click Search Options to enable it. Be aware that it will take some time for your documents to be indexed before you can conduct an accurate search.

(6) To edit the document, click its name in the Search Results task pane to open it.

(7) To create a new document that includes the contents of the original document, point to the document in the Search Results task pane, click the down arrow, and then click New From This File.

(8) Close the Search Results pane and work on the document.

> **! TIP:** To search quickly for a document whose name you know, choose Search from the Windows Start menu.

Editing Text

Whether you're creating a business letter, a financial report, or the Great American Novel, it's a sure bet that you're going to need to go back into your document and do some editing. Word provides a great variety of ways to edit. To edit existing content, you simply select it and make your changes.

Select and Modify Text

TIP: If you delete text by accident, immediately click the Undo button on the Standard toolbar to restore the deleted text.

SEE ALSO: For more information about different ways to select text, see "So Many Ways to Do It" on pages 16–17.

(1) Click at the beginning of the text that you want to delete.

(2) Drag the mouse over all the text to select it, and then release the mouse button.

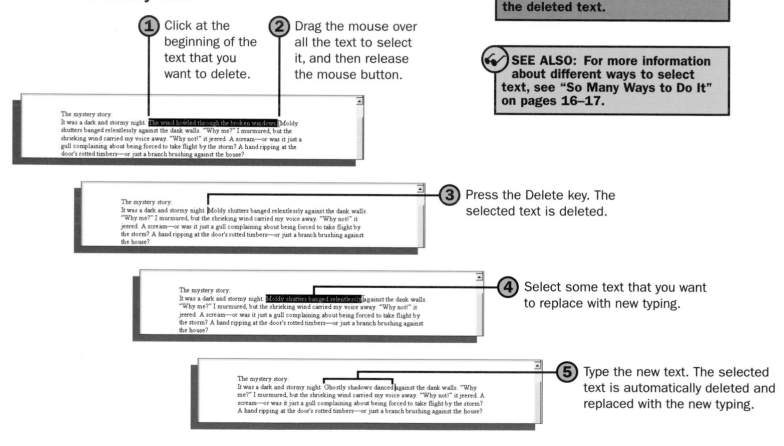

(3) Press the Delete key. The selected text is deleted.

(4) Select some text that you want to replace with new typing.

(5) Type the new text. The selected text is automatically deleted and replaced with the new typing.

Formatting Text ❀ NEW FEATURE

Rarely, except possibly in an e-mail message, is a document composed of just plain old text, with all the paragraphs in the same font and font size and with the same indents and line spacing. Word provides many predefined paragraph styles that you can use to give your documents that professional look.

> **! TIP:** If you don't see a style that appeals to you or that's appropriate for your document, click All Styles in the Show list at the bottom of the Styles And Formatting task pane.

Apply a Style

① Write your text without worrying about the formatting, and then click in the paragraph that you want to format.

② Click the Styles And Formatting button on the Formatting toolbar.

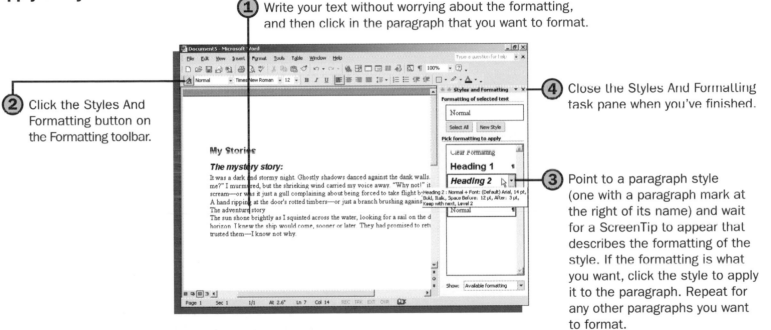

④ Close the Styles And Formatting task pane when you've finished.

③ Point to a paragraph style (one with a paragraph mark at the right of its name) and wait for a ScreenTip to appear that describes the formatting of the style. If the formatting is what you want, click the style to apply it to the paragraph. Repeat for any other paragraphs you want to format.

> **SEE ALSO:** For information about styles and different ways of formatting text and other content, see "Templates, Styles, Wizards, and Direct Formatting" on pages 26–27.
>
> For information about arranging each toolbar on a separate line, see "Managing Toolbars and Menus" on page 228.

> **✸ NEW FEATURE:** The Styles And Formatting task pane is a fast, easy, and visual way to apply styles and other formatting.

Moving and Copying Text

Word uses a tool called the *Clipboard* as a temporary holding area for text that you want to move or copy to another part of your document, to another document in the same program, or to a document in another program. You simply park your text on the Clipboard and then, when you're ready, you retrieve it and "paste" it into its new location. Word uses two different Clipboards: the Windows Clipboard, which stores the item that was most recently cut or copied; and the Office Clipboard, which can store as many as 24 different items, including the most recently cut or copied item. You'll probably use the Paste button when you're pasting the last item you cut or copied, and the Windows Clipboard when you want to move several different pieces of text from one place to another.

Cut or Copy Text

② Do either of the following:

- Click the Cut button to delete the selected text and store it on the Clipboard.
- Click the Copy button to keep the selected text where it is and place a copy on the Clipboard.

① Select the text to be cut or copied.

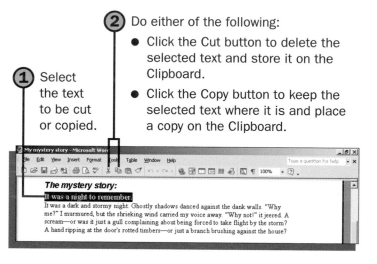

> **SEE ALSO:** For information about the many different ways to copy and move text, see "So Many Ways to Do It" on pages 16–17 and "Copying Information from Multiple Locations" on page 87.

> **TIP:** If you don't need to adjust the formatting of the inserted text, simply ignore the Actions button—it will go away as soon as you do anything else in your document.

Paste the Cut or Copied Text

① Click in your document where you want to insert the text.

② Click the Paste button.

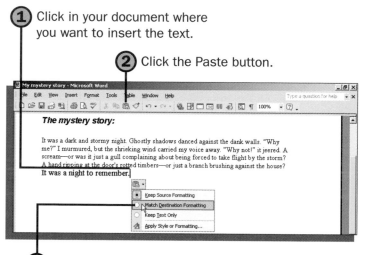

③ If the inserted text looks strange because it doesn't match the look (the formatting) of the surrounding text, click the Actions button that appears, and click the Match Destination Formatting option.

> **TIP:** If you don't see an Actions button when you paste text or drag text to a new location, choose Options from the Tools menu, and, on the View tab of the Options dialog box, select the Smart Tags check box. Click OK.

Copy and Paste Multiple Items

(1) In this document, or in any other Word or Office document, select and cut or copy the items you want. If necessary, switch to the document into which you want to paste some or all of the items you cut or copied.

(2) Click where you want to insert one of the items.

(3) Click the item to be inserted. Continue inserting, cutting, and copying text as necessary.

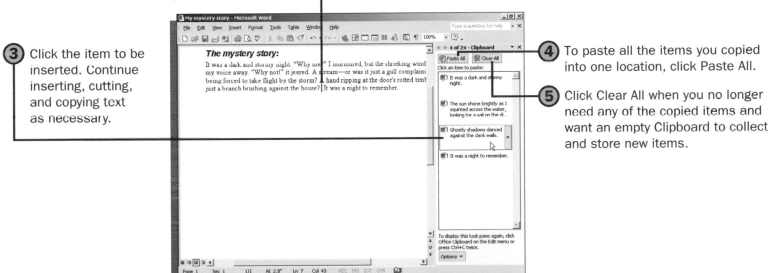

(4) To paste all the items you copied into one location, click Paste All.

(5) Click Clear All when you no longer need any of the copied items and want an empty Clipboard to collect and store new items.

! TIP: If the Clipboard task pane doesn't open automatically after you've copied two or more items, choose Office Clipboard from the Edit menu or double-click the Office Clipboard icon on the Windows taskbar.

! TIP: You can use both the Windows Clipboard and the Office Clipboard to store items other than text, including pictures, tables, and even data from Microsoft Excel spreadsheets.

! TIP: Although the Windows Clipboard is limited to storing only one item at a time, you can use it to transfer information among many different programs. The Office Clipboard works only with Office programs.

❄ NEW FEATURE: The Clipboard task pane provides quick access to and easy identification of all your copied items.

So Many Ways to Do It

Word offers you a variety of ways to do most things. You might, for example, be able to use a button, a menu item, a key combination, a task pane, or a mouse-click to accomplish the same result. Why are there so many choices? Well, one reason is that we all work differently. Given several choices, we usually do some experimenting, find the way that works best for us and that we're most comfortable with, and then stick with it. Another reason is that certain methods work best in certain situations.

Two procedures that you'll be using frequently—selecting text and moving or copying text—can be accomplished using quite a few different methods, some of which might cause you a bit of difficulty if you use them in the wrong situation. The tips we offer here will help you choose which method to use in which circumstances.

Try these common methods of selecting text and see which works best for you. Of course, there are other ways to select text, and, depending on whether and how you've customized Word, some selection methods might work a bit differently from those described here. For information about customizing Word, see section 14, "Customizing and Maintaining Word," starting on page 221.

Text-Selection Methods

To select	Use this method
Characters in a word	Drag the mouse over the characters.
A word	Double-click the word.
Several words	Drag the mouse over the words.
A sentence	Hold down the Ctrl key and click anywhere in the sentence.
A line of text	Move the pointer to the far left of the window, and click when you see a right-pointing arrow.
A paragraph	Move the pointer to the far left of the window, and double-click when you see a right-pointing arrow.
A long passage	Click at the beginning of the passage, and then hold down the Shift key and click at the end of the passage.
Non-adjacent blocks of text	Drag the mouse to select the first block. Hold down the Ctrl key and drag the mouse to select the second block.
A vertical block of text	Click at the top left corner of the text block. Hold down the Alt key and drag the mouse over the text block.
The entire document	Choose Select All from the Edit menu, or press Ctrl+A.

After you've selected the text, your next step might be to move it or copy it. Again, some methods are better than others, depending on the situation.

The process of moving or copying contents uses different tools, depending on what you want to do. When you use the F2 key or the Shift+F2 key combination, the selected material is stored in Word's short-term memory, where it's remembered only until you paste it into another location or execute any other Word activity.

The Cut and Copy buttons on the Standard toolbar store the selected material on the very single-minded Windows Clipboard, from where you can retrieve the information once or numerous times. The information you've stored on the Windows Clipboard stays there until you replace it with another item or shut down Windows. The Windows Clipboard is more than just a holding area, though—it's also a pathway through which you can transfer your cut or copied information to other documents or programs. Although the *Windows* Clipboard stores only one item at a time, the *Office* Clipboard stores up to 24 items, which you can retrieve one at a time or all at once. For more information about the Office Clipboard, see "Copying Information from Multiple Locations" on page 87.

If these seem like an overwhelming number of ways to accomplish the same tasks, get ready for a shock—there are even more ways. If you really want to explore the full range of different ways to do these tasks, take a stroll through Word's Help and try out some of the other methods.

Copying and Moving Methods

To do this	Use this method
Move a short distance	Drag the selection to the new location.
Copy a short distance	Hold down the Ctrl key, drag the selection to the new location, and release the Ctrl key.
Move a long distance or to a different document or program	Click the Cut button, click at the new location, and click the Paste button. OR press Ctrl+X, click at the new location, and press Ctrl+V.
Copy a long distance or to a different document or program	Click the Copy button, click at the new location, and click the Paste button. OR press Ctrl+C, click at the new location, and press Ctrl+V.
Copy several items and insert all at one place	Click the Copy button, select the next item, click the Copy button again, and repeat to copy up to 24 items. OR hold down the Ctrl key, select multiple items, and then click the Copy button. Click at the new location, and then click the Paste All button in the Clipboard task pane.
Move a long or short distance	Press the F2 key, click at the new location, and press Enter.
Copy a long or short distance	Press Shift+F2, click at the new location, and press Enter.

Correcting Your Spelling and Grammar

You can avoid the embarrassment of distributing a document full of misspellings or poor grammar even if you don't have a proof-reader or an editor at your disposal. Word comes to the rescue by discreetly pointing out your spelling errors and grammatical no-no's. When you see one of those helpful little squiggles under a word or phrase, you can choose what you want to do to correct the mistake—if it really is a mistake.

Correct a Spelling Error

① Right-click a red squiggle to see one or more suggestions for correcting the error.

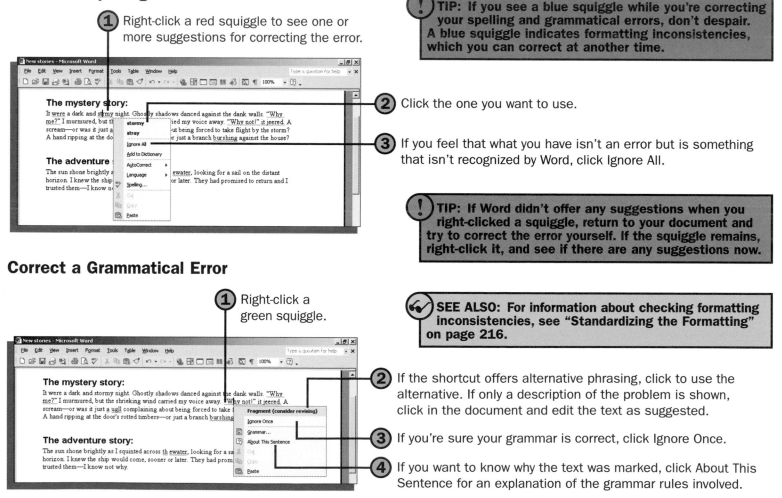

② Click the one you want to use.

③ If you feel that what you have isn't an error but is something that isn't recognized by Word, click Ignore All.

> **TIP:** If you see a blue squiggle while you're correcting your spelling and grammatical errors, don't despair. A blue squiggle indicates formatting inconsistencies, which you can correct at another time.

> **TIP:** If Word didn't offer any suggestions when you right-clicked a squiggle, return to your document and try to correct the error yourself. If the squiggle remains, right-click it, and see if there are any suggestions now.

Correct a Grammatical Error

① Right-click a green squiggle.

② If the shortcut offers alternative phrasing, click to use the alternative. If only a description of the problem is shown, click in the document and edit the text as suggested.

③ If you're sure your grammar is correct, click Ignore Once.

④ If you want to know why the text was marked, click About This Sentence for an explanation of the grammar rules involved.

> **SEE ALSO:** For information about checking formatting inconsistencies, see "Standardizing the Formatting" on page 216.

Printing a Document

E-mail and Web documents are bringing the paperless office closer to reality, but the most common way to distribute a finished document is still to print it. Printing is mostly a job for Windows—Word prepares your document, and then hands it off to Windows.

Print a Document

(1) Look over your document to make sure it's complete and free of errors. Then choose Print from the File menu.

TIP: If you don't need to change any settings in the Print dialog box, you can quickly print a document by clicking the Print button on the Standard toolbar.

TRY THIS: Complete your document, and click the Print Preview button on the Standard toolbar. Inspect the document to make sure it's laid out correctly. Click the Close button. Choose Print from the File menu, click the Options button, and note all the different ways you can print. Click OK, and print your document.

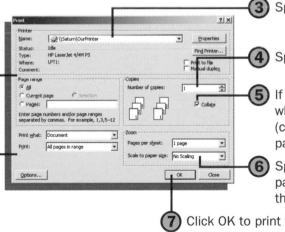

(2) Specify whether you want to print the entire document, a single page, some selected text, or a range of pages.

(3) Specify the printer to be used.

(4) Specify the number of copies to be printed.

(5) If you're printing multiple copies, specify whether the pages are to be printed in order (collated) or whether all copies of the same page are to be printed at one time.

(6) Specify a scaling size if you want to print on paper that's a different size from the paper the document was originally set up for.

(7) Click OK to print the document.

Getting Help

Nothing can replace this book, of course, but Word does provide you with other resources to help solve problems you might encounter. Word's Help system has several different ways to render assistance.

Interrogate Word

1 Click in the Ask A Question box, and type a word or phrase that describes a specific problem or an area in which you're having a problem. Press Enter.

2 In the list that appears, click the topic that most closely corresponds to your question.

3 Wait for the Microsoft Word Help window to appear. Read the topic and see whether it addresses your problem.

4 If not, use any of the three tabs to search for other solutions:
- Contents to see topics arranged by chapters
- Answer Wizard to ask another question
- Index to search for solutions based on a keyword

> **TIP:** If you're familiar with the Office Assistant and you miss it, you can make it appear by choosing Show The Office Assistant from the Help menu. To hide the Office Assistant again, right-click it, and choose Hide from the shortcut menu.

> **TRY THIS:** Press the Shift+F1 key combination to start What's This? help. Note that the mouse pointer now has a question mark attached to it. Click an item on one of Word's toolbars or menus. Now press Shift+F1 again, and click some text in your document. You'll receive all sorts of context-specific information.

Get More Help

① Choose Office On The Web from Word's Help menu, and connect to the Internet if you're not already connected. If necessary, follow the links to the Microsoft Office Assistance Center.

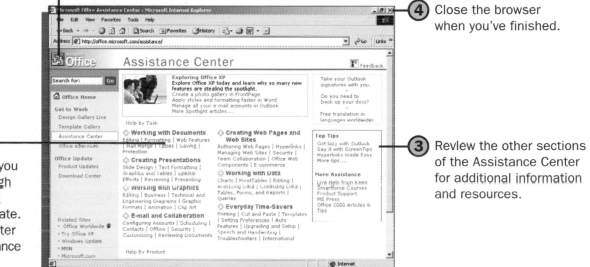

④ Close the browser when you've finished.

② Click the topic for which you need help. Browse through the list of topics, clicking those that seem appropriate. Click the Assistance Center link to return to the Assistance Center main page.

③ Review the other sections of the Assistance Center for additional information and resources.

> **! TIP:** The Assistance Center provides information about all the Office programs. To browse Word topics only, click the Word link in the Help By Product section of the Assistance Center.

> **! TIP:** For more help, consider using one of the Word newsgroups sponsored by Microsoft to review discussions or ask questions. To visit a newsgroup, in a newsreader such as Microsoft Outlook Express, add the news server *msnews.microsoft.com,* and look for newsgroups that start with *Microsoft.public.word.*

Using Word's Toolbars

Word offers many different toolbars, each designed for a specific purpose. When you get to know the toolbars and how to use them, you'll find them invaluable for getting your work done quickly and easily.

Display a Toolbar

① Point to Toolbars on the View menu.

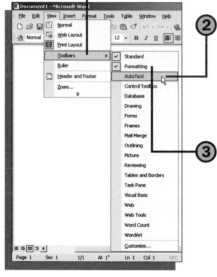

 On the submenu that appears, click the toolbar you want to use. If you're not sure which toolbar you need, consult the table at the right.

③ To hide a toolbar, click its name. A toolbar that's already displayed has a check mark next to it.

SEE ALSO: For information about modifying existing toolbars and creating your own toolbars, see "Rearranging Toolbar Buttons and Menus" on page 230 and "Customizing Toolbars and Menus" on page 232.

TIP: You can display the list of toolbars by right-clicking a blank spot on any toolbar.

Word's Most Useful Toolbars

Toolbar	Use for
Standard	File management and basic editing
Formatting	Font and paragraph formatting
AutoText	Inserting predefined text
Drawing	Inserting and formatting pictures, drawings, and nonstandard text elements
Outlining	Organizing and controlling the view of the document in Outline view
Picture	Inserting, formatting, and modifying pictures
Reviewing	Working with marked-up changes and comments
Tables And Borders	Inserting and modifying tables and borders
Web	Navigating on the Internet or your intranet; working with Web pages
Word Count	Counting characters, words, lines, and so on in your document
WordArt	Inserting and modifying special-effects text

3 Customizing Your Document

✳ NEW FEATURE

Even if you don't have the time, inclination, or experience to design the documents you use every day, you still can produce professional-looking, well-designed letters, memos, faxes, reports, brochures, and even a thesis or two. You do this by using templates, styles, and wizards—the principal tools Microsoft Word 2002 provides for creating, designing, and maintaining consistency throughout the documents you use every day. Depending upon your desired end result and how little or how much involvement you want in the design, you can use the predesigned elements, or you can create your own styles and templates or modify existing ones so that they're tailored more precisely to your needs.

Whether you're creating a long, detailed report or business proposal or simply changing the design of your company's letter template, you'll wonder how you ever managed to get your work completed on time without templates, styles, and wizards. For a detailed discussion of these useful tools, see "Templates, Styles, Wizards, and Direct Formatting" on page 26–27.

In this section, we'll also discuss the way you set up your pages: their orientation (that is, whether you want them to be printed in Landscape orientation, like the pages in this book, or in Portrait orientation, in which the pages are longer than they are wide); whether you're going to print your text on only one or on both sides of the paper; and—if your completed document is a book or a report that's going to be bound—what you need to do to accommodate the binding.

Composing Different Types of Documents

Word comes loaded with useful templates that you can use to quickly create your documents. When you start a new document based on a template, the document contains its own design elements, and the template's predefined styles ensure that all your paragraphs work together.

NEW FEATURE: The New Document task pane works as a control center. You can use it to edit an existing document, create a new blank document, create a new document based on an existing document, or create a new document based on a template.

Start the Document

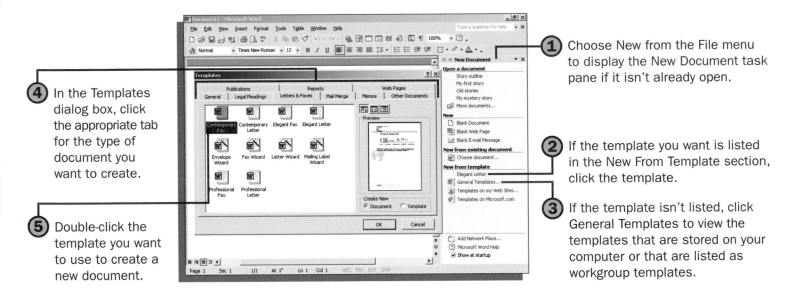

(1) Choose New from the File menu to display the New Document task pane if it isn't already open.

(2) If the template you want is listed in the New From Template section, click the template.

(3) If the template isn't listed, click General Templates to view the templates that are stored on your computer or that are listed as workgroup templates.

(4) In the Templates dialog box, click the appropriate tab for the type of document you want to create.

(5) Double-click the template you want to use to create a new document.

TIP: If you or someone in your company set up your templates to be stored on either your personal Web site or on a Microsoft SharePoint Team Web site, click Templates On My Web Sites to access those templates. To access additional templates prepared by Microsoft that weren't included with Word, click Templates On Microsoft.com.

TIP: Some items in the Templates dialog box are listed as "wizards." These are special tools that step you through a series of dialog boxes to help you create your document. In most cases, the wizards also provide the opportunity to select a specific template.

Complete the Document

(4) If the Show/Hide ¶ button on the Standard toolbar isn't already turned on, click it so that you can see all the elements in the template.

(3) Save the document with the file name you want, in the location you want.

(2) Read the placeholder text, if any, that tells you how to complete the template.

(5) Replace any placeholder text with your own text.

(6) If information such as the date is inserted automatically, don't modify the information—it was inserted using a Word file that's automatically updated and formatted.

(1) If you aren't already in Print Layout view, click the Print Layout View button.

(7) If there are paragraphs that tell you to "Click here...", do so, and then insert the appropriate text.

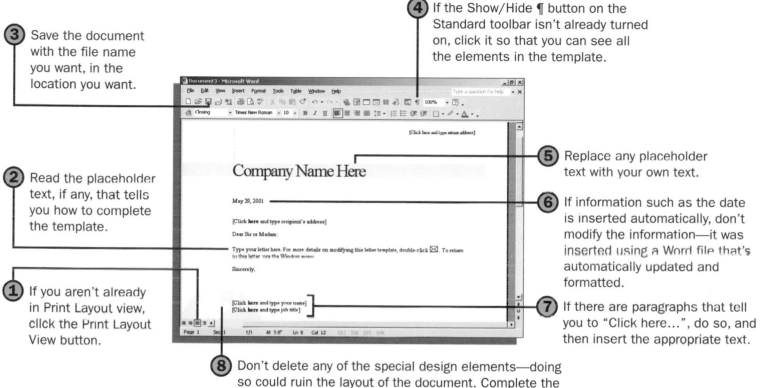

(8) Don't delete any of the special design elements—doing so could ruin the layout of the document. Complete the document, and then save, print, and distribute it.

CAUTION: Don't delete any paragraph marks—they contain your paragraph formatting. If you delete a paragraph mark, you'll lose any special formatting that was designed for that specific paragraph.

SEE ALSO: For information about modifying templates, see "Customizing a Template" on page 38.

For information about creating your own templates, see "Designing a Template" on page 40.

Templates, Styles, Wizards, and Direct Formatting

Templates and styles are invaluable. They're quick ways of applying formatting and layouts, and they help you maintain consistency throughout a document and throughout all documents of the same type. Wizards are interactive programs within Word that help you easily use styles and templates to create specialized documents. If a style doesn't supply exactly what you want, you can change the look by directly modifying the formatting.

Templates

A template is both a blueprint for your document and a container that holds the specialized tools you need to work on the document: styles, AutoText, toolbars, macros, page-layout specifications, and view settings. A template can also contain text, graphics, and any other elements that will always be included in the documents you create using that template. You can use a template as is, modify it to fit your needs, or create your own template.

Word always uses the Normal template, which contains Word's predefined styles and default content. When you make changes to this global template, the changes are available to all your documents. You can also use a specialized template that contains information specific to a certain type of document. In this case, the contents of the Normal template *and* the contents of the specialized template are available to your document. If there's a conflict (if the two have different formatting for a Heading 1 style, for example), the contents of the specialized template take precedence over those of the Normal template. For example, when you choose Blank Document from the New Document task pane, Word uses only the Normal template; when you choose a different type of document, Word uses the specialized template for that document *and* the Normal template.

Your templates can be located in a variety of places. The Normal template and the other templates that came with Word are usually stored on your computer, in the same folder as your personal settings. That way, each user of your computer has his or her own templates. Another set of templates, the Workgroup templates, might be stored in a network location so that everyone on that network has access to the same templates. That way, only one copy of a template needs to be customized, and everyone in the workgroup can use the same custom template. Microsoft also posts a large collection of templates on its Web site, and you can store templates on your own Web site.

Don't neglect your templates—templates, along with the styles they include, are your key to producing professional-looking documents with an absolute minimum of effort.

Styles

A style is a definition of the way an item is formatted. Word comes with an abundance of predefined styles. To view them, open a new blank document, and click the Styles And Formatting button on the Formatting toolbar. In the Styles And Formatting task pane, choose All Styles from the Show list, and scroll through the list. A paragraph mark at the right of the style name denotes a paragraph style, an underlined "a" denotes a character style, a grid denotes a table style, and a blank area denotes a list style. You can use a style as is, redefine its formatting, or create your own style.

By using a style, you can apply consistent—and, if necessary, complex—formatting with a quick click! Word provides four different types of styles:

- A *paragraph style* is the blueprint for the look of a paragraph—the font and its size; the line spacing; the way the text is indented from the margins by using left, right, or first-line indents; the types of tab stops and their positions; the borders; and even the paragraph's position on the page. The formatting applied with a paragraph style applies to the entire paragraph.

- A *character style* defines the look of one or more characters (letters or numbers), and applies only to the characters to which you apply that style.

- A *table style* defines the look of a table—its borders, shading, and character fonts. If you apply a table style to standard text, the table style creates a table and places the text in the table. If you apply a table style to an existing table, the formatting of the table changes to that style. Using a table style is similar to using the Table AutoFormat command on the Table menu, except that you can customize a table style and apply it to only part of the table if you want.

- A *list style* defines the type of bullets or the numbering scheme used in a list. You can add a list style to an existing paragraph style or table style so that the layout and formatting remain consistent in your document.

Wizards

Wizards really live up to their name! They use the templates and styles you have, but they hide from your view the macros, fields, and whatever other tools they need, and simply step you painlessly through the creation of a document. You make choices and provide information, and Word's wizards work their magic behind the scenes, quietly taking care of all the details and allowing you to concentrate on the content.

You can't create your own wizards or modify existing wizards, and sometimes you might even find it easiest to complete your work without using a wizard. However, if you're working your way through a complex procedure or doing something you've never done before, and if there's a wizard available, *use it!* You'll find that a wizard reduces a difficult task to a few simple steps.

Direct Formatting

Although it makes sense to use styles whenever you can, sometimes it's quicker and easier to apply direct formatting to your document. Direct formatting means that you select what you want to format and then use the tools on the Formatting toolbar or those on the Format menu to apply the formatting you want to the selection. The main disadvantage of using direct formatting is that you're likely to introduce formatting inconsistencies into your document. Fortunately, Word provides several tools to help you inspect and modify any inconsistencies. These tools include a feature that automatically detects and marks formatting inconsistencies; a task pane that compares the formatting of selected text; and the Styles And Formatting task pane, in which you can quickly modify your formatting if necessary.

Formatting Your Document ⊕ NEW FEATURE

Word offers you many ways to format the content of your document. However, we think the easiest way to turn out a good-looking document is to create the content of the document first, without worrying about any formatting, and then to go back through the document using styles to apply the formatting you want.

Apply Preset Formatting

① After you've created your document based on the appropriate template, click the Styles And Formatting button.

A heading paragraph style ——

A phrase using a character style ——

Paragraphs using a list style ——

A table using a table style ——

② In your document, click in a paragraph or a table; or select a series of characters, a word, or a group of words to be formatted.

③ In the Styles And Formatting task pane, click the style you want to apply. If the style you want to use isn't listed, click All Styles in the Show list to see a long list of all the styles available from your template. Then locate and click the style or the formatting you want to use. Continue applying styles until you're happy with the look of the document.

Reapply Custom Formatting

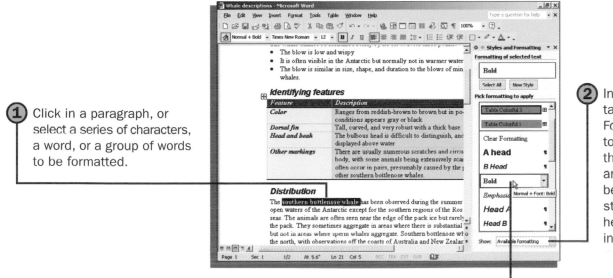

(1) Click in a paragraph, or select a series of characters, a word, or a group of words to be formatted.

(2) In the Styles And Formatting task pane, click Available Formatting in the Show list to see any custom formatting that has already been used, any styles that have already been used, and your custom styles and the common heading styles available in the template.

(3) Click the formatting you want to apply.

TRY THIS: You can "steal" font formatting from a paragraph style without applying the style to the entire paragraph. Type some text in a document, and then select a word in a sentence. Display the Styles And Formatting task pane, and click the Heading 1 style. Select another word in the document, and click the Heading 2 style. Continue experimenting with different styles. Finally, select the entire paragraph, and click Clear Formatting in the Styles And Formatting task pane to restore the paragraph to its original state.

SEE ALSO: For information about applying formatting that isn't part of an existing style, see "Custom-Formatting Your Text" on page 30 and "Custom-Formatting a Paragraph" on page 32.

Custom-Formatting Your Text

Sometimes, as creativity flows from brain to computer, you'll want to create a special look for certain characters or words in a paragraph. You might want to change the size of the characters or use a particularly attractive font. You might want a few words to be bolder than the rest of the text to emphasize their importance. Or perhaps you want to distinguish a quotation by placing it in italics. Word gives you the tools to quickly convey a feeling or set the tone of a message.

Change the Font or Font Size

(1) Select the text to be formatted.

(2) Click the down arrow at the right of the Font list on the Formatting toolbar.

(3) Scroll through the list to find the font you want to use. Click the font.

(4) Click the down arrow at the right of the Font Size list on the Formatting toolbar. Click the font size you want to use. If the size isn't listed, type the size you want in the box.

! TIP: In most cases, you'll want to use a font that displays the TrueType symbol (a double "T") at the left of its name. TrueType fonts look the same on the screen as when they're printed, so you can see an accurate representation of what your printed document will look like.

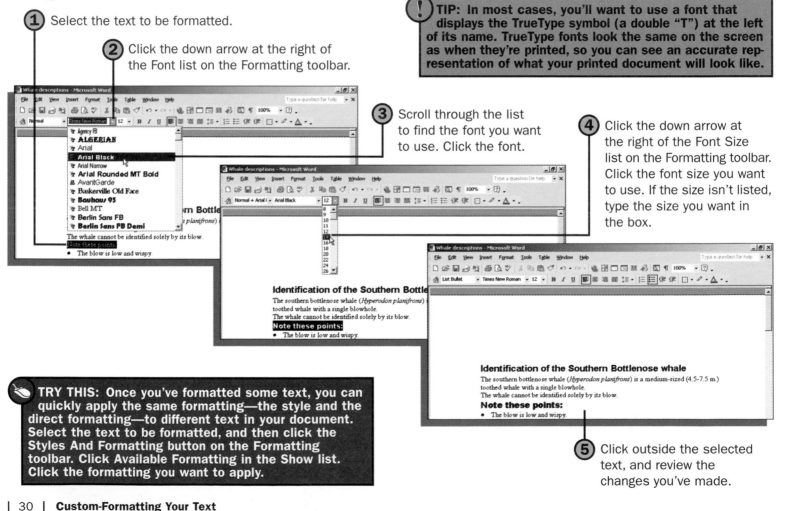

✍ TRY THIS: Once you've formatted some text, you can quickly apply the same formatting—the style and the direct formatting—to different text in your document. Select the text to be formatted, and then click the Styles And Formatting button on the Formatting toolbar. Click Available Formatting in the Show list. Click the formatting you want to apply.

(5) Click outside the selected text, and review the changes you've made.

Apply Emphasis

(1) Select the text to be formatted.

(2) Click an emphasis button on the Formatting toolbar. If you want to apply more than one characteristic (for example, both bold and italic), click the second emphasis button.

(3) If you don't see the emphasis you want to apply, choose Font from the Format menu.

SEE ALSO: For information about applying character formatting that you've already applied to other text in your document, see "Formatting Your Document" on page 28.

For information about creating your own styles, see "Creating Your Own Styles" on page 42.

(4) On the Font tab of the Font dialog box, select the check box or boxes to apply the emphasis or the effect you want.

(5) Click OK.

(6) Click outside the selected text, and review your formatting changes.

TIP: Word provides a few character styles, but most of them are intended for use with Web pages or are used for special purposes, such as page numbering. If you use a certain character style frequently, consider creating your own character style.

Custom-Formatting a Paragraph

Sometimes, when none of the existing paragraph styles is right for you, you'll create a custom style to achieve the look you want. However, if this is the only instance of the paragraph you'll ever need, you can design the formatting for that one-time-only paragraph.

Modify a Paragraph

(1) Select the entire paragraph you want to format.

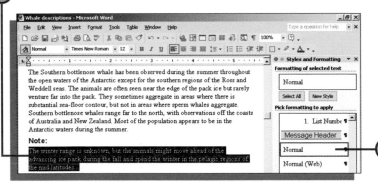

TIP: If you're not sure which screen elements are which, point to each item and wait for the ScreenTip to tell you the item's name. If a ScreenTip doesn't appear, choose Options from the Tools menu. On the View tab, select the ScreenTips check box, and click OK.

TIP: If the ruler isn't displayed, choose Ruler from the View menu.

(2) Use the Styles And Formatting task pane to apply a style that's as close as possible to the way you want the paragraph to look. Close the Styles And Formatting task pane.

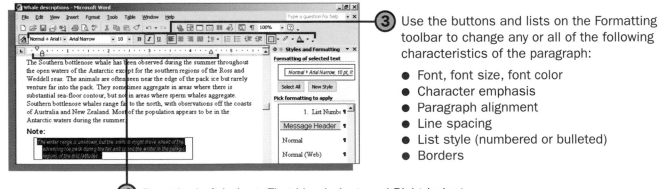

(3) Use the buttons and lists on the Formatting toolbar to change any or all of the following characteristics of the paragraph:

- Font, font size, font color
- Character emphasis
- Paragraph alignment
- Line spacing
- List style (numbered or bulleted)
- Borders

(4) Drag the Left Indent, First-Line Indent, and Right Indent markers to set the indents for the paragraph. Click outside the paragraph, and review your formatting.

Formatting a Document Automatically

If you have an unformatted or undeniably ugly-looking document—perhaps a hodgepodge of material you cut and pasted from several sources, or a file in plain text that someone sent you—you can tell Word to clean it up for you. Be aware, though, that although Word does a pretty good job, you'll still need to review the document, and you might want to tweak the formatting a bit to bring it up to your own high standards.

> **TIP:** To control what Word does when it formats a document, click the Options button in the AutoFormat dialog box. To apply a specific template to the document, click the AutoFormat And Review Each Change option before you click OK. Then, in the AutoFormat dialog box, click the Style Gallery button, and use the Style Gallery to choose the template you want.

AutoFormat a Document

(2) Choose AutoFormat from the Format menu.

(1) Open the document if it isn't already open.

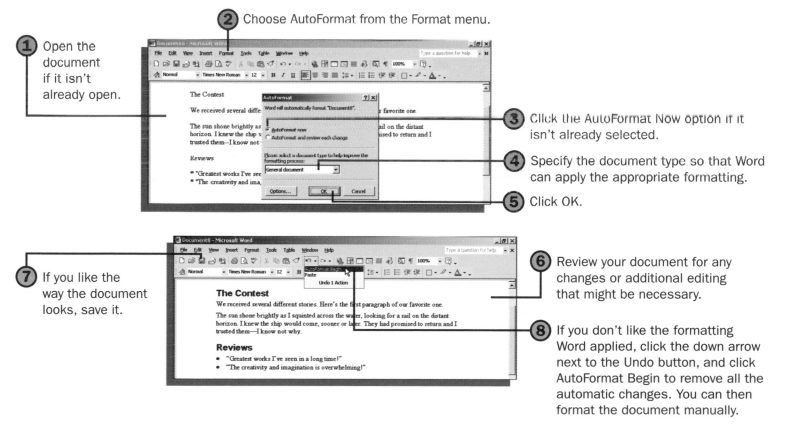

(3) Click the AutoFormat Now option if it isn't already selected.

(4) Specify the document type so that Word can apply the appropriate formatting.

(5) Click OK.

(6) Review your document for any changes or additional editing that might be necessary.

(7) If you like the way the document looks, save it.

(8) If you don't like the formatting Word applied, click the down arrow next to the Undo button, and click AutoFormat Begin to remove all the automatic changes. You can then format the document manually.

Setting Up the Page

When you create a document that will be printed, you need to tell Word how you want the page to be set up—what size paper you're using, whether the page will be printed in landscape or in portrait orientation, the size of the margins, and so on. If the document is going to be printed on both sides of the paper or is to be bound, you can tell Word to accommodate those design elements. A good template will usually set up the specifics for you, but you might need to readjust the settings a bit to get everything exactly right.

Set Up a Standard Page

(2) On the Paper tab, verify that the correct paper size is selected. If it isn't, specify the size of the paper you're using. If the paper size isn't listed, click Custom Size in the Paper Size list, and specify the dimensions of the paper.

(1) Choose Page Setup from the File menu to display the Page Setup dialog box.

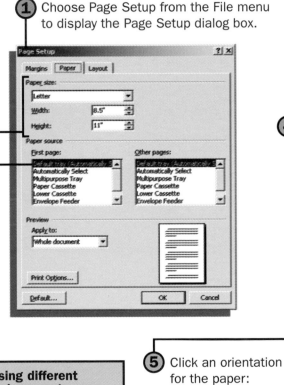

(3) If you're using a printer that has multiple paper trays, specify the tray for the first page (for example, the tray that contains the letterhead paper) and the tray for all subsequent pages.

TIP: The *gutter* is the extra space you add to the margin where the document is to be bound so that the text won't be hidden by the binding.

(4) On the Margins tab, specify the dimensions of the margins.

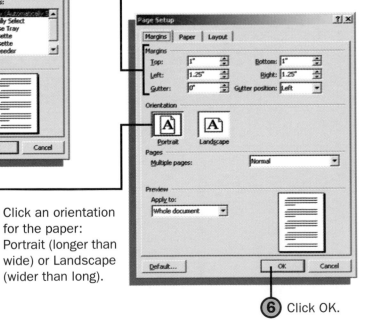

(5) Click an orientation for the paper: Portrait (longer than wide) or Landscape (wider than long).

SEE ALSO: For information about using different headers and footers in a two-sided document, see "Creating Variable Running Heads" on page 82.

For information about printing your document on both sides of a sheet of paper, see "Printing on Both Sides of the Paper" on page 94.

(6) Click OK.

Set Up for a Two-Sided Document

1 Choose Page Setup from the File menu to display the Page Setup dialog box.

2 On the Margins tab, click Mirror Margins in the Multiple Pages list.

4 Click OK.

3 Set the document's side margins using the Inside and Outside boxes. The Inside margin will be on the left side of odd-numbered (right-hand, or *recto*) pages and on the right side of even-numbered (left-hand, or *verso*) pages.

! **TIP:** You can apply a gutter to any document layout. However, you can specify the gutter location (left or top) only if you're printing a single page on a sheet of paper (that is, Normal is specified in the Multiple Pages list). In all other cases, Word uses the default location for the gutter for the type of layout you choose. Use the preview to see the placement of the gutter.

Set Up for a Bound Document

1 Choose Page Setup from the File menu to display the Page Setup dialog box.

2 On the Margins tab, specify a value for the gutter.

3 If the document is set up as Normal for Multiple Pages, specify whether the gutter (and therefore the binding) is to be on the left side or at the top of the page.

4 Click OK.

Formatting as You Compose

Some people like to create the content of a document first and then go back and format it. Others, however, prefer to do the formatting while they're creating the content. When you're typing, the easiest way to apply styles or direct formatting is to use special keyboard shortcuts so that you don't need to take your hands off the keyboard. Word can give you some extra help by automatically formatting some text for you, provided you've told it to do so.

Format Your Text

1 Start typing the content of your document. Make sure that nothing is selected and that the insertion point is in the paragraph you want to format. Press the keyboard shortcut for the style you want, or use the Styles And Formatting task pane to specify a style.

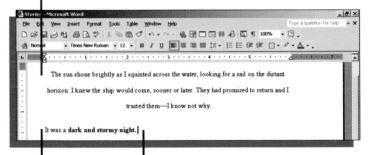

3 After you've finished typing the text to be formatted, press the same keyboard shortcut or click the same formatting tool to turn off the formatting.

2 To start using direct character formatting, use the keyboard shortcut to turn on the formatting you want, or click a tool on the Formatting toolbar. Then type your text.

Common Formatting Keyboard Shortcuts

Formatting	Keyboard Shortcut
Bold	Ctrl+B
Italic	Ctrl+I
Underline a single letter	Ctrl+U
Underline a whole word	Ctrl+Shift+W
Small capital letters	Ctrl+Shift+K
Superscript	Ctrl+Shift++ (plus sign)
Subscript	Ctrl+= (equal sign)
Single line spacing	Ctrl+1
1.5 line spacing	Ctrl+5
Double line spacing	Ctrl+2
Blank line before a paragraph	Ctrl+0 (zero)
Center a paragraph	Ctrl+E
Left-align a paragraph	Ctrl+L
Right-align a paragraph	Ctrl+R
Justify a paragraph	Ctrl+J
Heading 1 style	Alt+Ctrl+1
Heading 2 style	Alt+Ctrl+2
Heading 3 style	Alt+Ctrl+3
Normal style	Ctrl+Shift+S
List style	Ctrl+Shift+L

TIP: Word provides many more keyboard shortcuts than those listed here. Type keyboard shortcuts in the Ask A Question box, and press Enter. You can also define your own keyboard shortcut for a style when you create or modify a style.

TIP: You can use keyboard shortcuts to format existing text. To do so, select the text, and then use the keyboard shortcuts instead of the tools on the Formatting toolbar or the commands on the Format menu.

Set the Automatic Changes

(1) Choose AutoCorrect Options from the Tools menu to display the AutoCorrect dialog box.

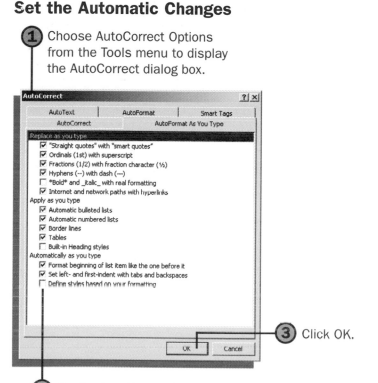

(3) Click OK.

(2) On the AutoFormat As You Type tab, select the check boxes for the AutoFormat options you want to use, and clear the check boxes for the options you don't want to use.

Control the Changes

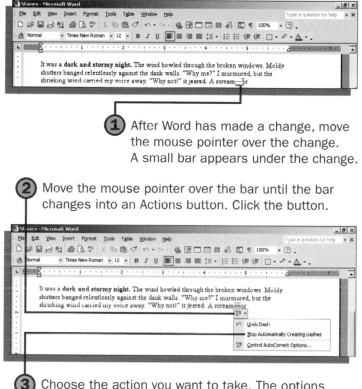

(1) After Word has made a change, move the mouse pointer over the change. A small bar appears under the change.

(2) Move the mouse pointer over the bar until the bar changes into an Actions button. Click the button.

(3) Choose the action you want to take. The options are different for different AutoFormat actions.

TRY THIS: Make sure that all the options on the AutoFormat As You Type tab are turned on. Type * _Fruit_. _Apples and Oranges_. **Press Enter, and type** Grain. Wheat and Rye. **Press Enter, turn off the Bullets button on the Formatting toolbar, type** ---- **and press Enter. Then type** +----+----+ **and press Enter. Now try to figure out which AutoFormat As You Type feature caused which effect!**

TIP: To find out what an option in a dialog box is used for, click the little Help button (the one with a question mark on it) at the top right of the dialog box. Then click the check box or button for the option in question to see a description of the option.

Customizing a Template

Word provides templates that are useful for many different purposes. However, they're generic templates that might not include every element you need. If you use a template frequently, you can create a more personalized document from the template—and save lots of time—by creating a new, customized template from the existing template.

✋ **CAUTION:** If you're sharing a template with other people, make sure no one else is using the template when you modify it and that any changes you make won't adversely affect the other users.

Open the Template

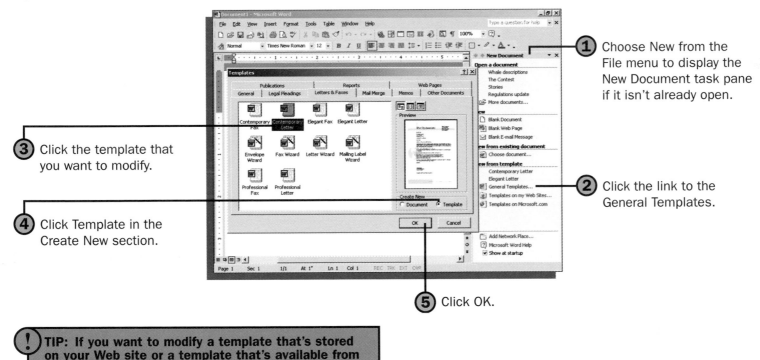

① Choose New from the File menu to display the New Document task pane if it isn't already open.

② Click the link to the General Templates.

③ Click the template that you want to modify.

④ Click Template in the Create New section.

⑤ Click OK.

❗ **TIP:** If you want to modify a template that's stored on your Web site or a template that's available from Microsoft.com, you can't open the template as a template. Instead, open it as a document, make your modifications, and then save it as a template.

Modify the Template

(1) Click the Save button on the Standard toolbar, type a unique and descriptive file name for your new template, and click Save. The template will be saved in your personal Templates folder and will appear on the General tab of the Templates dialog box.

! TIP: Most paragraph styles are based on the Normal style, so when you make any changes to the Normal style, those changes will also take place in the other styles.

(2) Replace the placeholder text with any text that will be common to all documents based on this new template.

(3) Add any new text or other page elements.

(4) Redefine or create your own paragraph styles and character styles.

(5) Save and close the template. Create a document based on the new template to confirm that the template is correct. (In the Templates dialog box, be sure to specify that you're creating a document and not a new template.)

! TIP: You can have the template appear on a new tab of the Templates dialog box. To do so, when you save the template, create a new folder in the Templates folder, using a unique name. If you want the template to appear on an existing tab, name the folder with the name of the existing tab. Save the template in the new folder.

✓ SEE ALSO: For information about starting a document based on a template, see "Composing Different Types of Documents" on page 24.

Designing a Template

Sometimes an existing template just doesn't do the job for you, no matter how much you modify it. If that's the case, you'll want to create a template from scratch. The easiest way to do this is to use an existing document and set it up as a template. If you don't have an existing document that incorporates all the special elements you need, create one, and then save and close it. Then review the entire document to determine whether the design really works. You'll be using a copy of the document as the basis for your template's design, so if you don't like the resulting template, you can simply delete it and then revise it, using the same document.

Create the Design

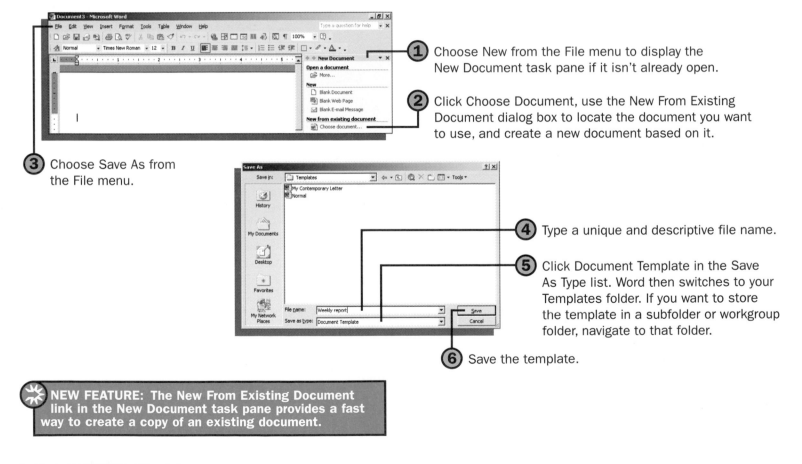

1. Choose New from the File menu to display the New Document task pane if it isn't already open.

2. Click Choose Document, use the New From Existing Document dialog box to locate the document you want to use, and create a new document based on it.

3. Choose Save As from the File menu.

4. Type a unique and descriptive file name.

5. Click Document Template in the Save As Type list. Word then switches to your Templates folder. If you want to store the template in a subfolder or workgroup folder, navigate to that folder.

6. Save the template.

NEW FEATURE: The New From Existing Document link in the New Document task pane provides a fast way to create a copy of an existing document.

Customize the Content

(1) Click the Show/Hide ¶ button on the Standard toolbar if it isn't already turned on.

(5) Click the Save button on the Standard toolbar.

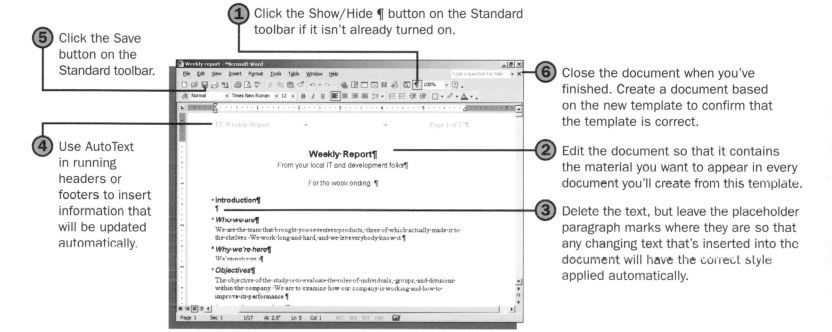

(6) Close the document when you've finished. Create a document based on the new template to confirm that the template is correct.

(4) Use AutoText in running headers or footers to insert information that will be updated automatically.

(2) Edit the document so that it contains the material you want to appear in every document you'll create from this template.

(3) Delete the text, but leave the placeholder paragraph marks where they are so that any changing text that's inserted into the document will have the correct style applied automatically.

TIP: To include the date and time and have them updated each time you create a new document, choose Date And Time from the Insert menu, click the format you want to use, and select the Update Automatically check box.

SEE ALSO: For information about working with headers and footers, see "Numbering Pages and Creating Running Heads" on page 81 and "Creating Variable Running Heads" on page 82.

For information about using AutoText, see "Inserting Frequently Used Text" on page 182.

CAUTION: A date or time that's set to update automatically is useful in a template but can sometimes cause problems in a completed document by updating when you don't want it to. To stop it from ever updating again, click the date or time, and press Ctrl+Shift+F9.

Creating Your Own Styles

Whether you're creating a new template or modifying an existing one, you might find that none of the existing styles is right for your document. If that's the case, you can create your own style and define all its elements in a few quick steps. If one style almost works, and you don't want to go through the effort of creating an entirely new style, you can modify that style.

Create a Style

(3) Click Paragraph to create a paragraph style, or click Character to create a character style.

(4) Click the style from which this style will be cloned.

(5) For a paragraph style, click the style that will automatically be applied to the paragraph that follows a paragraph with this style.

(6) Use the formatting tools to specify how this style differs from the style on which it's based.

> **SEE ALSO:** For information about creating and modifying table styles, see "Customizing the Look of a Table" on page 111.
>
> For information about creating and modifying list styles, see "Customizing a List" on page 120.
>
> For information about specifying a language in a style, see "Proofing in Another Language" on page 208.

(2) Type a name for the style you're going to create.

(1) Click the Styles And Formatting button on the Formatting toolbar to display the Styles And Formatting task pane if it isn't already open. Click New Style.

(9) Click OK.

(8) Select this check box to add the style to the document's template, or leave the check box cleared to create the style in the current document only.

(7) Click to apply additional formatting to the style. For example, you can include additional font specifications, add another language, or designate a keyboard shortcut to apply the style. For a paragraph style, you can specify the paragraph design in greater detail: set tabs; add borders; or use absolute positioning (frame), heading numbering, and so on.

Modify a Style in a Document

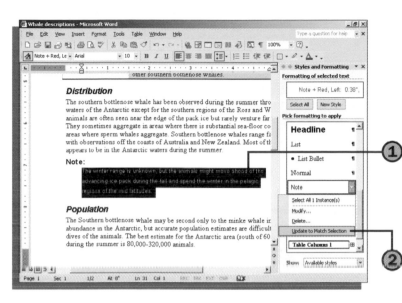

(1) Create a paragraph, or type some text based on the style you want to modify. Select the entire paragraph to modify a paragraph style, or select the text to modify a character style. Format the paragraph or text to look the way you want, using the direct formatting tools on the Formatting toolbar or those on the Format menu.

(2) Point to the style in the Styles And Formatting task pane. Click the down arrow that appears, and click Update To Match Selection.

Specify Style Changes

(1) Point to the style in the Styles And Formatting task pane. Click the down arrow that appears, and click Modify to display the Modify Style dialog box.

(2) Use the settings in the dialog box to make changes to the style. (You can't change the style *type*—that is, a paragraph style can't become a character style, and vice versa.) Be sure to select the Add To Template check box if you want to add the change to the document's template.

(3) Click OK.

Switching Templates

Every document is based on a template. When you start a plain, blank document, its design is based on the Normal template. Different templates, however, provide different styles and formatting, as well as tools such as AutoText and macros. If you have an existing document that might be improved if it were based on a different template, you can simply switch templates and update the styles to match those of the new template.

TRY THIS: To see a preview of the way your document will look with a different template, choose Theme from the Format menu. In the Theme dialog box, click the Style Gallery button. In the Style Gallery, with Document selected in the Preview section, click a template name to see how your document will look with that template's formatting. If you want to attach the template to the document, double-click the template name.

Switch Templates

(1) Choose Templates And Add-Ins from the Tools menu to display the Templates And Add-Ins dialog box.

(2) Click Attach.

(5) Select this check box so that the styles in your document will be updated to match the style definitions in the new template.

(3) Use the Attach Template dialog box to locate the template you want to use.

(4) Double-click the template.

(6) Click OK.

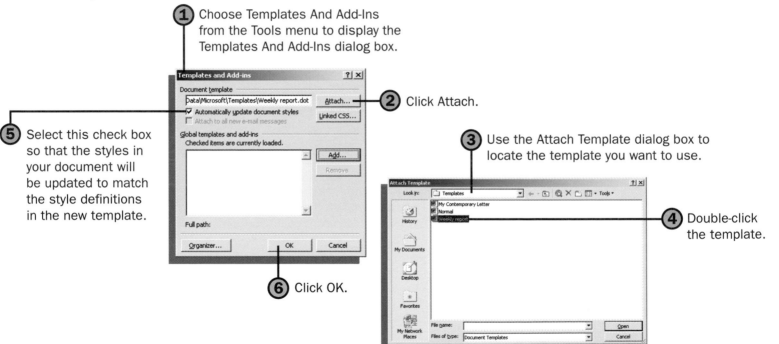

4 Writing a Letter

✳ NEW FEATURE

Despite the fact that so much of our daily correspondence is of the instant and virtual variety, written and read on screen via e-mail, there are still times when we need to write letters that get printed on actual paper, placed in actual envelopes, and sent by "snail mail." Using the tools that Microsoft Word 2002 provides, you can create well-designed, professional-looking business letters; letters to family and friends that reflect your individuality; and—quick as a wink with the mail merge feature—stacks of personalized form letters and envelopes.

So what do you need to know about those letter-writing tools? The quickest and easiest one is the Letter Wizard—you answer a few questions, and the wizard sets up a format that's ready for you to type your letter. If you want to make some changes, a click or two brings the wizard in with some alternative choices. To add a level of originality and sophistication to your letters—creating a watermark, for example, or designing your own letterhead—you can use templates and styles, which we've discussed throughout section 3, "Customizing Your Document," starting on page 23. And last but not least, there's the mail merge feature—a marvelous time-saver when you need to send the same information to a few individuals or to a large group of people. You provide a main document and a data source (names and addresses, for example), and Word combines, or *merges,* the information into a new, personalized document. You can create form letters, envelopes, mailing labels, awards, and so on, as well as incorporate data from Microsoft Excel and Microsoft Access into mail-merged documents.

Creating a Letter

When you want to write a letter, you can decide which of three different methods you prefer. You can format each line as you write it; you can use a letter template; or you can use Word's Letter Wizard. In most cases, we think the Letter Wizard is the easiest way to go. You make a few choices and fill in a few blanks, and Word creates a letter format that's ready and waiting for you to insert your message.

Start the Letter

 Start a new document. Point to Letters And Mailings on the Tools menu, and choose Letter Wizard from the submenu.

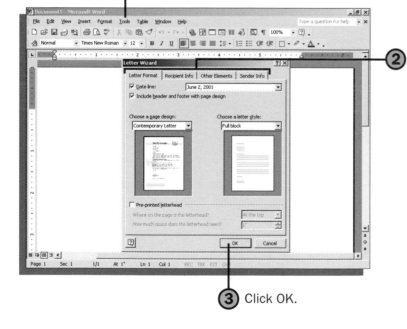

③ Click OK.

!TIP: Although the Letter Wizard is undeniably handy, there are times when it's just easier to insert the information directly into the letter. To create a letter without using the Letter Wizard, simply start a document based on a letter template.

SEE ALSO: For information about starting a document based on a specific template, see "Composing Different Types of Documents" on page 24.

!TIP: If the template you want to use isn't listed in the Page Design list (for example, if it's located on a Web site), start a document based on the template before you start the Letter Wizard.

② Complete the following items on each tab of the wizard:

- On the Letter Format tab, define the basic layout by choosing a page design (the template) and a letter style. The Page Design list should contain all your letter templates except for any that are stored in a remote location such as a Web site.

- On the Recipient Info tab, specify the recipient's name and address and an appropriate salutation style.

- On the Other Elements tab, select the check boxes for any additional elements you want to include, and enter the required specific information for each element.

- On the Sender Info tab, verify your return address, and specify the letter's closing elements.

TRY THIS: If the Office Assistant is installed and active on your computer, put it to work for you. Start a blank document, type Dear John (or the appropriate name), and press Enter. Click the Get Help option, and there's the Letter Wizard, ready and waiting for you.

Complete the Letter

1 Replace the placeholder text with your own text.

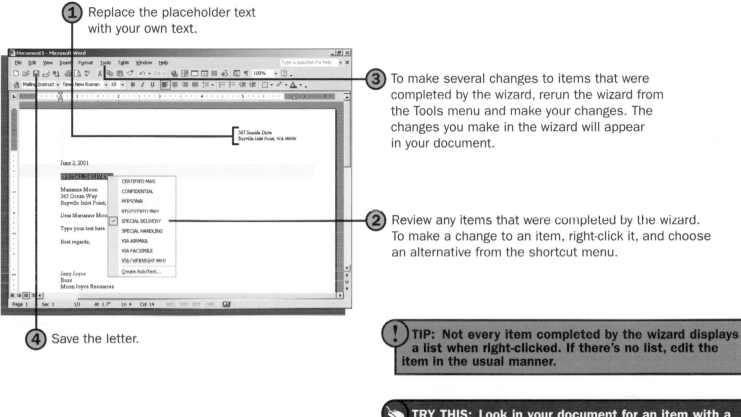

3 To make several changes to items that were completed by the wizard, rerun the wizard from the Tools menu and make your changes. The changes you make in the wizard will appear in your document.

2 Review any items that were completed by the wizard. To make a change to an item, right-click it, and choose an alternative from the shortcut menu.

4 Save the letter.

> **!** **TIP:** Not every item completed by the wizard displays a list when right-clicked. If there's no list, edit the item in the usual manner.

> **!** **TIP:** Many of the items inserted by the wizard are *fields*. A field usually becomes shaded when you click inside it, letting you know that it acts differently from your normal text.

> **TRY THIS:** Look in your document for an item with a purplish-red dotted underline, which indicates a smart tag. Point to the item, and then click the Smart Tag Actions button that appears to see what options you have. A smart tag contains information relevant to the type of text it's associated with.

Creating Your Own Letterhead

Instead of using preprinted letterhead stationery, you can create your own letterhead in your template, and the letterhead will be printed on the first page of your document whenever you use that template. By placing the letterhead in the first-page header, you won't need to worry about margins, the position of the first paragraph, and so on.

Create a First-Page Header

1 Create a new template based on a letter template or on an existing letter document. Edit the new template so that it contains only the elements you want.

2 Choose Page Setup from the File menu, and click the Layout tab.

3 Select this check box.

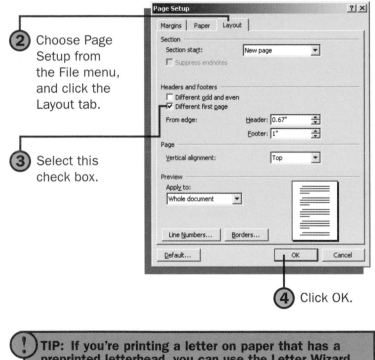

4 Click OK.

Create a Letterhead

1 Choose Header And Footer from the View menu.

2 Create your letterhead, using paragraph and font formatting.

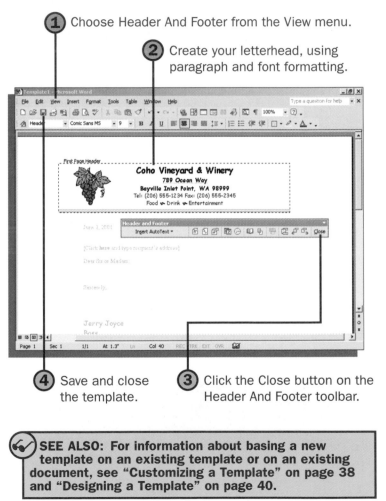

4 Save and close the template.

3 Click the Close button on the Header And Footer toolbar.

> **TIP:** If you're printing a letter on paper that has a preprinted letterhead, you can use the Letter Wizard to specify the size and location of the letterhead so that the text of your letter doesn't print on top of the letterhead. Some custom templates can also be designed to allow space for the letterhead.

> **SEE ALSO:** For information about basing a new template on an existing template or on an existing document, see "Customizing a Template" on page 38 and "Designing a Template" on page 40.

Designing for Letterhead Stationery

If you use paper with a preprinted letterhead for the first page of your letter, you can set up a template that not only allows the correct amount of blank space for the letterhead but starts the printing of subsequent pages at the top of the page. If your printer has more than one paper tray, you can specify that the letterhead paper is to be used only for the first page of the letter.

Design the Template

1. Determine how much space the letterhead requires. On a piece of letterhead paper, measure the distance from the top of the page to where you want the top of the first paragraph to start.

2. Open the letter template or create a new template based on a letter template. Name and save the template.

8. Right-click in the first paragraph of the template, and choose Paragraph from the shortcut menu.

3. Choose Page Setup from the File menu, and click the Paper tab.

6. On the Margins tab, specify the size of the top margin.

4. Specify the source of your letterhead paper.

5. Specify the source of your standard paper.

7. Click OK.

9. In the Before box, enter the space required for the letterhead. This value is determined by subtracting the size of the top margin from the space you measured on the letterhead paper. If the Before box uses *pt* (points) for the measurement unit, and if your measurement is in inches or centimeters, replace the *pt* with *in* for inches or *cm* for centimeters.

10. Click OK, and save and close your template.

Adding a Watermark ⊕ NEW FEATURE

A *watermark* is a picture or some text (a company logo, for example) that sits "behind" the main text. It appears on every printed page as if it were part of the paper. You can create a picture watermark or a text watermark, but you can't have both on the same page.

TIP: To have the same watermark appear in every document that you create using a particular template, create the watermark in that template.

Create a Text Watermark

TIP: To remove a watermark from a document, open the Printed Watermark dialog box and click the No Watermark option.

(1) Point to Background on the Format menu, and choose Printed Watermark from the submenu to display the Printed Watermark dialog box.

(2) Click the Text Watermark option.

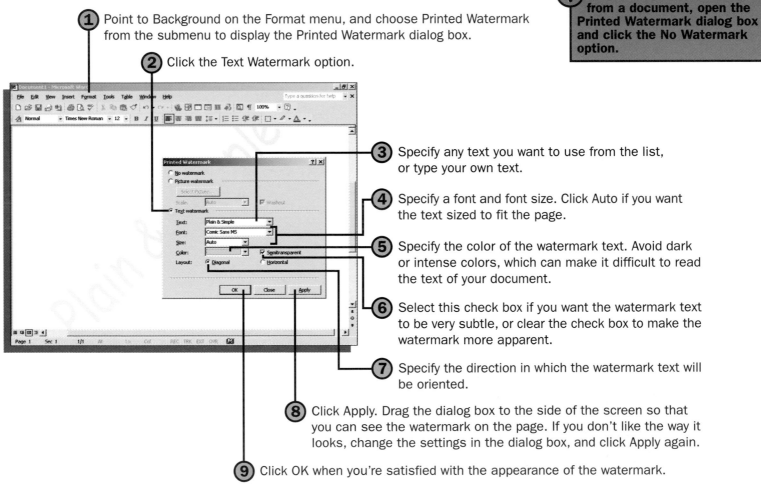

(3) Specify any text you want to use from the list, or type your own text.

(4) Specify a font and font size. Click Auto if you want the text sized to fit the page.

(5) Specify the color of the watermark text. Avoid dark or intense colors, which can make it difficult to read the text of your document.

(6) Select this check box if you want the watermark text to be very subtle, or clear the check box to make the watermark more apparent.

(7) Specify the direction in which the watermark text will be oriented.

(8) Click Apply. Drag the dialog box to the side of the screen so that you can see the watermark on the page. If you don't like the way it looks, change the settings in the dialog box, and click Apply again.

(9) Click OK when you're satisfied with the appearance of the watermark.

Create a Picture Watermark

1 Point to Background on the Format menu, and choose Printed Watermark from the submenu to display the Printed Watermark dialog box.

2 Click the Picture Watermark option.

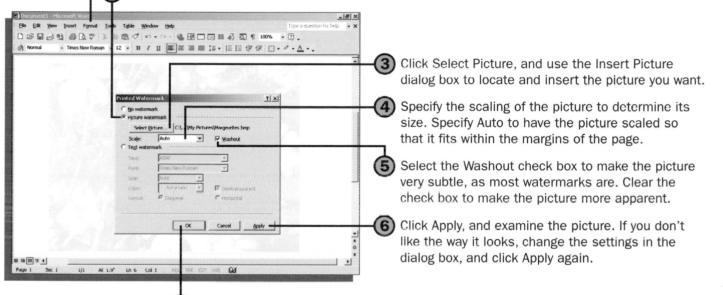

3 Click Select Picture, and use the Insert Picture dialog box to locate and insert the picture you want.

4 Specify the scaling of the picture to determine its size. Specify Auto to have the picture scaled so that it fits within the margins of the page.

5 Select the Washout check box to make the picture very subtle, as most watermarks are. Clear the check box to make the picture more apparent.

6 Click Apply, and examine the picture. If you don't like the way it looks, change the settings in the dialog box, and click Apply again.

7 Click OK when you're satisfied with the appearance of the watermark. Now add some text to the document to see whether you like the way the watermark looks behind the text. If necessary, open the Printed Watermark dialog box again, and adjust the settings.

> **TIP:** A watermark is used for printed documents only. All the other options on the Background submenu are for formatting the background of online documents and are visible only when Word is set to Web Layout view.

> **SEE ALSO:** For information about using the background settings for online documents, see "Creating an Online Document" on page 158.

> **TRY THIS:** Insert a picture watermark, and close the dialog box. Choose Header And Footer from the View menu. Click the picture, and use the Picture toolbar to modify the picture any way you want. Drag the sizing handles (the little squares that appear around a picture when you click it) to change the picture's size. Click Close on the Header And Footer toolbar when you've finished.

Printing an Envelope

When you've taken the time and trouble to create a professional-looking letter or other document, you don't want to ruin the good impression with a handwritten envelope! Word makes it easy for you to create crisp, businesslike printed envelopes. You can easily include your return address, and, in the United States, you can add electronic postage and a postal bar code. If you already have the mailing address in your letter, Word usually detects it and copies it to the Envelopes And Labels dialog box. You can also type the address directly in the dialog box.

Add the Address

1 Point to Letters And Mailings on the Tools menu, and choose Envelopes And Labels from the submenu to display the Envelopes And Labels dialog box.

2 If a delivery address is displayed on the Envelopes tab, verify that it's correct.

3 If no delivery address is shown, or if you want to use a different address, type the address. If the address is in your Microsoft Outlook Contacts list, click the Insert Address button.

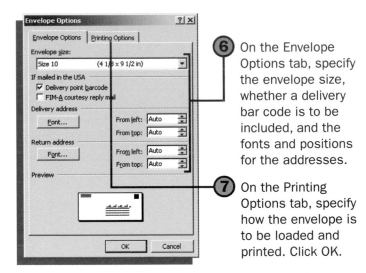

6 On the Envelope Options tab, specify the envelope size, whether a delivery bar code is to be included, and the fonts and positions for the addresses.

7 On the Printing Options tab, specify how the envelope is to be loaded and printed. Click OK.

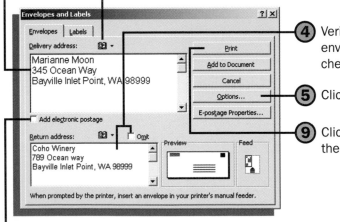

4 Verify that the return address is correct. If you're using an envelope with a preprinted return address, select the Omit check box so that the return address won't be printed.

5 Click Options.

9 Click to print the envelope.

> **!** **TIP:** Your return address is based on the user information Word has stored for you. To review this information, choose Options from the Tools menu, click the User Information tab, and change the information. If you want to change only the return address, edit it in the Envelopes And Labels dialog box, and Word will make the change for you in the user information.

8 If you have Electronic Postage (E-Postage) software installed, select this check box to use electronic postage. Click the E-Postage Properties button to make changes to your e-postage setup.

Printing a Mailing Label

Whether you need to print a single mailing label or a full page of mailing labels, Word has a tool that takes care of most of the details for you. All you need to do is specify the type of label you're using, the address, and how you want the labels printed. Word does the rest for you.

> **SEE ALSO:** For information about mail merge, see "Mail Merge: The Power and the Pain" on pages 54–55 and "Printing Envelopes from a Mailing List" on page 58.

Print a Label

(1) Make a note of the manufacturer and design number of the labels you'll be using. If you're going to print only one label, figure out which label on the sheet you're going to use. Later you'll need to specify the label by row (the horizontal line of labels) and by column (the vertical line of labels). Insert the sheet of labels into your printer (usually in the manual feed tray, if there is one).

(7) Select this check box to add a delivery bar code to the address. Not all labels have room for a bar code, so this option might not be available.

(6) Click the appropriate option to print a whole page of identical labels or only one label on the sheet of labels. If you want to print only one label, specify the label by row and column.

(2) Point to Letters And Mailings on the Tools menu, and choose Envelopes And Labels from the submenu to display the Envelopes And Labels dialog box. Click the Labels tab.

(3) Use the proposed address, type a new one, or click the Address Book button to insert an address from your Outlook Contacts list. To insert your return address, select the Use Return Address check box.

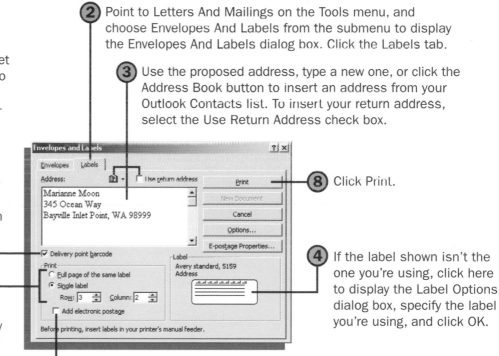

(8) Click Print.

(4) If the label shown isn't the one you're using, click here to display the Label Options dialog box, specify the label you're using, and click OK.

(5) Select this check box if you have electronic-postage software installed and want to use electronic postage on the label.

> **TIP:** If you need to print many different mailing labels, consider using the mail merge feature.

Mail Merge: The Power and the Pain

Mail merge is a tool that combines two different parts into a sleek and well-crafted whole—a series of identical printed documents (form letters, for example) with the appropriate information (individual names and addresses) inserted automatically into each document. The two parts are a *master document* and a *data source.* The master document is the template (although not a template in the Word-document sense) that lays out your document and contains text or other items that never change. The master document also contains instructions to insert data from a data source into each document. The data source is a uniform collection of information from one of a number of sources.

Mail merge is an almost unbelievable time-saver once you've set it up, and its power can be awesome. But—and here's the rub—you must be willing to deal with the complexities of *fields* and *conditional expressions.* The good news is that the mail merge feature is extremely *scalable*—that is, it's easy to do a simple, basic mail merge, but the process becomes increasingly demanding as your mail merge becomes more complex. If, for example, you simply want to address a stack of envelopes to people whose addresses are contained in a Word table, an Excel worksheet, or your Outlook Contacts list, you can just jump in and do it with little preparation and a great likelihood of success.

If you want to go beyond the basics—for example, printing letters and envelopes that are grouped by a specific city or postal code—you'll need to venture into a bit of data management and selective merging. And if you want to get even more deeply involved—using conditional content, for example, whereby certain text is included only when some data value meets or exceeds a certain threshold—you'll find yourself wandering around Word's fields. Once you get involved in complex mail merges, you'll need to exercise caution by conducting some testing of your setup. You'll want to make sure there's

no major error that will cause you to toss out all those printed letters or envelopes, or, even worse, send them out only to discover too late that the merge made a horrible mess of your intentions.

Managing the Data

In many types of mail merge there's no need for you to manipulate the data—you simply specify the data source and create the merged documents from the existing data. In other situations, however, you'll want either to sort the data according to a certain parameter (ZIP code or other postal code, for example) or exclude data that doesn't meet specific criteria (someone who didn't contribute enough money, for example).

Word can use data from many different sources. For some types of data, it's often easiest to modify the data in its original program and then do a simple mail merge in Word without worrying about data manipulation. For example, if you're using a list of addresses in Excel and you want to print envelopes grouped by city, you can sort the data by city in Excel. Or if you want to send a message to only the top contributors, and all your data is in an Access database, you can run a query in Access and use the results of the query for your mail merge.

However, Word provides data-manipulation tools, and these are especially useful for data from sources that you can't manipulate. When you specify a data source in the Mail Merge Wizard, you can decide (in Word, rather than in the source program) which data fields are to be used, and, by sorting the data by one or more of the data fields, you can also decide how the data records are to be grouped. For example, you might want to sort all the data first by city and then by ZIP code or other postal code so that the final documents will already be sorted for you when you print them. Another way to manipulate the data is to *filter* it—that is, specifying criteria that must be met in order for the data to be included. For example, you could set the criteria to send a letter only to contributors who live in a specific city and whose contributions exceed a certain amount of money. If you're using data from an Outlook Contacts list or from a large database used for many purposes, you'll find these features particularly useful.

Setting Conditional Content

One of the real powers of mail merge is the ability it gives you to tailor the content of a document based on some data stored in your mailing list. For example, you might offer a tour of your company to individuals who have invested a large amount of money in the company, and offer only a free brochure to the small investors. If you have an entry in your data file for the level of investment, you can use that data to control the content of your document.

Conditional content is controlled by using the IF Word field. To use this field, you place it in your document where you want the conditional text to appear by clicking the Insert Word Field button on the Mail Merge toolbar, and then clicking If...Then...Else in the list that appears. In the Insert Word Field: IF dialog box, you specify the data field that lists the value to be tested (for example, amount of investment), the comparison (for example, Greater Than Or Equal To), and the value (for example, 5000). Then you insert the text to be used if the comparison is true ("Please call to arrange a tour.") and the text to be used if the comparison is not true ("Please call to receive your full-color brochure.").

It's More than Letters

The Mail Merge feature can do more than create form letters and address envelopes. By using the buttons on the Mail Merge toolbar, you can send your merged documents by e-mail or as faxes. You can create almost any type of document by using a specific template or creating a design from scratch.

All Word needs is a data document with some data fields in it. With mail merge, you can create mailing labels and address books, awards and parts lists, different versions of exams, and catalogs designed for specific geographical areas or demographic populations. The uses for mail merge are limited only by your imagination, your willingness to experiment with different data fields and Word fields, and your decision as to whether mail merge would be faster than manually creating individual documents.

The Pain of Mail Merge

Mail merge is certainly powerful, but it's also a bit tricky. The Mail Merge task pane, and the specially designed tasks it contains—creating letters or envelopes, for example—simplifies the process. However, any inconsistencies or errors in the data and any typographic or layout errors in the master document can produce some very surprising results. Fortunately, the Mail Merge Wizard and the tools on the Mail Merge toolbar let you preview the results of your mail merge on the screen; conduct a simulated merge, which reports any errors in the merge; or print a sampling of your documents for a visual check of the finished product.

If you do find a problem in a merge, carefully track down the source of the problem—is it a problem in the data source, in the master document, or in the way you sorted or filtered the data? Once you've determined the source of the problem, correct it, and then test the merge again. Don't assume, however, that the merge will have no further problems. Your fix might not have completely fixed the problem or might have caused a different problem. There could be other problems that you haven't found yet. Don't despair! Just be aware that setting up a mail merge that works correctly might take a while. Once you've perfected it, though, you'll be amazed by the speed with which you can accomplish your mailings.

Creating a Form Letter

"Mail merge"—a dreaded phrase in the world of word processing! Not only does it conjure up an image of piles of junk mail, but associated words such as "fields" and "conditional statements" add to the intimidation factor. However, with just a little effort—and a lot of help from Word—when you need to send nearly identical letters to numerous people, you can create your own mail-merged documents and personalized form letters.

> **! TIP:** Word provides several templates designed for creating form letters and other mail-merged documents. When you open one of these templates, the Mail Merge task pane opens, and you'll find some fields already inserted in your document.

Set Up Your Letter

(1) Create your letter as you would any other letter, leaving blank any parts of the letter you want to be completed with data from your mailing list. Save the letter.

(2) Point to Letters And Mailings on the Tools menu, and choose Mail Merge Wizard from the submenu to open the Mail Merge task pane.

(3) Complete the first two steps of the wizard, clicking Next to move to each new step. Make sure that Letters is selected as the document type and that you're using the current document as your starting document.

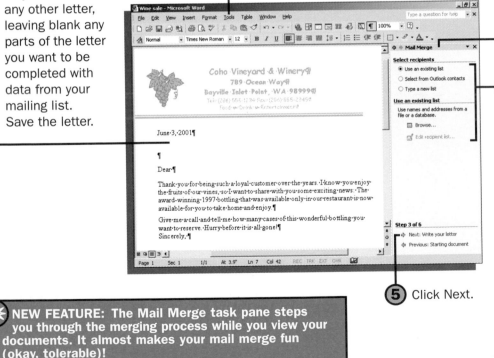

(4) Specify the type of data you want to use for your mailing list:

- Data that exists in a file Word can read. Click Browse to locate and specify the file. To see what type of data sources you can use, open the Files Of Type list in the Select Data Source dialog box, and review the list.

- Data from your Outlook Contacts list. Click Choose Contacts Folder to specify the folder, and review the data in that folder.

- Data you enter to create a new list. Click Create to start entering data.

(5) Click Next.

> **✹ NEW FEATURE:** The Mail Merge task pane steps you through the merging process while you view your documents. It almost makes your mail merge fun (okay, tolerable)!

Specify the Data to Be Merged

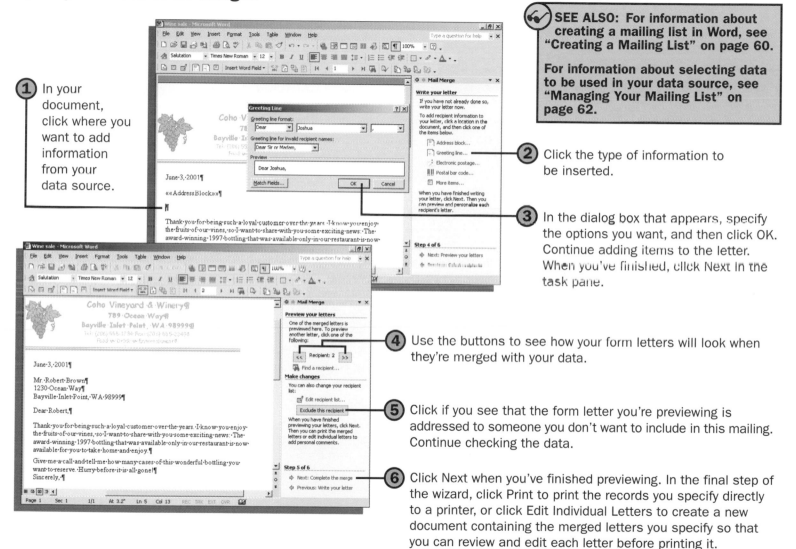

1 In your document, click where you want to add information from your data source.

SEE ALSO: For information about creating a mailing list in Word, see "Creating a Mailing List" on page 60.

For information about selecting data to be used in your data source, see "Managing Your Mailing List" on page 62.

2 Click the type of information to be inserted.

3 In the dialog box that appears, specify the options you want, and then click OK. Continue adding items to the letter. When you've finished, click Next in the task pane.

4 Use the buttons to see how your form letters will look when they're merged with your data.

5 Click if you see that the form letter you're previewing is addressed to someone you don't want to include in this mailing. Continue checking the data.

6 Click Next when you've finished previewing. In the final step of the wizard, click Print to print the records you specify directly to a printer, or click Edit Individual Letters to create a new document containing the merged letters you specify so that you can review and edit each letter before printing it.

Printing Envelopes from a Mailing List

When you have a stack of envelopes to be addressed, whether they're for a party or a corporate promotion, you can automate the process by using the mail merge feature to address and print the envelopes you need from your list of recipients.

Set Up the Envelope

1 Create and then save a new, blank document. Point to Letters And Mailings on the Tools menu, and choose Mail Merge Wizard from the submenu to open the Mail Merge task pane.

> **TIP:** If you chose Options from the Tools menu and entered your own address on the User Information tab of the Options dialog box, that address will appear as the return address on the envelope. If you're using envelopes with a preprinted return address, delete the return address from the letter in step 4 of the Mail Merge Wizard.

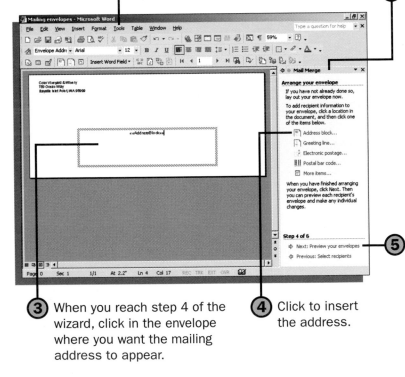

2 Complete steps 1 through 3 of the Mail Merge Wizard, clicking Next to move to each new step. In the wizard, make sure to

- Specify Envelopes as the document type.
- Specify whether to set up the open document for envelopes or to use an existing document that has been set up for a custom envelope design.
- Set the dimensions of the envelope, the fonts you want to use to print the return address and the mailing address, and the orientation of the envelope in your printer.
- Specify the source of your mailing list. Click Browse to locate the data file for an existing list, click Contacts Folder to specify the correct Contacts list, or click Create to enter data and create a new list.

3 When you reach step 4 of the wizard, click in the envelope where you want the mailing address to appear.

4 Click to insert the address.

5 If you want other items added to the envelope, click where you want each item located on the envelope, and then click the item. When you've finished, click Next.

Complete the Merge

① Review the envelope to make sure that it's set up the way you want it and that the address appears correctly.

TIP: After you've attached the mailing list to the document, it stays attached, so the next time you open the document, you'll be ready to execute your mail merge immediately.

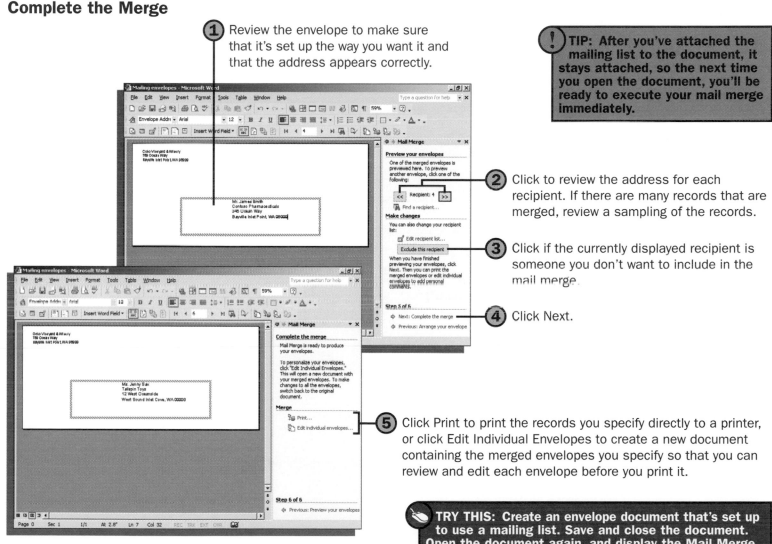

② Click to review the address for each recipient. If there are many records that are merged, review a sampling of the records.

③ Click if the currently displayed recipient is someone you don't want to include in the mail merge.

④ Click Next.

⑤ Click Print to print the records you specify directly to a printer, or click Edit Individual Envelopes to create a new document containing the merged envelopes you specify so that you can review and edit each envelope before you print it.

TRY THIS: Create an envelope document that's set up to use a mailing list. Save and close the document. Open the document again, and display the Mail Merge toolbar if it isn't already displayed. Use the toolbar to preview your envelopes, and then send the merged envelopes to a printer or to a new document.

Creating a Mailing List

If you want to create a mail merge for completing form letters, addressing envelopes, or conducting some other type of basic mail merge, you need a data document to use for the mailing list. If you don't already have the information in a file, you can easily create your own mailing list.

Set Up the List

> **NEW FEATURE:** Word stores the data you enter directly in a database format that provides considerable power for managing and sorting the data. (In previous versions of Word, the information was stored in a Word table.) You can edit the data file by using the tools in the Mail Merge Wizard or on the Mail Merge toolbar, or by opening the database in Access.

(1) Start creating your mail-merged document. Point to Letters And Mailings on the Tools menu, and choose Mail Merge Wizard from the submenu to open the Mail Merge task pane. Complete the first two steps of the wizard.

(2) Click the Type A New List option, and then click Create.

(5) Click to add a field.

(6) Type the name of a field you want to add, and click OK. Continue adding any fields you need.

(4) Select any field that you don't need to include in your list, and click Delete. Continue deleting any fields you don't need.

(3) Click to set up the fields the way you want them.

(8) Click OK when you've finished.

> **TIP:** You can still use a Word table to store your data. To do so, start a new document, create a table with the field headings in the top row, and then fill in the data for each record. When you save the document, verify that nothing but the table is contained in the document.

(7) To reorganize the list, select a field, and click either button to re-order the list.

Create Your List

(1) Click in the top field, and type the information. Press Tab to move to the next field, and enter that information. Continue through the form until you've entered all the information. You can leave some fields blank, but make sure that you've included information for the items that are necessary to complete your mail merge.

(2) Click to save the current record and start a new record. Complete the information in the data fields. Continue completing fields and clicking New Entry to start each new record until all your data has been entered.

SEE ALSO: For information about managing your data in the Mail Merge Recipients dialog box, see "Managing Your Mailing List" on page 62.

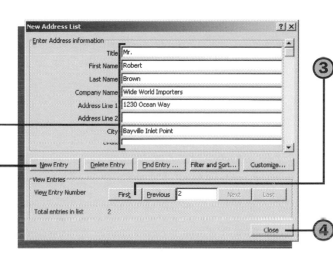

(3) To review your entries, click First, review the data in the first data record, and then click Next to see the next record. You can edit any of the data, or you can click the Delete Entry button to remove an entry.

(4) When you've finished, click Close. In the Save Address List dialog box, type a name for the file, and click Save.

(5) Use the Mail Merge Recipients dialog box to review the records and to sort or filter the files used in the mail merge. Click OK when you've finished, and complete the mail merge as you would any other mail merge.

> **TIP:** By default, Word stores your data documents in the My Data Sources folder. When you open a data source, Word always looks in the My Data Sources folder first. To avoid hunting through your folders, save your data file in the My Data Sources folder if possible. If you must store it in another location, consider placing a shortcut to the file in the My Data Sources folder.

Managing Your Mailing List

When you're using the Mail Merge Wizard to create a letter or to address envelopes, you can modify the data to group the information by similar items or to select which data records are included.

Manage the Data

(1) Start creating your mail-merged document. Point to Letters And Mailings on the Tools menu, and choose Mail Merge Wizard from the submenu to open the Mail Merge task pane. Complete the first two steps of the wizard. In step 3 of the wizard, after you've specified the source of your list of recipients, the Mail Merge Recipients dialog box appears.

(2) To remove a record from the merge, clear the check box for that record.

(3) To sort the records by a particular field, click the field's name. Click the field's name again to sort it in reverse order.

(4) To limit which records are included based on the contents of the field, click the down arrow next to the field's name, and specify the value that you want to use as the criterion to include a field.

(!) TIP: To edit the data in your list, click the Edit button in the Mail Merge Recipients dialog box. If the button is grayed and unavailable, update the data in the source program, and then click the Update button in the dialog box.

(5) To create your own query and set criteria to specify which records are included, click the down arrow next to any field name, and click Advanced to display the Filter And Sort dialog box.

(6) Use the Filter Records tab to create the conditional query. When you've finished, click OK.

(7) Click OK when you've finished, and then proceed through the Mail Merge Wizard to complete the mail merge.

(!) TIP: To quickly manage the data at any time, click the Mail Merge Recipients button on the Mail Merge toolbar.

5 Working with E-Mail and Faxes

The ability to communicate electronically is one of a computer's most used and most valued features. In fact, many of us find it difficult to remember a time when e-mail and faxes didn't exist!

In this section, we'll discuss the way Microsoft Word 2002 and Microsoft Outlook work together to enhance the power and flexibility of your e-mail. For example, you can format your e-mail messages with your favorite fonts and colors, you can design a signature that reflects your personality and that can be added automatically to your messages, you can choose or create your own e-mail stationery, and you can enclose files—or *attachments*—with your messages. But you don't *have* to send a document as an attachment—if you prefer, you can send the Word document itself simply by clicking a button that adds an e-mail header to the document. Just enter the recipient's address, add a few comments or an introductory message if you want, and quickly send the document on its way!

If you have faxing software installed on your computer, you can use Word to send faxes directly from your computer rather than using a separate fax machine. The Fax Wizard walks you step by step through the setup process, after which you use the faxing software to send the fax. And even if you don't have faxing software or hardware on your computer, you can use Word's templates or the Fax Wizard to create fax cover sheets to accompany the faxes you send from a fax machine.

Using Word for Your E-Mail Messages

If you're using Microsoft Outlook as your e-mail program,
you can use the power of Word to compose and read your e-mail
messages. Doing so allows you to use Word's invaluable spelling-
and grammar-checking features, the AutoCorrect and AutoFormat
options, and even Word's smart tags.

Configure Outlook

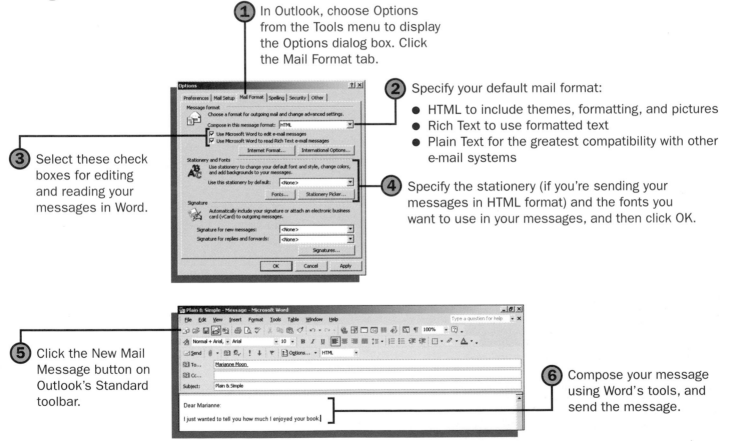

1 In Outlook, choose Options from the Tools menu to display the Options dialog box. Click the Mail Format tab.

2 Specify your default mail format:
- HTML to include themes, formatting, and pictures
- Rich Text to use formatted text
- Plain Text for the greatest compatibility with other e-mail systems

3 Select these check boxes for editing and reading your messages in Word.

4 Specify the stationery (if you're sending your messages in HTML format) and the fonts you want to use in your messages, and then click OK.

5 Click the New Mail Message button on Outlook's Standard toolbar.

6 Compose your message using Word's tools, and send the message.

Creating an E-Mail Message

If Outlook is set up on your computer, you don't need to switch from Word to Outlook to send a message. All you need to do is start an e-mail message in Word, complete it, and send it on its way. It's that simple!

Send a Message

CAUTION: Although you can compose an e-mail message in Word when Outlook isn't running, you can't send the message right away. When you click the Send button, the message is stored in the Outbox, and you can send it only when Outlook is running.

(1) Choose New from the File menu to display the New Document task pane if it isn't already open.

SEE ALSO: For information about sending an existing document by e-mail, see "Sending a Document as E-Mail" on page 68.

(2) Click to start a new mail message.

(5) Use the buttons on the toolbar to specify any items that you want to include with the message and to specify the formatting and settings for the message.

(3) Start typing the recipient's name. Word might complete the name for you from your Contacts list. If the name isn't correct, or if Word didn't complete the name for you, continue typing. To add another name, press the Right arrow key if the name is selected, type a comma or a semicolon, and start typing the next name. When you've added all the names, press Tab to move to the CC field, complete it, press Tab again, type a subject, and press Tab again to move to the body of your text.

(4) Type your message.

(6) Click to send the message.

Setting the Default Formatting for Your E-Mail Messages

When you use Word to compose your e-mail messages, you can format the way your messages look. Be aware, though, that no matter how gorgeous a message looks when you send it, it might not look the same when it's received! For that to happen, the recipient must have an e-mail program such as Outlook or Outlook Express that can display your formatting in all its glory.

> **TIP:** Outlook and Word communicate with each other, so when you set a theme, a font, or a signature in the E-Mail Options dialog box in Word, those same elements will be set in Outlook. If you modify any settings on the Mail Format tab of the Options dialog box in Outlook, those settings will be changed in Word.

Format the Message

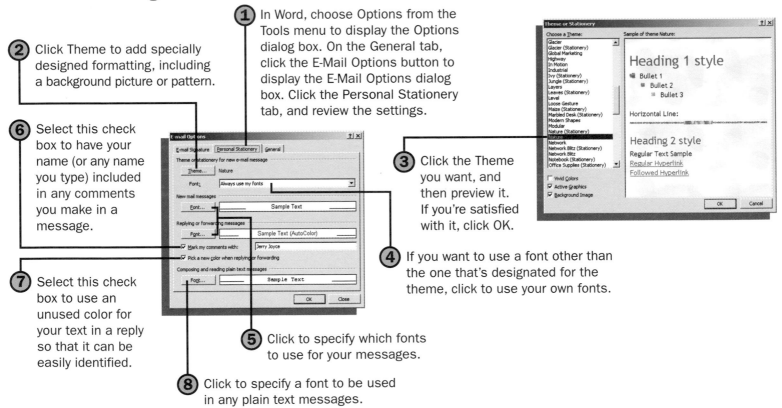

(1) In Word, choose Options from the Tools menu to display the Options dialog box. On the General tab, click the E-Mail Options button to display the E-Mail Options dialog box. Click the Personal Stationery tab, and review the settings.

(2) Click Theme to add specially designed formatting, including a background picture or pattern.

(3) Click the Theme you want, and then preview it. If you're satisfied with it, click OK.

(4) If you want to use a font other than the one that's designated for the theme, click to use your own fonts.

(5) Click to specify which fonts to use for your messages.

(6) Select this check box to have your name (or any name you type) included in any comments you make in a message.

(7) Select this check box to use an unused color for your text in a reply so that it can be easily identified.

(8) Click to specify a font to be used in any plain text messages.

Add Your Signature

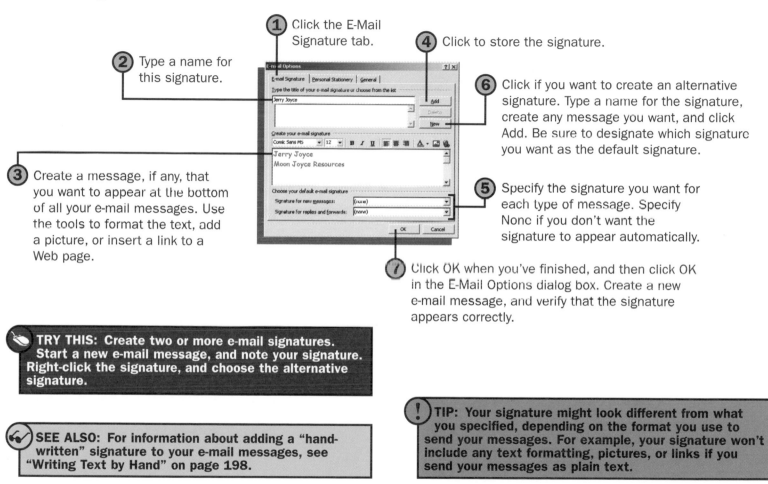

1 Click the E-Mail Signature tab.

2 Type a name for this signature.

4 Click to store the signature.

6 Click if you want to create an alternative signature. Type a name for the signature, create any message you want, and click Add. Be sure to designate which signature you want as the default signature.

3 Create a message, if any, that you want to appear at the bottom of all your e-mail messages. Use the tools to format the text, add a picture, or insert a link to a Web page.

5 Specify the signature you want for each type of message. Specify None if you don't want the signature to appear automatically.

7 Click OK when you've finished, and then click OK in the E-Mail Options dialog box. Create a new e-mail message, and verify that the signature appears correctly.

> **TRY THIS:** Create two or more e-mail signatures. Start a new e-mail message, and note your signature. Right-click the signature, and choose the alternative signature.

> **SEE ALSO:** For information about adding a "handwritten" signature to your e-mail messages, see "Writing Text by Hand" on page 198.

> **TIP:** Your signature might look different from what you specified, depending on the format you use to send your messages. For example, your signature won't include any text formatting, pictures, or links if you send your messages as plain text.

Sending a Document as E-Mail

If there's a document that you want to send out to friends or coworkers, you can easily transform it into a formatted e-mail message. To do this, you add an e-mail header to the document and then send a copy of the entire document as the body of the message. You can also add a brief introduction to the document if you want.

TIP: When you send a document as an e-mail message, the mailing information is saved with the document. The next time you open the document and click the E-Mail button, the addressing information is still there, along with the date and time the message was sent. It's a great way to keep track of when and to whom you sent certain documents.

Send the Text

1 In Word, create and save a document, or open an existing document.

2 Click the E-Mail button to display the e-mail header.

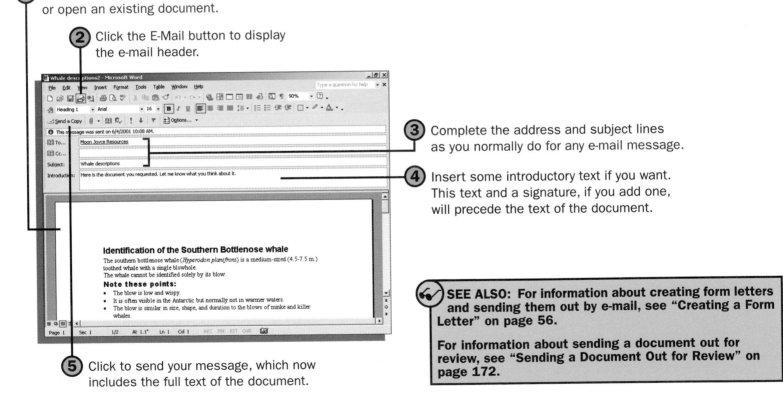

3 Complete the address and subject lines as you normally do for any e-mail message.

4 Insert some introductory text if you want. This text and a signature, if you add one, will precede the text of the document.

SEE ALSO: For information about creating form letters and sending them out by e-mail, see "Creating a Form Letter" on page 56.

For information about sending a document out for review, see "Sending a Document Out for Review" on page 172.

5 Click to send your message, which now includes the full text of the document.

Sending a Document File by E-Mail

If you want to make sure that the content and formatting of a Word document are preserved when you send the document out by e-mail, you can attach a copy of the document as a Word file. That way, regardless of the e-mail program the recipient is using, he or she should be able to save the attachment and receive your document with all its elements intact.

> **TIP:** If you see Mail Recipient (As Text) instead of Mail Recipient (As Attachment) on the Send To submenu of the File menu, choose Options from the Tools menu, and, on the General tab, select the Mail As Attachment check box, and click OK. (If the check box is cleared, the text of the document will be copied and inserted into the mail message.)

Send the File

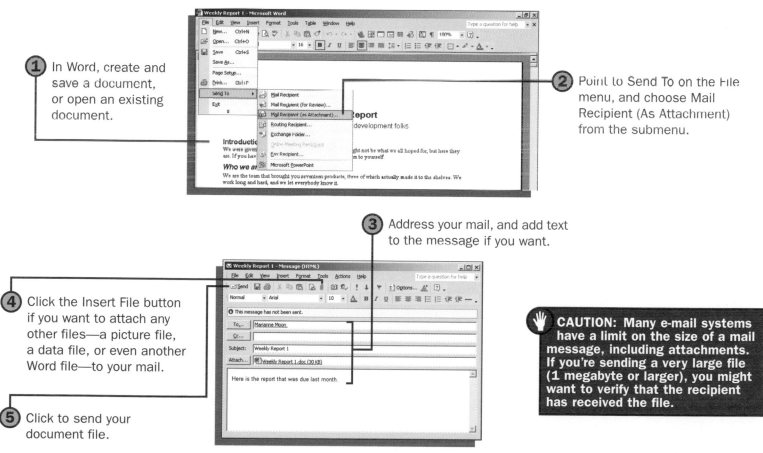

1 In Word, create and save a document, or open an existing document.

2 Point to Send To on the File menu, and choose Mail Recipient (As Attachment) from the submenu.

3 Address your mail, and add text to the message if you want.

4 Click the Insert File button if you want to attach any other files—a picture file, a data file, or even another Word file—to your mail.

5 Click to send your document file.

> **CAUTION:** Many e-mail systems have a limit on the size of a mail message, including attachments. If you're sending a very large file (1 megabyte or larger), you might want to verify that the recipient has received the file.

Controlling Hidden Content in E-Mail Messages

When you use Word to compose your e-mail messages, Word might add some hidden content so that the messages can be easily viewed and edited. Although these enhancements are useful, they can increase the size of your messages. You can control the hidden content of your messages, depending on how your messages are used.

TIP: If you exclude the enhancements from your messages but occasionally have to send a message that needs the extra information, create the message as a Word document and then send the document as an attachment in your message.

Set the Options

(2) Select this check box to reduce the size of your e-mail messages if you're sending your mail in HTML format and you don't expect your messages to be substantially altered by the recipients. However, if some of your HTML messages are likely to be substantially edited in Microsoft Office programs by the recipients, clear this check box.

(1) In Word, choose Options from the Tools menu to display the Options dialog box. On the General tab, click the E-Mail Options button to display the E-Mail Options dialog box. Click the General tab if it isn't already displayed.

(3) Select this check box to reduce the size of your e-mail messages only if all the recipients are using a mail program that supports Cascading Style Sheets. If the recipients don't use Outlook and Word, there's a good chance they'll have problems with your messages if this check box is selected.

E-mail Options

E-mail Signature | Personal Stationery | General

HTML options

☐ Filter HTML before sending
Reduce the size of the message by removing formatting information used by some Office features. Filtering does not change text or basic formatting.

☐ Rely on CSS for font formatting
Remove extra font formatting information from the message. The message will display differently in email programs that do not support Cascading Style Sheets.

☑ Save smart tags in e-mail
Save smart tags in the e-mail message so they can be used by the recipient.

OK   Cancel

(4) Select this check box if all your recipients are using Outlook 2002 and you want them to have access to all the smart tags in your messages.

(5) Click OK when you've finished, and then click OK to close the Options dialog box.

TIP: When you send a message as plain text, no extra information is included in the document, so the E-Mail Options settings don't affect the content of the message.

SEE ALSO: For information about sending a document as an attachment, see "Sending a Document File by E-Mail" on page 69.

Sending a Document as a Fax

If you have faxing hardware and software installed on your computer or available over your network, you should be able to fax a document directly from Word. Before you try this, however, make sure your faxing program works correctly, using the software that came with it or using the faxing tools built into your operating system. If your computer doesn't have faxing capabilities, you can still use the Fax Wizard to create a cover sheet to accompany the document when you send it from a separate fax machine.

Send a Fax

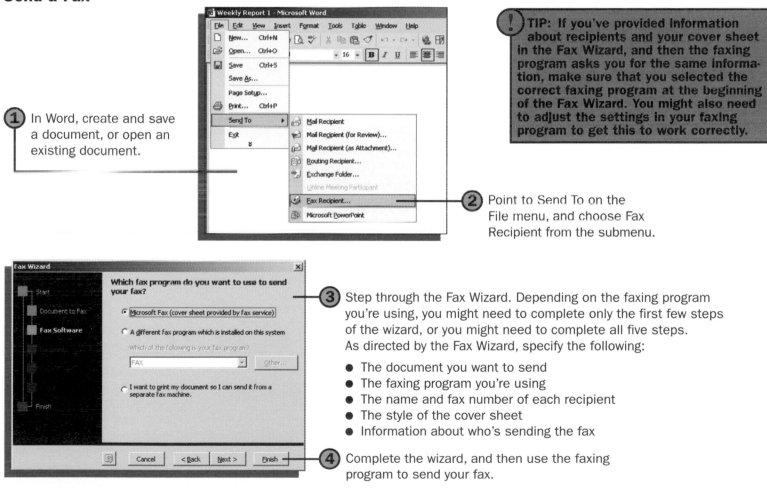

1 In Word, create and save a document, or open an existing document.

> **TIP:** If you've provided information about recipients and your cover sheet in the Fax Wizard, and then the faxing program asks you for the same information, make sure that you selected the correct faxing program at the beginning of the Fax Wizard. You might also need to adjust the settings in your faxing program to get this to work correctly.

2 Point to Send To on the File menu, and choose Fax Recipient from the submenu.

3 Step through the Fax Wizard. Depending on the faxing program you're using, you might need to complete only the first few steps of the wizard, or you might need to complete all five steps. As directed by the Fax Wizard, specify the following:

- The document you want to send
- The faxing program you're using
- The name and fax number of each recipient
- The style of the cover sheet
- Information about who's sending the fax

4 Complete the wizard, and then use the faxing program to send your fax.

Creating a Fax Cover Sheet

Word includes several templates for creating fax cover (or transmittal) sheets. After you've created the cover sheet document, you can print it out to be sent on a separate fax machine or, if your computer is set up to send faxes directly, from your computer.

> **TIP: Microsoft Fax Service is often configured so that you can't use your own cover sheet. By creating a cover sheet in Word and sending it as a normal document, you can bypass this restriction.**

Create a Cover Sheet

1 Choose New from the File menu to display the New Document task pane if it isn't already open. Click General Templates to display the Templates dialog box. On the Letters & Faxes tab, double-click the fax cover sheet you want.

3 Choose Print from the File menu.

2 Replace the placeholder text with the information you want to include.

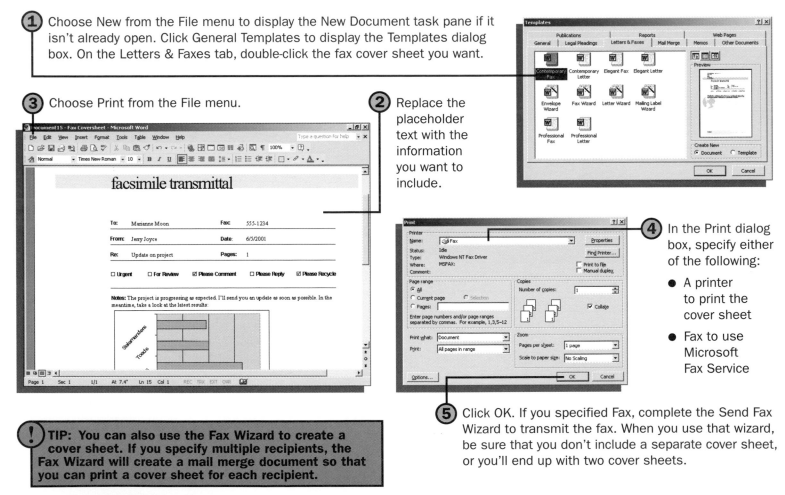

4 In the Print dialog box, specify either of the following:

- A printer to print the cover sheet
- Fax to use Microsoft Fax Service

5 Click OK. If you specified Fax, complete the Send Fax Wizard to transmit the fax. When you use that wizard, be sure that you don't include a separate cover sheet, or you'll end up with two cover sheets.

> **TIP: You can also use the Fax Wizard to create a cover sheet. If you specify multiple recipients, the Fax Wizard will create a mail merge document so that you can print a cover sheet for each recipient.**

6 Creating a Long Document

What's the difference between creating a long document and creating a short document? Well, a long document can give you a much bigger headache, for one thing! If your long document is simply pages and pages of text with absolutely nothing else—no headings, no graphics, no sections—the only difference between it and a short document might be that you'd add page numbers. Many long documents, however, contain elements such as tables, graphics, several levels of headings, footnotes, and so on. When a document contains so many elements, it's important to organize those elements in a consistent manner so that your readers can understand how and where to find the information they need. Using the Styles And Formatting task pane, you can quickly apply styles to create a clearly understandable hierarchy of headings, and you can format body text, captions, and other elements to give your document a unified appearance. Microsoft Word 2002 can help you divide a long document into chapters or sections, add running heads, and number the pages. Word also provides many style choices for tables of contents and indexes, and walks you easily through the creation of either or both.

A long document involves a lot of planning and many revisions. Unexpected things happen: for example, the marketing people change the name of the product you're writing about. You're presenting your report at a big meeting in the morning. It'll take all night to make those changes. Don't panic! You won't have to work until the wee small hours, because Word can make the changes for you in just a few minutes. Using Word's powerful tools, your long-document headaches will be long gone!

Organizing with Styles

Paragraph styles do more than quickly apply formatting to paragraphs; they also assign an *outline level* to each paragraph in a document. Word uses these levels to understand how you're organizing the document—which paragraphs are headings, which are subheadings, and which are text. You can use Word's defined outline hierarchy, or you can create your own structure by defining the outline levels for your styles.

SEE ALSO: For information about creating styles, see "Creating Your Own Styles" on page 42.

For information about using Outline view to look at your heading hierarchy, see "Reorganizing a Document" on page 78.

For information about transferring styles between templates and documents, see "Transferring Styles, AutoText, and Macros" on page 238.

Create a Heading Hierarchy

1 Start Word and open your document if it isn't already open. Switch to Normal view.

2 Choose Options from the Tools menu.

4 Click the Styles And Formatting button to display the Styles And Formatting task pane if it isn't already open.

5 Click in a paragraph.

3 On the View tab of the Options dialog box, select this check box, and click OK.

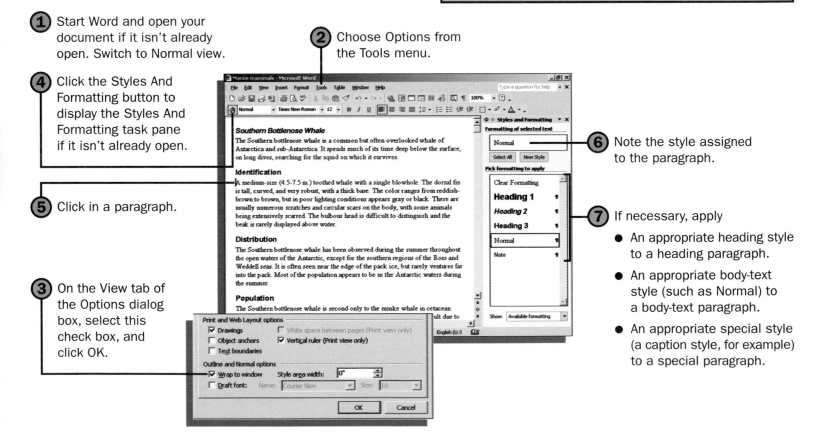

6 Note the style assigned to the paragraph.

7 If necessary, apply

- An appropriate heading style to a heading paragraph.
- An appropriate body-text style (such as Normal) to a body-text paragraph.
- An appropriate special style (a caption style, for example) to a special paragraph.

Define a Style as a Heading

① Click in a paragraph whose style you want to define as a heading in an outline.

② Point to the style, click the down arrow, and choose Modify from the menu that appears.

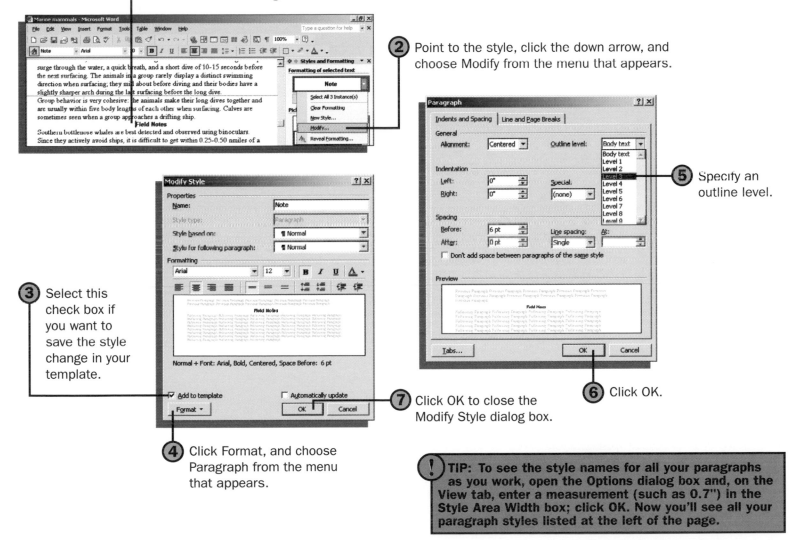

③ Select this check box if you want to save the style change in your template.

⑤ Specify an outline level.

④ Click Format, and choose Paragraph from the menu that appears.

⑦ Click OK to close the Modify Style dialog box.

⑥ Click OK.

> **TIP:** To see the style names for all your paragraphs as you work, open the Options dialog box and, on the View tab, enter a measurement (such as 0.7") in the Style Area Width box; click OK. Now you'll see all your paragraph styles listed at the left of the page.

Finding Topics in a Document

The longer a document becomes, the more difficult it can be to find a specific topic within it. This is when you'll really appreciate Word's Document Map. When you display the Document Map, you can see an outline view of your document, and, with a click or two, you can jump to the appropriate topic. The outline structure is based on the heading levels assigned to the styles you used.

TRY THIS: Drag the border between the Document Map and the text area to see more or less of the Document Map.

Navigate with the Document Map

(1) Click the Document Map button.

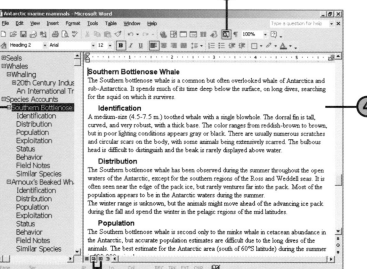

(3) Click a topic. Click a plus sign to expand the headings directly below it. Click a minus sign to collapse the headings directly below it. When you click a topic, the document jumps to that topic.

(4) Review the material. If necessary, use the Document Map to locate and review other topics. When you've finished locating and reviewing topics, click the Document Map button again to hide the Document Map.

(2) Switch to the view you want to use:

- Web Layout view to easily view all the content of the document
- Print Layout view to see the formatting and line breaks that will be used in a printed document

TIP: Point to a topic to see its full text if the heading is too long to be displayed completely in the Document Map area.

SEE ALSO: For information about structuring your document, see "Organizing with Styles" on page 74.

Numbering Headings

It's a commonly accepted practice to number each heading level in certain long documents so that when the document is being reviewed or is under discussion at a meeting, it's easy to refer to the relevant sections. Word uses the outline-level setting for each style as the basis for the numbering hierarchy.

SEE ALSO: For information about modifying a style, see "Modify a Style in a Document" on page 43.

For information about setting outline levels, see "Organizing with Styles" on page 74.

Number the Headings

TIP: To number all the lines in a document, choose Page Layout from the File menu, and click the Line Numbers button on the Layout tab.

(3) Choose Bullets And Numbering from the Format menu.

(2) Click in the first heading paragraph.

(1) Verify that all the headings have the correct heading styles applied.

(4) Click the Outline Numbered tab.

(5) Click one of the numbering schemes shown in the bottom row.

(6) Click OK.

(7) Verify that your document headings are numbered correctly. If you don't like the numbering scheme, click the Undo button on the Standard toolbar.

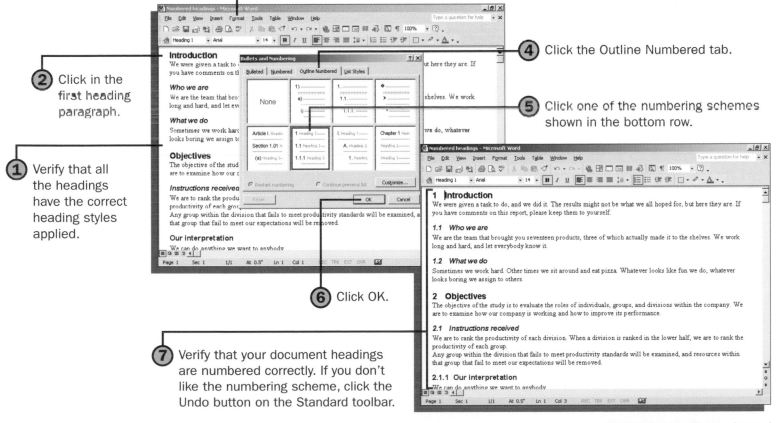

Reorganizing a Document

Outline view provides a powerful way for you to view the structure of your document and to rearrange the order of presentation of topics in the document. The outline structure assumes that you've used specific styles to organize your document into a hierarchy of topics and subtopics.

> **TRY THIS:** Drag a topic's plus or minus sign to the left to quickly promote the topic's outline level, to the right to demote it, or to the far right to turn it into body text. Changing the outline level also changes the style that's assigned to that paragraph.

View a Document's Outline

(1) Start Word, and open your document if it isn't already open. Switch to Outline view.

(4) Click to change the outline level of a heading by promoting it one level, demoting it one level, or specifying the outline level.

(5) Click to expand or collapse the content under the heading.

(2) Specify which levels of headings are to be displayed.

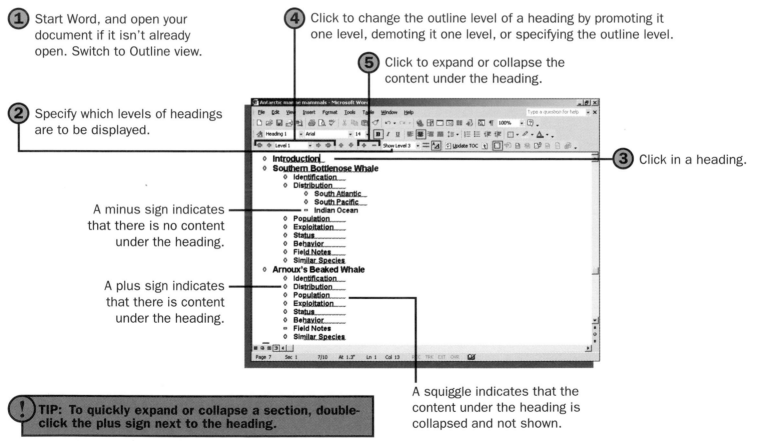

(3) Click in a heading.

A minus sign indicates that there is no content under the heading.

A plus sign indicates that there is content under the heading.

A squiggle indicates that the content under the heading is collapsed and not shown.

> **TIP:** To quickly expand or collapse a section, double-click the plus sign next to the heading.

Move a Paragraph

1 Expand the outline so that the paragraph you want to move and the area into which you want to move it are both displayed.

2 Click in the paragraph that you want to move.

3 Click to move the paragraph up or down in the document.

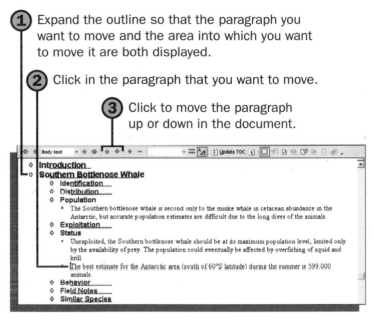

Move a Section

1 Click the plus sign to select the entire section.

2 Click to move the topic up or down in the document.

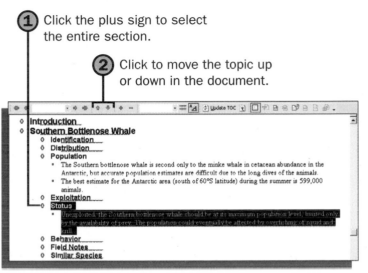

> ✋ **CAUTION:** Be very careful about editing text in Outline view. For example, if the text of a section is collapsed under its heading, you might think that you're deleting only the heading, but you're actually deleting all the text in that section.

> ❗ **TIP:** When you select and move a section, all the paragraphs in that section are moved, including those that haven't been expanded and displayed.

> ❗ **TIP:** To quickly move a section, click the plus sign next to the heading, and then drag the heading up or down in the document.

Browsing Through Your Document

When you're editing or proofreading a document, you often do so in stages: you might check the tables, for example, and then the graphics, and so on. You can browse through your document, jumping to the next occurrence of a specific element, with the help of a tiny button that does a big job. Use the table at the right to achieve the results you want.

Browse by Element

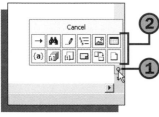

2 Click the type of element you're looking for.

1 Click the Select Browse Object button at the bottom of the vertical scroll bar.

3 Click the appropriate button to go to the next or previous occurrence of the element.

4 Continue clicking the buttons to move through the document, locating each instance of the element you want to review.

 SEE ALSO: For information about using the Document Map to find topics in a long document, see "Finding Topics in a Document" on page 76.

Elements of the Select Browse Object Button

Use this button	To do this
→	Display the Go To tab of the Find And Replace dialog box.
🔍	Display the Find tab of the Find And Replace dialog box.
✏	Go to the next or previous edit.
☰	Go to the next or previous heading.
🖼	Go to the next or previous graphic.
▭	Go to the next or previous table.
{a}	Go to the next or previous field.
📑	Go to the next or previous endnote.
📄	Go to the next or previous footnote.
🗏	Go to the next or previous comment.
🗔	Go to the next or previous section.
🗋	Go to the next or previous page.

Numbering Pages and Creating Running Heads

In addition to page numbers, a long document usually has some type of identifying text—called a *running head*—at the top or bottom of each page of the document. All you do is create the running head once, and Word places it on the pages you designate. For the sake of consistency, we're using the term running head for the heading itself, and the terms *header* and *footer* to describe the running head's position on the page. Note that on the screen you can see the headers and footers on your page only in Print Layout view or in Print Preview.

Create a Header

1 Choose Header And Footer from the View menu.

2 Type the text you want for the header in the Header area. Use tabs, paragraph spacing and alignment, and font settings to customize the layout.

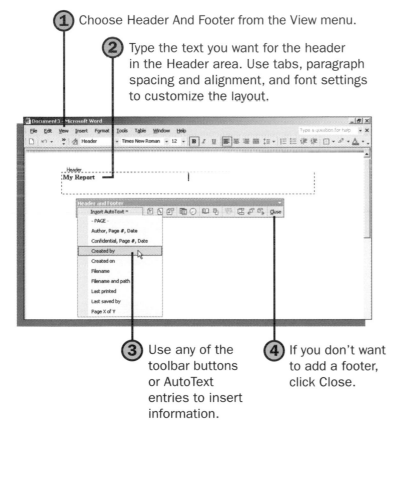

3 Use any of the toolbar buttons or AutoText entries to insert information.

4 If you don't want to add a footer, click Close.

Create a Footer

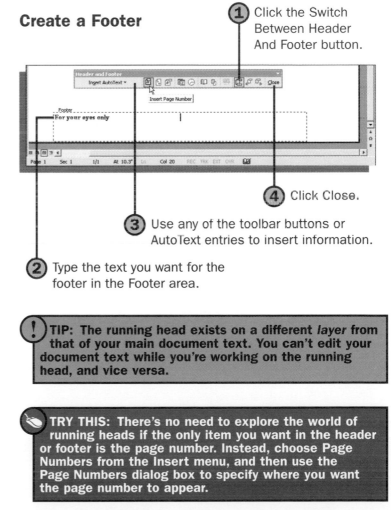

1 Click the Switch Between Header And Footer button.

4 Click Close.

3 Use any of the toolbar buttons or AutoText entries to insert information.

2 Type the text you want for the footer in the Footer area.

> **! TIP:** The running head exists on a different *layer* from that of your main document text. You can't edit your document text while you're working on the running head, and vice versa.

> **TRY THIS:** There's no need to explore the world of running heads if the only item you want in the header or footer is the page number. Instead, choose Page Numbers from the Insert menu, and then use the Page Numbers dialog box to specify where you want the page number to appear.

Creating Variable Running Heads

Look through most books (but not this one, which has what are called "dictionary style" running heads) and you'll see that the odd- and even-numbered pages often have alternating running heads. This is a fairly standard design, especially for double-sided documents, and you can set it up quite easily in Word. Running heads are visible on the screen when you look at your document in Print Layout view or Print Preview, and they appear on designated pages of the printed document.

Specify Different Headers or Footers

! **TIP:** It's fairly standard practice not to use a running head on the first page of a document or the first page of each chapter in a book. Leave the first-page header and footer areas blank to omit the running head.

① With your document open, choose Page Setup from the File menu to display the Page Setup dialog box. Click the Layout tab if it isn't already displayed.

② Select this check box for different odd- and even-page running heads.

④ Click OK.

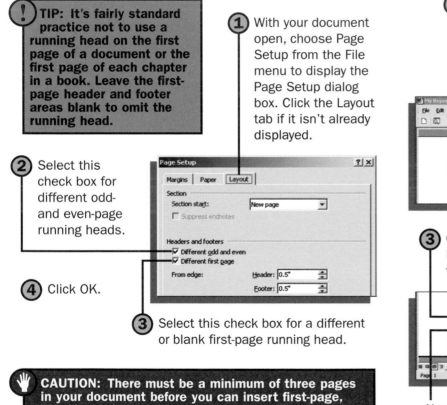

③ Select this check box for a different or blank first-page running head.

✋ **CAUTION:** There must be a minimum of three pages in your document before you can insert first-page, odd-page, and even-page running heads. If your document doesn't have three pages, press Ctrl+Enter twice to create two virtual extra pages. You can delete these manual page breaks later.

Create a First-Page Running Head

① With the insertion point at the beginning of the document, choose Header And Footer from the View menu.

Use any formatting and alignment you want.

② Enter the header information.

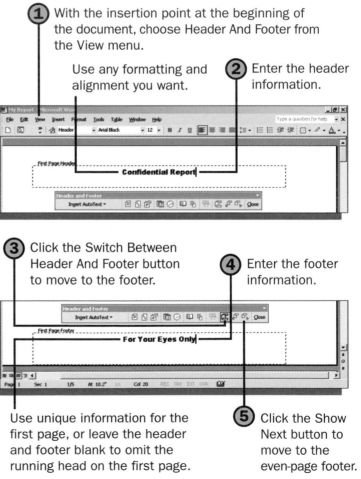

③ Click the Switch Between Header And Footer button to move to the footer.

④ Enter the footer information.

Use unique information for the first page, or leave the header and footer blank to omit the running head on the first page.

⑤ Click the Show Next button to move to the even-page footer.

Create an Even-Page Running Head

1 Enter the footer information. Place the text on the left side so that it will appear on the outside edge of an even-numbered (left-hand, or *verso*) page.

2 Click the Switch Between Header And Footer button to move to the even-page header.

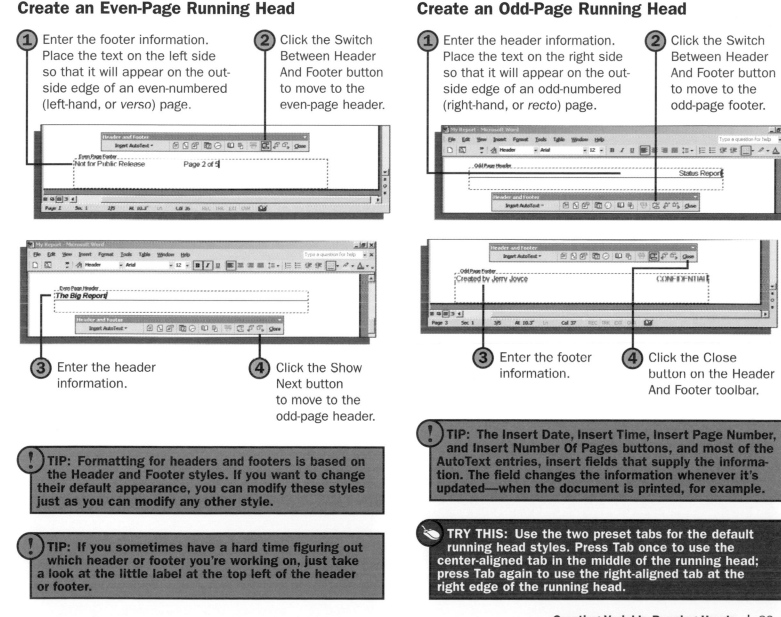

3 Enter the header information.

4 Click the Show Next button to move to the odd-page header.

> **TIP:** Formatting for headers and footers is based on the Header and Footer styles. If you want to change their default appearance, you can modify these styles just as you can modify any other style.

> **TIP:** If you sometimes have a hard time figuring out which header or footer you're working on, just take a look at the little label at the top left of the header or footer.

Create an Odd-Page Running Head

1 Enter the header information. Place the text on the right side so that it will appear on the outside edge of an odd-numbered (right-hand, or *recto*) page.

2 Click the Switch Between Header And Footer button to move to the odd-page footer.

3 Enter the footer information.

4 Click the Close button on the Header And Footer toolbar.

> **TIP:** The Insert Date, Insert Time, Insert Page Number, and Insert Number Of Pages buttons, and most of the AutoText entries, insert fields that supply the information. The field changes the information whenever it's updated—when the document is printed, for example.

> **TRY THIS:** Use the two preset tabs for the default running head styles. Press Tab once to use the center-aligned tab in the middle of the running head; press Tab again to use the right-aligned tab at the right edge of the running head.

Finding Text

If you're not sure where to find some text in your document, Word can locate it for you. You can broaden the search so that Word finds similar words, or you can narrow the search to a designated part of the document or to text that uses specific formatting.

> ! **TIP:** To limit the search to only a specific part of a document, select that part of the document before you open the Find And Replace dialog box.

Find Text One Instance at a Time

(1) Choose Find from the Edit menu to display the Find And Replace dialog box.

(2) Type the text you want to find.

(3) Click Find Next. Continue to click Find Next to move through the document, finding each instance of the text.

Find All Instances of Text

(1) Select this check box to find and select, or highlight, every instance of the text.

(2) Specify Main Document to search the entire document.

(3) Click Find All to view every instance of the selected text.

> **TRY THIS:** If you choose to select all instances of certain text but then you edit only one instance, all the other instances of the text will no longer be selected. To edit each instance of the text, search for each instance, make your edit, and then click Find Next to go to the next instance of the text to edit it.

> ! **TIP:** When you use the Find Next command, the Select Browse Object button at the bottom of the vertical scroll bar automatically uses the information you entered in the Find And Replace dialog box. To find text again after you've closed the dialog box, click the Next Find/GoTo button below the Select Browse Object button.

Modify the Search

(1) Click the More button, if it's displayed, to show the full dialog box.

(3) Select the check box or check boxes you need to customize the search:

- Match Case to find only text that exactly matches the capitalization of the text in the Find What box

- Find Whole Words Only to find text only if the matching text consists of whole words, not parts of words

- Use Wildcards to use certain characters as wildcard characters

- Sounds Like to find words that sound the same but are spelled differently (*their* and *there*, for example)

- Find All Word Forms to find all words that are forms of the word (its plural or its past tense, for example) in the Find What box

(2) Click Up, Down, or All to specify whether all or part of the document is to be searched. (This option is available only if the Highlight All Items Found In check box isn't selected.)

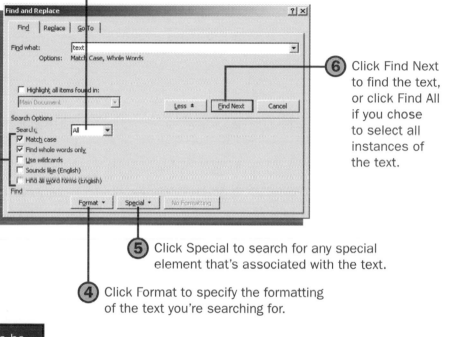

(6) Click Find Next to find the text, or click Find All if you chose to select all instances of the text.

(5) Click Special to search for any special element that's associated with the text.

(4) Click Format to specify the formatting of the text you're searching for.

TRY THIS: In your document, type To be or not to be is asked too often. **In the Find What box, type** o?t **and select the Use Wildcards check box. Click Find Next until the entire selection has been searched. Then change the Find What text to** o*t **and repeat the search. Then use** to **as the search text, select the Sounds Like check box, and search the document. Finally, use** is **as the search text, select the Find All Word Forms check box, and search the document. Note the different results.**

TIP: "Wildcard" characters are used to represent other characters. The most commonly used wildcards are ? and *. The ? wildcard represents any single character, and the * wildcard represents any number of characters. For a complete list of wildcards, select the Use Wildcards check box, and click the Special button.

Replacing Text

When you need to replace a word or phrase with a different word or phrase in several places in your document, let Word do it for you. It's a great way to use Word's speed and power to make quick work of those tedious document-wide changes.

Replace Text

1 Choose Replace from the Edit menu to display the Find And Replace dialog box with the Replace tab displayed. Click the More button, if it's displayed, to show the full dialog box.

2 Type the text you want to find.

5 Type the replacement text. Use the Format button to specify any formatting the replacement text should have. Use the Special button to specify a non-text element.

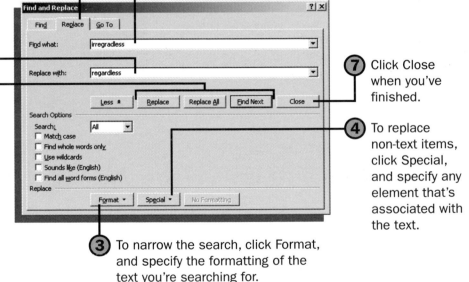

7 Click Close when you've finished.

6 Click one of the following:

- Replace to replace the found text and find the next instance of the search text
- Replace All to replace all instances of the search text with the replacement text
- Find Next to find the next instance of the search text without replacing it

4 To replace non-text items, click Special, and specify any element that's associated with the text.

3 To narrow the search, click Format, and specify the formatting of the text you're searching for.

SEE ALSO: For information about broadening or narrowing a search, see "Finding Text" on page 84.

For information about replacing formatting only, see "Standardizing the Formatting" on page 216.

TIP: If you used the Replace All button and the results aren't what you expected, click the Undo button on the Standard toolbar. You can then try the replacement again, this time with more specific search parameters.

Copying Information from Multiple Locations

If you need to move items within your document, or copy information from other Word documents or from other Microsoft Office documents, the Office Clipboard is a handy tool. It's similar to the Windows Clipboard, but, unlike the Windows Clipboard, it can contain up to 24 different items (provided they were all copied from Office documents). Once you've copied the items and placed them on the Clipboard, you can insert a single item, or you can insert all the items at once.

Copy and Insert Content

(1) Choose Office Clipboard from the Edit menu to display the Clipboard task pane if it isn't already open.

(2) Click Clear All if you don't want to use any of the content currently shown on the Clipboard.

(4) Click at the location where you want to insert the content.

(5) Click Paste All to insert all the items on the Clipboard into your document.

(6) Click a single item to insert only that item.

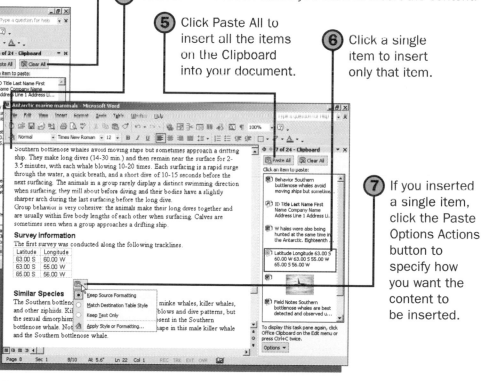

(3) Locate and select the content you want to copy from any Office document, and click the Copy button on the Standard toolbar. To move an item, click the Cut button on the Standard toolbar. Continue collecting content from multiple locations in the document, or from different documents.

(7) If you inserted a single item, click the Paste Options Actions button to specify how you want the content to be inserted.

(8) Continue collecting and inserting text as you need it. If there's an item you don't need on the Clipboard, point to the item, click the down arrow, and choose Delete from the menu that appears.

Creating Chapters

A long document is usually divided into chapters or sections, each of which should begin on an odd-numbered (right-hand, or recto) page. Word will start your chapters or sections on odd-numbered pages, and will create running heads to your specifications.

 SEE ALSO: For information about running heads, see "Numbering Pages and Creating Running Heads" on page 81 and "Creating Variable Running Heads" on page 82.

Start a New Chapter

1 In the document you want to divide into different chapters, place the insertion point at the beginning of the paragraph that starts a new chapter.

2 Choose Break from the Insert menu to display the Break dialog box.

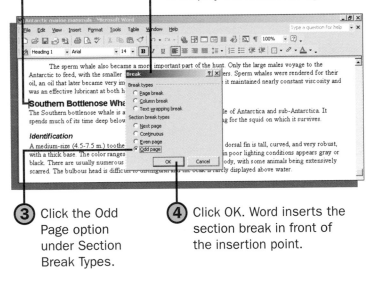

3 Click the Odd Page option under Section Break Types.

4 Click OK. Word inserts the section break in front of the insertion point.

> **! TIP:** When you use an Odd Page section break to start a new chapter, note that if the previous section of your document ended on an odd-numbered page, Word will insert a blank even-numbered page so that your chapter will start on the odd-numbered page, as is customary.

Change the Running Heads

1 Choose Header And Footer from the View menu to display your header and the Header And Footer toolbar. Any text in the header comes from the previous header.

2 Click the Same As Previous button to turn it off and disconnect the header from the previous header.

3 Replace the old header text with the text for your new running head.

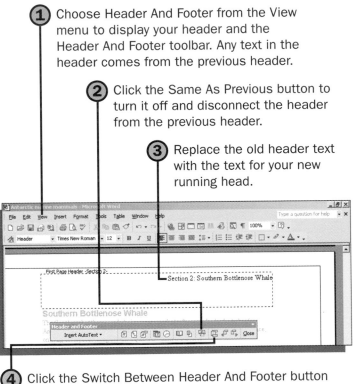

4 Click the Switch Between Header And Footer button to move to the footer, and repeat steps 2 and 3 for the footer. If the document is set for a different running head on the first page, or for different running heads on odd- and even-numbered pages, repeat steps 2 and 3 for those running heads. Click Close when you've finished.

Changing Page Orientation Within a Document

Different parts of a long document sometimes require different layouts. For example, although most of the document's text is in portrait orientation, there might be one or two pages that contain tables, figures, or other special elements that need to be set up in landscape orientation. By dividing the document into sections, you can set up each section with its own orientation.

Change the Page Orientation

1 Select the part of the document whose page orientation you want to change.

2 Choose Page Setup from the File menu, and click the Margins tab.

3 Click the orientation you want.

4 Specify Selected Text.

5 Click OK.

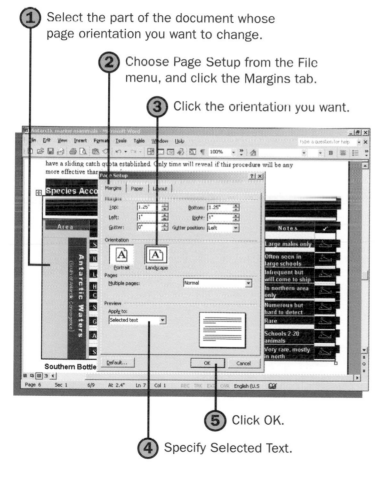

6 Click the Print Preview button to preview your text.

7 Click the Multiple Pages button, and choose to view three or more pages.

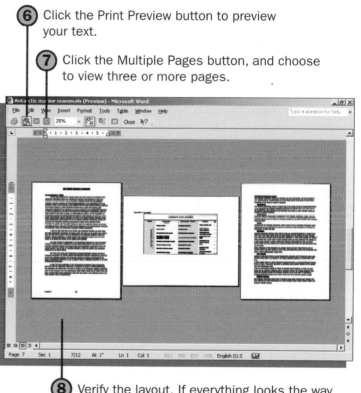

8 Verify the layout. If everything looks the way you want, close Print Preview and continue working on the document.

> **! TIP:** When you change the orientation of selected text, you're actually creating two new sections: one section for the selected text and another for the text that follows the selection.

Changing Margins Within a Document

In most cases, a document has one set of margins, and you use paragraph indents to control the layout of individual paragraphs. Sometimes, though, a long document might have one or more large sections that need different margins. Setting different margins for different sections is a chore that would be much too time consuming and tedious to do using paragraph indents. Instead, you can set each section to start on a new page, or to start on the same page as a section that has different margins.

Change the Margins

(1) Select the part of the document whose margins you want to change.

(2) Choose Page Setup from the File menu, and click the Margins tab.

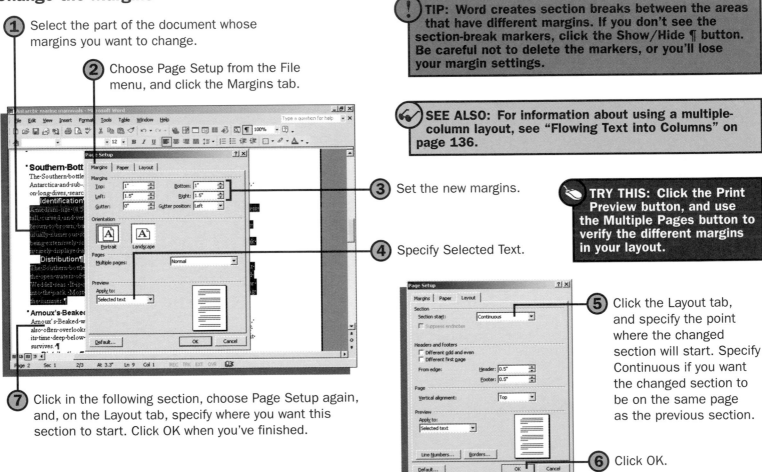

(3) Set the new margins.

(4) Specify Selected Text.

(7) Click in the following section, choose Page Setup again, and, on the Layout tab, specify where you want this section to start. Click OK when you've finished.

TIP: Word creates section breaks between the areas that have different margins. If you don't see the section-break markers, click the Show/Hide ¶ button. Be careful not to delete the markers, or you'll lose your margin settings.

SEE ALSO: For information about using a multiple-column layout, see "Flowing Text into Columns" on page 136.

TRY THIS: Click the Print Preview button, and use the Multiple Pages button to verify the different margins in your layout.

(5) Click the Layout tab, and specify the point where the changed section will start. Specify Continuous if you want the changed section to be on the same page as the previous section.

(6) Click OK.

Creating a Table of Contents

Provided your document is organized by styles, it's a snap to have Word create a well-organized table of contents for you. You design your table of contents by selecting a format and designating which levels are assigned to the headings. Word can adjust the appearance of the table of contents depending on how you're viewing it.

In Web Layout view, for example, the table can consist of links, but in Print Layout view or Print Preview it looks like a table of contents you'd see in a book. Either way, when your document is viewed on line, the table of contents is active, with links to the headings listed in your table.

Create a Table of Contents

(2) Select a check box to display the page numbers either next to corresponding entries in the table of contents or aligned at the right side of the page. If you want the page numbers right-aligned, specify a style for the tab leader that's placed between the entry and the page number.

(1) With the insertion point located in your document where you want the table of contents to appear, point to Reference on the Insert menu, and choose Index And Tables from the submenu to display the Index And Tables dialog box. Click the Table Of Contents tab.

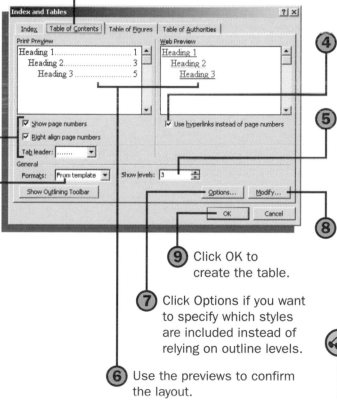

(4) Select this check box to display links in Web Layout view, or clear the check box if page numbers are to be displayed.

(5) Specify the lowest outline level to be included in the table of contents. Paragraphs whose style has been assigned an outline level that's included within this range will appear in the table.

(3) Specify the style of the table of contents. (Some styles will cause some of the layout options to be unavailable.)

(8) Click Modify if you want to change the formatting of the styles used in the table of contents. (You can modify only the styles that come from the template.)

(9) Click OK to create the table.

(7) Click Options if you want to specify which styles are included instead of relying on outline levels.

(6) Use the previews to confirm the layout.

> **(!) TIP:** To update the table of contents after you've made changes to your document, click the Update TOC button on the Outlining toolbar.

> **(✓) SEE ALSO:** For information about assigning outlining levels to styles, see "Organizing with Styles" on page 74.

Creating an Index

If you're not blessed with the expertise of a professional indexer, Word is the next best thing. It simplifies and automates the complex and arduous mechanics of indexing. Word places a hidden-text tag next to each indexed item, so no matter how the page numbers change, the index is kept current. Your index can include multiple levels, cross-references, and even a range of pages when an indexed item extends beyond a single page.

TRY THIS: To cross-reference a related entry but still include a page number, tag the entry twice—once using "See also" in the Cross-Reference box, and again with the Current Page option selected.

Tag the Entries

(1) Point to Reference on the Insert menu, and choose Index And Tables from the submenu to display the Index And Tables dialog box. Click the Mark Entry button on the Index tab to display the Mark Index Entry dialog box.

(2) Click the Show/Hide ¶ button on the Standard toolbar if it isn't already turned on.

(3) In your document, select the text you want to index.

(4) Click the Mark Index Entry dialog box to make it active. The text you selected appears in the Main Entry box. Modify the wording or capitalization of the main entry, if necessary.

(5) Type any subentries. To specify more than one level of subentry, separate subentry levels with colons.

(6) Specify options as follows:

- Click Cross-Reference, and type the topic to be cross-referenced.

- Click Current Page to list the page number next to the entry.

- Click Page Range, and select the bookmark that marks the entire text of the entry. The text must be bookmarked (see facing page) before it can be included as an entry.

(7) Click in the document, find your next index entry, and repeat steps 3 through 6.

(8) When you've finished, click Close, and save the document.

CAUTION: When you're creating an index or a table of contents, keep in mind that Word doesn't search text boxes for content.

Bookmark a Page Range

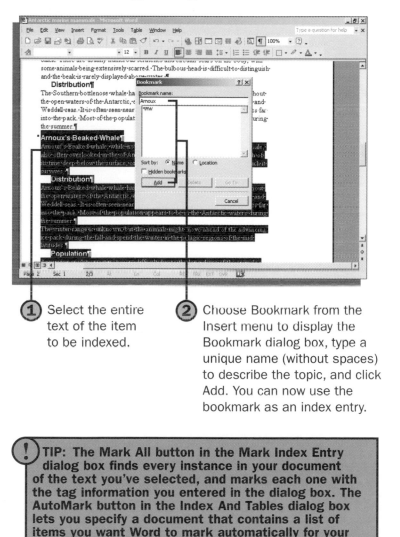

1 Select the entire text of the item to be indexed.

2 Choose Bookmark from the Insert menu to display the Bookmark dialog box, type a unique name (without spaces) to describe the topic, and click Add. You can now use the bookmark as an index entry.

> **!** **TIP:** The Mark All button in the Mark Index Entry dialog box finds every instance in your document of the text you've selected, and marks each one with the tag information you entered in the dialog box. The AutoMark button in the Index And Tables dialog box lets you specify a document that contains a list of items you want Word to mark automatically for your index. If you use either of these automated techniques, you'll need to go through your document and carefully verify these index entries.

Compile the Index

1 Press Ctrl+End to move to the end of the document. Point to Reference on the Insert menu, and choose Index And Tables from the submenu to display the Index And Tables dialog box. Click the Index tab.

2 Select this check box if the page numbers for your index entries are aligned at the right side of the page, and specify the style of the tab leader that's placed between the text and the page number.

3 Specify the style of the index. (Some styles will cause some of the layout options to be unavailable.)

4 Click to specify the type of index you want.

5 Specify the number of columns you want.

6 Specify the language of the index. In most cases, only your default language is available.

7 Click Modify if you want to change the styles used in formatting the index. (You can modify only the styles that come from the template.)

8 Use the preview to verify the layout.

9 Click OK to create your index.

Printing on Both Sides of the Paper

When your document is complete and ready to be printed, you can make it look very professional—and save paper at the same time—by printing on both sides of the paper. This is called *duplex printing,* and many network printers do it automatically. Other printers, however, aren't designed to print on both sides of the paper. Fortunately, with a little help from Word, you should be able to manually configure your non-duplex printer to print on both sides of the paper.

Print on Both Sides

1 Complete and save your document. Make sure you've set up the document for two-sided printing.

2 Choose Print from the File menu to display the Print dialog box.

3 Specify the correct printer. (Make sure this printer doesn't have duplex capabilities.)

✋ **CAUTION: Check your printer manual before you try to print on both sides of the paper. Some printers, especially certain color printers, can have big problems when you try printing on paper that has already been printed on one side.**

! **TIP: Figuring out how to reload the paper is always an adventure! Try printing only a page or two to see whether you've reloaded the paper correctly.**

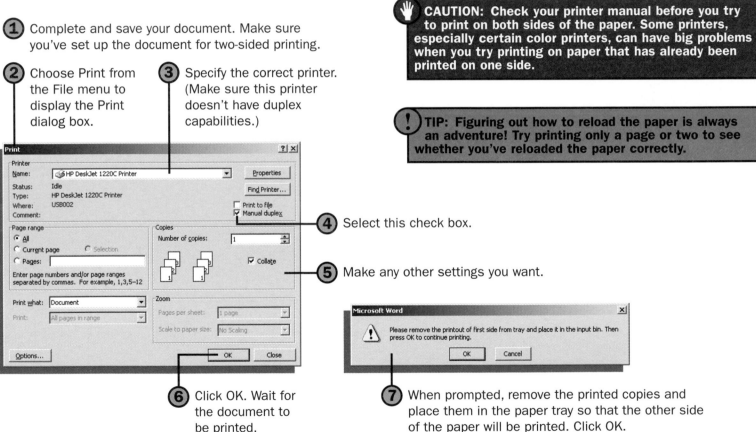

4 Select this check box.

5 Make any other settings you want.

6 Click OK. Wait for the document to be printed.

7 When prompted, remove the printed copies and place them in the paper tray so that the other side of the paper will be printed. Click OK.

7 Creating a Technical Document

✳ NEW FEATURE

Elsewhere in this book we've discussed standard documents, long documents, and working with elements other than text. A technical document can integrate some or all of these elements while still having its own set of requirements. Conversely, elements of a technical document can be incorporated into a nontechnical document. In reality, few elements are unique to any one type of document, and you can use the techniques we describe throughout this book to achieve the results you want regardless of the headings under which you find them.

So what *is* a technical document anyway? It could be a doctoral dissertation, a high-school paper, a scientific report, your company's quarterly financial statement, or an annual report to stockholders. It could be an ongoing analysis of a medical experiment, the written specifications for an architectural design, a grade-school teacher's compilation of test scores, or a comparison of various sets of data. What all these examples have in common is that they must present a lot of sometimes complicated information in a format that's inviting rather than daunting, that's organized for ease of reference rather than confusion, and that conveys the information with simplicity and clarity so that it can be understood by a receptive and interested audience.

In this section, you'll find descriptions of the tools and procedures that will help you design and put together some of the elements—footnotes, equations, charts, diagrams, and so on—that are often found in technical documents. You'll also learn how to add captions to tables and figures, number the lines in a document, and create cross-references.

Inserting Special Characters

With at least 101 keys at your fingertips, you'd think that every character you could possibly need would be available on your keyboard. But what about the accented characters in other languages? Different currency symbols? Mathematical symbols? You'd need a keyboard with thousands of keys! As you can see in the illustration, Microsoft Word 2002 gives you a huge assortment of symbols and special characters, and provides several ways to insert them into your documents.

Insert a Character

①	With the insertion point located where you want to insert the character, choose Symbol from the Insert menu, and click the Symbols tab. (If the character you want is displayed, select it, and then skip to step 5.)

②	Click Normal Text to insert a character from the font you're currently using, or click a specific font. Click one of the symbol fonts for nonstandard characters.

③	Click the character's category if it's displayed.

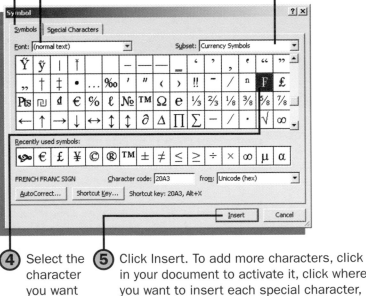

④	Select the character you want to use.

⑤	Click Insert. To add more characters, click in your document to activate it, click where you want to insert each special character, and then select and insert the character.

Insert a Typographic Character

①	Click the Special Characters tab.

②	Double-click the character you want to insert.

③	Click Close after you've inserted the special characters and symbols you want.

> **!** **TIP: Some of the characters in the Symbol dialog box might not be supported by all fonts and printers. If you see an empty box instead of a symbol in your document, try using a different font. If you see the symbol on your screen but it doesn't print, try using only the TrueType fonts that came with Word.**

Creating Footnotes

Word makes it so easy to add footnotes to a document! Word can mark the footnoted material for you with an automatic series of numbers or symbols, or you can insert your own choice of symbols. When you leave it to Word to insert the footnote number, it updates the number whenever you add or delete a footnote. Word also figures out how much space is required at the bottom of the page for the footnote, and when a footnote is too long for the page, Word automatically continues it on the next page. How clever!

Insert a Footnote

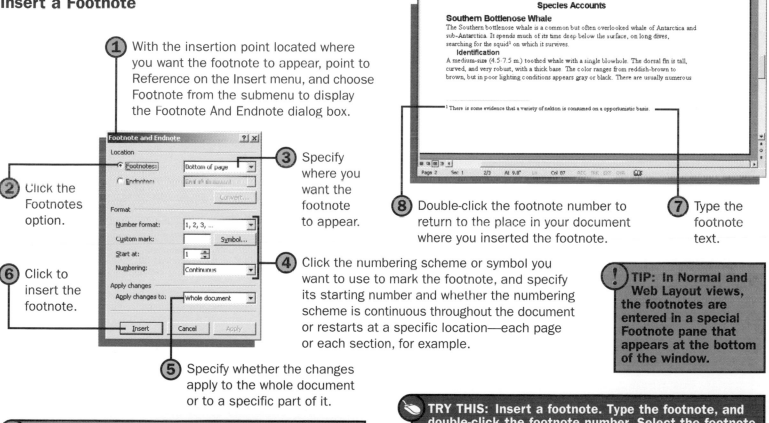

(1) With the insertion point located where you want the footnote to appear, point to Reference on the Insert menu, and choose Footnote from the submenu to display the Footnote And Endnote dialog box.

(2) Click the Footnotes option.

(3) Specify where you want the footnote to appear.

(6) Click to insert the footnote.

(4) Click the numbering scheme or symbol you want to use to mark the footnote, and specify its starting number and whether the numbering scheme is continuous throughout the document or restarts at a specific location—each page or each section, for example.

(5) Specify whether the changes apply to the whole document or to a specific part of it.

(8) Double-click the footnote number to return to the place in your document where you inserted the footnote.

(7) Type the footnote text.

TIP: In Normal and Web Layout views, the footnotes are entered in a special Footnote pane that appears at the bottom of the window.

TIP: Endnotes are just like footnotes, except that endnotes appear all together at the end of a document (or the end of a section) instead of at the foot of each page. Use the Convert button to change footnotes into endnotes, and vice versa.

TRY THIS: Insert a footnote. Type the footnote, and double-click the footnote number. Select the footnote reference number in the document, and cut it (press Ctrl+X). The footnote is gone. Click elsewhere in your document, and paste the footnote reference number to restore the footnote (press Ctrl+V). Double-click the footnote reference number, and edit the footnote.

Creating an Equation

It can be difficult to construct mathematical equations on a computer. For simple equations, you can generally use standard characters and formatting, but for more complex equations, you'll want to use Microsoft Equation Editor 3.0. Be aware, though, that you're simply *constructing* the equation. Word doesn't do any calculations based on the equation.

> **! TIP:** To create a formula or an equation that uses exponents or other forms of superscripts and subscripts as the only special elements, you can skip the Equation Editor and simply format the text with superscripts (press Ctrl+Shift+=) or subscripts (press Ctrl+=).

Create an Equation

(1) Choose Object from the Insert menu, and, on the Create New tab, click Microsoft Equation 3.0 in the list.

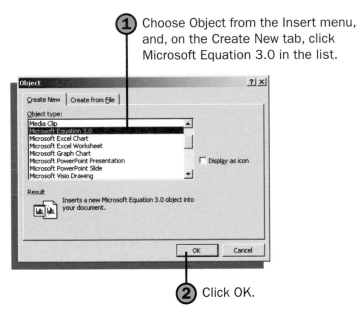

(2) Click OK.

(3) Use the template menus to insert the symbols with the correct configuration, and use the keyboard to enter characters, keeping these points in mind:

- Work from left to right.
- Use Tab and Shift+Tab to move to different elements and levels.

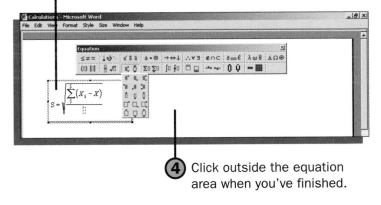

(4) Click outside the equation area when you've finished.

> **SEE ALSO:** For information about installing Equation Editor if it doesn't appear in the Object Type list, see "Adding or Removing Components" on page 222.

Inserting a Diagram ⊛ NEW FEATURE

Word provides the following six types of diagrams to illustrate relationships and processes: the Organization Chart, the Cycle Diagram, the Radial Diagram, the Pyramid Diagram, the Venn Diagram, and the Target Diagram. All you need to do is choose the appropriate diagram and then use the tools to customize it for your use.

Create a Diagram

(1) Choose Diagram from the Insert menu to display the Diagram Gallery dialog box.

(2) Double click a diagram type to start creating your diagram.

Sizing handles

Adds another diagram element.

Re-orders the elements.

Changes the size and scaling of the diagram.

Changes the style of the diagram.

Changes the type of diagram.

Sets text wrapping.

(4) Use the toolbar to modify the diagram. To modify an individual item, choose AutoLayout from the Layout menu to turn off the option, and then use the sizing handles around the item to resize or move it.

(3) Follow the instructions on the screen to enter your text. Continue adding text to complete the diagram.

(5) When the diagram is complete, click outside the diagram area, and continue working on your document.

TRY THIS: Enhance your diagram by adding your own AutoShapes from the Drawing toolbar, which appears when you start creating a diagram. Then add a background to the diagram by double-clicking the diagram, and, on the Colors And Lines tab of the Format Diagram dialog box, set the fill color.

TIP: The Organization Chart has a slightly different toolbar from that of the other diagrams, but it works in much the same way. However, although you can switch the same information among the five other diagrams, depending on which style you prefer, you can't convert the Organization Chart into another diagram style.

Inserting Excel Data

Microsoft Excel is a great tool for collecting and analyzing data, but the information contained in an Excel worksheet is often easier to understand when it's presented along with some explanations or supplemental information. To that end, you can integrate Excel information into a Word document by copying the data from Excel into the Word document. You can include the Excel data in one of several ways. If the Excel information is static—that is, your data collection is complete and the numbers won't change—you can insert the data into a Word document as a table or as text. If your data collection and analysis are still in progress and the information might change, you can link the data to the original Excel file so that any changes to the Excel data will appear in the Word document. If, however, the data or analysis might change but you won't be able to access the original Excel file, or you don't want the original Excel file to be changed or played around with by anyone else who has access to it, you can copy the entire Excel worksheet into your Word document, where you can still use the worksheet features to adjust the data.

Copy the Data

(1) In the Excel worksheet, select and copy the cells you want.

(2) In Word, click the Paste button to insert the data.

> **!** **TIP: If you want to link to the original Excel file, make sure that you name and save the file before you copy and link to it.**

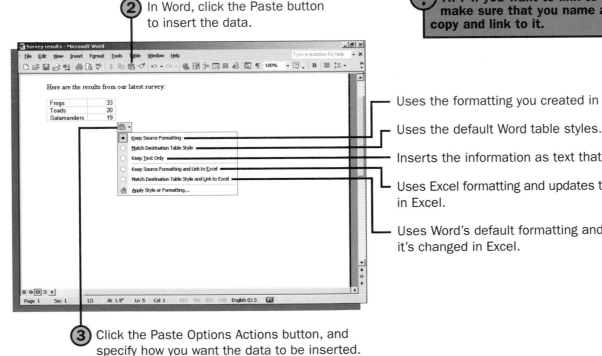

Uses the formatting you created in the Excel worksheet.

Uses the default Word table styles.

Inserts the information as text that isn't displayed in a table.

Uses Excel formatting and updates the data when it's changed in Excel.

Uses Word's default formatting and updates the data when it's changed in Excel.

(3) Click the Paste Options Actions button, and specify how you want the data to be inserted.

Insert All the Data

(1) In the Excel worksheet, select and copy the cells you want.

(2) In Word, choose Paste Special from the Edit menu to display the Paste Special dialog box.

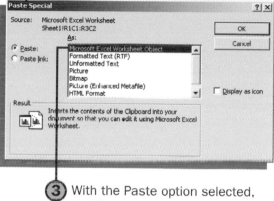

(3) With the Paste option selected, double-click the Excel object.

(4) Double-click the inserted table to edit the data.

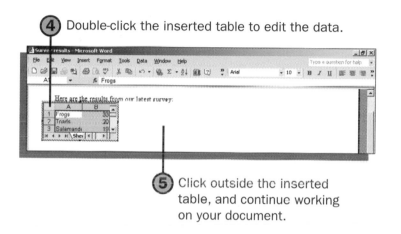

(5) Click outside the inserted table, and continue working on your document.

TRY THIS: Insert the Excel object. Click it to select it, and drag a sizing handle. Note that the size of the text increases. Double-click the object to activate it, and drag a sizing handle. Note that the number of rows and columns that are displayed has changed. Click outside the object to deactivate it.

TIP: To work with the entire worksheet in Excel instead of in the Word window, right-click the table in your Word document, point to Worksheet Object on the shortcut menu, and choose Open from the submenu. In Excel, after you've worked with the data, choose Update from the File menu, and then close Excel.

Inserting an Excel Chart

If you have the final results of your data in an Excel worksheet but you want to display the data as a chart, you can copy the chart into your Word document. Once you've done so, the chart resides in Word, so you can edit it as necessary, and you no longer need the original Excel document.

Insert a Chart

 In Excel, create and format your chart. Select the chart and copy it.

 In Word, click the Paste button to insert the chart.

TIP: Excel provides many powerful formatting tools, so make sure you've formatted the chart so that it looks the way you want before you insert it. You might need to change the size of the inserted chart to clearly see all the formatting that you've used.

CAUTION: If you're linking to the Excel chart, make sure that you've named and saved the Excel file before you insert it.

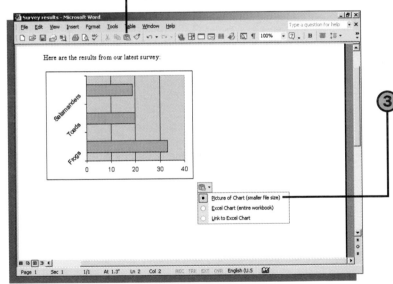

(3) Click the Paste Options Actions button that appears, and click an option to specify how you want the chart to be inserted:

- Picture Of Chart if you're not going to edit the chart and its data

- Excel Chart to incorporate all the Excel data so that you can edit the data without access to the original Excel file

- Link To Excel Chart if you'll need to edit the data and you have access to the original Excel file

Adding Captions to Tables and Figures

Figures, tables, equations, and other similar elements in a technical document often need captions that number these elements consecutively and provide identifying, qualifying, and explanatory text. Word can label and number these items and can keep track of the numbering so that if you add or delete an item in the sequence, Word will automatically renumber the entire sequence.

> **TIP:** Click the AutoCaption button if you want Word to automatically number certain types of items, such as Excel charts or bitmap pictures, when you insert them into your document. If you do use the AutoCaption feature, be sure to check your document carefully to verify that each item you want to have a caption actually has one.

Create a Caption

(1) Select the item to be captioned.

(2) Point to Reference on the Insert menu, and choose Caption from the submenu.

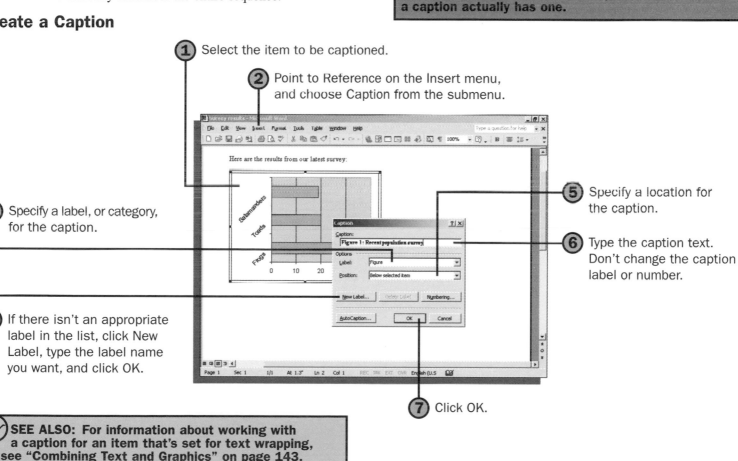

(3) Specify a label, or category, for the caption.

(4) If there isn't an appropriate label in the list, click New Label, type the label name you want, and click OK.

(5) Specify a location for the caption.

(6) Type the caption text. Don't change the caption label or number.

(7) Click OK.

> **SEE ALSO:** For information about working with a caption for an item that's set for text wrapping, see "Combining Text and Graphics" on page 143.

Creating a Table of Figures

A technical document often contains a table that lists all the figures or illustrations that appear in the document. Word can generate a table of figures for you. You can also use the method described here to generate a table of equations, a table of captions, or a table of tables.

CAUTION: Note that if you created a caption as part of a figure, and both the figure and the caption have been set for text wrapping, Word won't include that caption in the table.

Compile the Table

(1) With captions added to all your figures, click in the document where you want the table of figures to appear. Point to Reference on the Insert menu, and choose Index And Tables from the submenu. Click the Table Of Figures tab.

(2) Select a check box to display the page numbers either next to corresponding entries in the table or aligned at the right side of the page. If you want the page numbers right-aligned, specify a style for the tab leader that's placed between the entry and the page number.

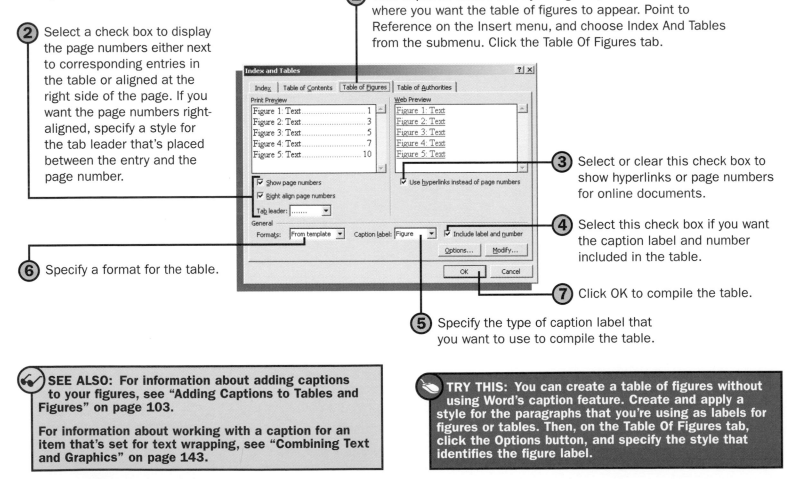

(3) Select or clear this check box to show hyperlinks or page numbers for online documents.

(4) Select this check box if you want the caption label and number included in the table.

(6) Specify a format for the table.

(7) Click OK to compile the table.

(5) Specify the type of caption label that you want to use to compile the table.

SEE ALSO: For information about adding captions to your figures, see "Adding Captions to Tables and Figures" on page 103.

For information about working with a caption for an item that's set for text wrapping, see "Combining Text and Graphics" on page 143.

TRY THIS: You can create a table of figures without using Word's caption feature. Create and apply a style for the paragraphs that you're using as labels for figures or tables. Then, on the Table Of Figures tab, click the Options button, and specify the style that identifies the figure label.

Numbering Lines

It's a nice convenience to be able to number the lines in a technical document for easy reference when the document is being reviewed or discussed. Word will number the lines for you in whatever increments you want, and will skip any paragraphs in which you *don't* want the line numbering to appear.

> **SEE ALSO:** For information about adding numbers to headings only, see "Numbering Headings" on page 77.

Number a Document

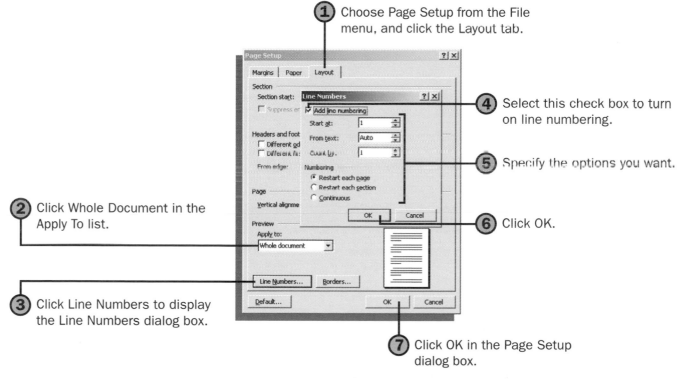

① Choose Page Setup from the File menu, and click the Layout tab.

④ Select this check box to turn on line numbering.

⑤ Specify the options you want.

② Click Whole Document in the Apply To list.

⑥ Click OK.

③ Click Line Numbers to display the Line Numbers dialog box.

⑦ Click OK in the Page Setup dialog box.

> **TIP:** To exclude a paragraph from the numbering sequence, choose Paragraph from the Format menu, and, on the Line And Page Breaks tab, select the Suppress Line Numbers check box.

> **TRY THIS:** After you've inserted the line numbers, open the Styles And Formatting task pane, and change the font, font size, or font color for the Line Number character style.

Creating Cross-References

Cross-references are valuable tools in a long and informative document, but you have to be *extremely* well organized if you're planning to insert them manually, especially if you do a lot of editing and rewriting. It's much easier to let Word do the work for you! Word will keep track of all your cross-references and will keep all the information current. Word can even insert your cross-references as hyperlinks in an online document.

> **TRY THIS:** Create a cross-reference to a heading. Type For more information, see , **open the Cross-Reference dialog box, and insert the heading text. Click in the document, add a space, type** on page , **and use the Cross-Reference dialog box to insert the page number for the heading.**

Create a Cross-Reference

(1) Type the beginning text of your cross-reference.

(5) Select this check box if you want to create a hyperlink to the section of the document being cross-referenced. (A hyperlink is useful only when a document is being read on line.)

(2) Point to Reference on the Insert menu, and choose Cross-Reference from the submenu to display the Cross-Reference dialog box.

(6) Select the cross-reference.

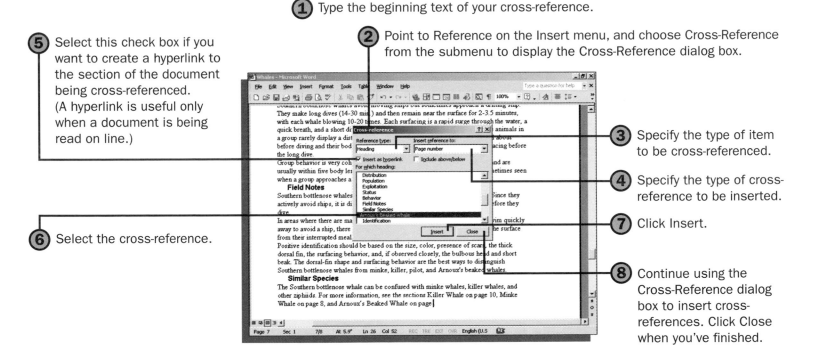

(3) Specify the type of item to be cross-referenced.

(4) Specify the type of cross-reference to be inserted.

(7) Click Insert.

(8) Continue using the Cross-Reference dialog box to insert cross-references. Click Close when you've finished.

> **TIP:** If you insert a cross-reference as a hyperlink, consider formatting the text with the Hyperlink text style. To use a hyperlink to jump to a topic, hold down the Ctrl key and click the hyperlink.

> **SEE ALSO:** For information about creating a book-mark, see "Bookmark a Page Range" on page 93.

8 Organizing with Tables and Lists

Tables are powerful organizational and layout tools that can contain text, pictures, hyperlinks, numbers, and even other tables. If you're familiar with the old way of using tabs to align the columns in a table, forget it! What with proportional fonts and complex layouts, a tab-based table can turn into a misaligned, confusing mess. A Word table provides a spreadsheet-like environment of columns, rows, and cells, into which you insert your content. But the similarity to spreadsheets ends there— Microsoft Word 2002 gives you powerful formatting choices (although it doesn't have the mathematical capabilities that a spreadsheet provides).

Word gives you several ways to create and manage tables. The simplest way? Let Word do it for you! Word creates a generic table, and then, after you add your information, Word can format the table for you, using whichever table style you specify. If you don't like the table styles Word provides, you can design your own customized styles and can dress them up with stripes, shading, and so on. If you don't know how many columns or rows you need when you start the table, you can easily add or delete them as you work.

If you'd prefer your information to be presented as a list rather than as a table, you can choose among a variety of styles of bulleted or numbered lists, or you can design your own list styles. You can create multilevel lists and nested lists, and Word will help you by jumping in and renumbering any items that you move around in a numbered list.

What a great way to organize your information!

Creating a Table

If you think of tables merely as containers for numbers, think again. Tables are a superb way to organize almost any kind of information, and Word makes it so easy. You can draw your table with a little onscreen pencil if you want, but it's easier and faster to let Word do the work for you. Just specify the number of rows and columns you want in your table, and Word will create them for you. Then you can put your content into the cells, adding more rows and columns if you need to, or changing their sizes to make everything fit.

Create a Table

TIP: To convert existing text into a table, select the text, point to Convert on the Table menu, and choose Text To Table from the submenu. Use the options in the Convert Text To Table dialog box to create the table you want.

(1) Click the Insert Table button. Move the mouse pointer to select the number of rows and columns you want in your table. Click to insert the table.

(2) Click in the first cell, and insert your content.

(3) Press Tab to move to the next cell, and add your content. (Press Enter only to start a new paragraph inside a table cell.) Continue pressing Tab to complete your table.

(4) If you've reached the end of your table but you still need to enter more items, press Tab, and Word will create a new row.

TRY THIS: Move the mouse pointer just above the table. When the pointer turns into a small downward-pointing arrow, click, and you'll select the entire column. Move the mouse pointer over another column, hold down the Ctrl key, and click to select a second column. Move the mouse pointer to the left of the table, and click to select an entire row. With columns or rows selected, you can delete all the text or change the formatting of all the selected cells at one time.

TIP: To move to the previous cell, press Shift+Tab. To insert a tab inside a table cell, press Ctrl+Tab.

Format a Table

① Click anywhere inside the table.

② Choose Table AutoFormat from the Table menu to display the Table AutoFormat dialog box.

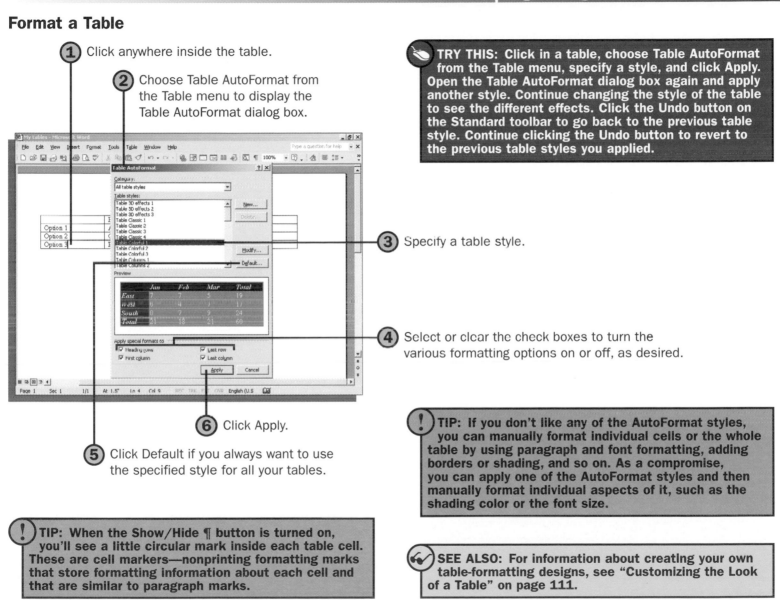

③ Specify a table style.

④ Select or clear the check boxes to turn the various formatting options on or off, as desired.

⑥ Click Apply.

⑤ Click Default if you always want to use the specified style for all your tables.

> **TRY THIS:** Click in a table, choose Table AutoFormat from the Table menu, specify a style, and click Apply. Open the Table AutoFormat dialog box again and apply another style. Continue changing the style of the table to see the different effects. Click the Undo button on the Standard toolbar to go back to the previous table style. Continue clicking the Undo button to revert to the previous table styles you applied.

> **TIP:** If you don't like any of the AutoFormat styles, you can manually format individual cells or the whole table by using paragraph and font formatting, adding borders or shading, and so on. As a compromise, you can apply one of the AutoFormat styles and then manually format individual aspects of it, such as the shading color or the font size.

> **TIP:** When the Show/Hide ¶ button is turned on, you'll see a little circular mark inside each table cell. These are cell markers—nonprinting formatting marks that store formatting information about each cell and that are similar to paragraph marks.

> **SEE ALSO:** For information about creating your own table-formatting designs, see "Customizing the Look of a Table" on page 111.

The Anatomy of a Table

Move box appears when the mouse pointer is positioned over the table in Print Layout and Web Layout views.

Table cells in a row are merged into a single cell.

Different borders can be used to define areas.

Text is vertically aligned.

Text can be horizontal or vertical.

Some cells in a column are merged into a single cell.

Shading

There can be more than one paragraph in a cell. The text and paragraphs in one cell can have different formatting.

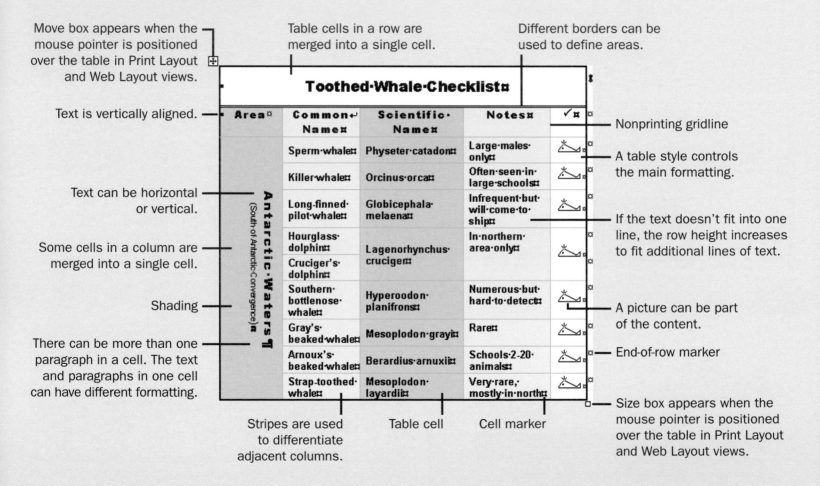

Nonprinting gridline

A table style controls the main formatting.

If the text doesn't fit into one line, the row height increases to fit additional lines of text.

A picture can be part of the content.

End-of-row marker

Size box appears when the mouse pointer is positioned over the table in Print Layout and Web Layout views.

Stripes are used to differentiate adjacent columns.

Table cell

Cell marker

Customizing the Look of a Table ⊕ NEW FEATURE

Word provides numerous formatting styles for tables, but what can
you do if you don't like any of the designs? You can create your
own customized table style, and then you can apply the same
formatting to other tables simply by applying that table style.

Define Your Style

(1) Create your table. With the insertion point in
the table, choose Table AutoFormat from the
Table menu. Review the existing table styles,
noting the name of the style that's most like
the one you want to use.

NEW FEATURE: Table styles are similar to other types
of styles. They can be applied from either the Table
AutoFormat dialog box or the Styles And Formatting
task pane. The styles include a formatting feature called
Stripes, which lets you format the table with colors
alternating by column or row. Click the Format button
to define a striped pattern.

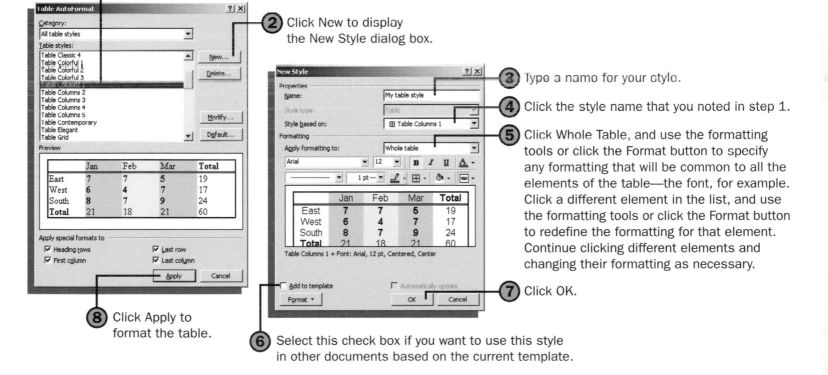

(2) Click New to display
the New Style dialog box.

(3) Type a name for your style.

(4) Click the style name that you noted in step 1.

(5) Click Whole Table, and use the formatting
tools or click the Format button to specify
any formatting that will be common to all the
elements of the table—the font, for example.
Click a different element in the list, and use
the formatting tools or click the Format button
to redefine the formatting for that element.
Continue clicking different elements and
changing their formatting as necessary.

(7) Click OK.

(8) Click Apply to
format the table.

(6) Select this check box if you want to use this style
in other documents based on the current template.

Adding or Deleting Rows and Columns

You can modify an existing table by adding or deleting rows and columns anywhere in the table.

Add to the Table

1 Click in the table next to where you want to add a row or column.

2 Point to Insert on the Table menu, and, from the submenu, choose what you want to add.

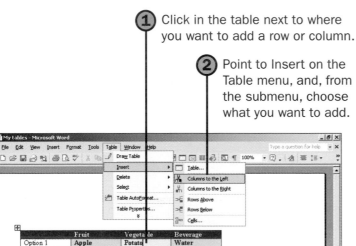

TIP: To delete the content of a row or column without deleting the row or column itself, select the row or column, and press the Delete key.

CAUTION: If you want to delete content from a row or column without deleting the row or column, make sure your selection doesn't extend outside the table. If it does, you'll delete whatever part of the table is selected, as well as its content.

Delete from the Table

1 Click in a table cell that's in the row or column you want to delete.

2 Point to Delete on the Table menu, and, from the submenu, choose what you want to delete.

TRY THIS: Create a table with three columns and three rows. Click in the top left cell. Drag the mouse to the right to select the first two cells. Point to Insert on the Table menu, and choose Columns To The Left from the submenu. With the new columns selected, point to Insert on the Table menu, and choose Rows Above from the submenu. Note that the number of rows or columns that are inserted is based on the number of rows or columns in which cells were selected. Now try deleting rows and columns to revert to the size of the original table.

Positioning Elements in a Table

You can align the text in a table in several ways. Although you can use paragraph formatting to provide some alignments, there are special tools available in a table for more varieties of alignment.

Align the Text

1 Create and format your table.

2 Click in the cell, or select the cells, to which you want to apply a specific alignment.

3 Click the Tables And Borders button on the Standard toolbar to display the Tables And Borders toolbar if it isn't already displayed.

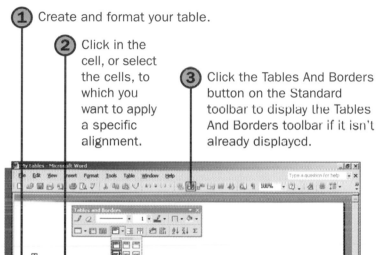

4 Click the Align button, and then click the alignment you want to apply.

> **SEE ALSO:** For information about formatting a table, see "Format a Table" on page 109.
>
> For information about changing the size of cells to accommodate sideways text, see "Customizing a Table Layout" on page 114.

Set the Text Direction

1 Click in the cell, or select the cells, to which you want to apply a specific text direction.

2 Click the Change Text Direction button. If the direction of the text isn't what you want, click the button again.

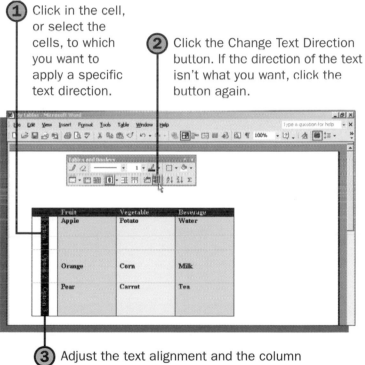

3 Adjust the text alignment and the column and row dimensions as necessary.

> **TRY THIS:** Select an entire column or row of a table that will contain decimal numbers. Choose Tabs from the Format menu, and, in the Tabs dialog box, set a decimal tab in the cell. Click OK, and your numbers will be aligned by their decimal points.

Customizing a Table Layout

A Word table can be more than just a grid of equally sized rows and columns. You can change the width of the columns or the height of rows, for example, or draw new cell boundaries and erase old ones. Word gives you a great deal of flexibility in the layout of your table.

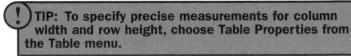

TIP: To specify precise measurements for column width and row height, choose Table Properties from the Table menu.

Change the Table Size

1 In Print Layout view, move the mouse pointer over the table to make the Size box appear.

2 Drag the Size box to change the size of the table.

TRY THIS: Make sure the ruler is displayed. Move the mouse pointer over a cell boundary. Hold down the Alt key while you drag the cell boundary. Note that the ruler shows the distance between the boundaries.

Change the Row or Column Size

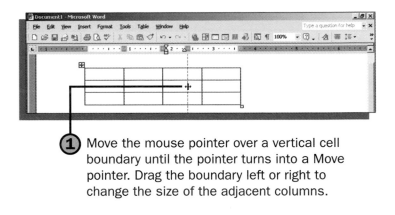

1 Move the mouse pointer over a vertical cell boundary until the pointer turns into a Move pointer. Drag the boundary left or right to change the size of the adjacent columns.

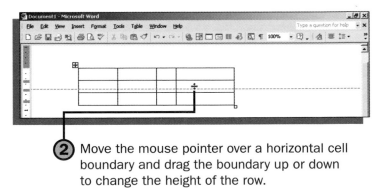

2 Move the mouse pointer over a horizontal cell boundary and drag the boundary up or down to change the height of the row.

Divide One Cell into Two

② Click the Draw Table button if it isn't already turned on. (You'll see a little pencil pointer on your screen when the button is turned on.)

① Click the Tables And Borders button on the Standard toolbar to display the Tables And Borders toolbar if it isn't already displayed.

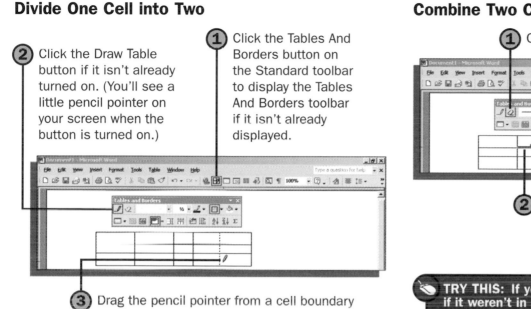

③ Drag the pencil pointer from a cell boundary to the opposite boundary. Add as many cell boundaries as you need. Click the Draw Table button to turn it off when you've finished.

TIP: To delete several cell boundaries, drag the Eraser pointer to include all of them.

CAUTION: When you're working on a table using the Draw Table and the Eraser tools, it's difficult to achieve a high degree of precision. It's easy, for example, to accidentally add boundaries you don't want or delete ones you do want. Carefully inspect your table after you add or delete a boundary. You can remedy an error by clicking the Undo button on the Standard toolbar.

Combine Two Cells into One

① Click the Eraser button.

② Click a cell boundary to delete it and merge the two cells. Click the Eraser button to turn it off when you've finished.

TRY THIS: If you think your content might look better if it weren't in a table after all, you can quickly restore it to standard text. To do so, click in the table, point to Convert on the Table menu, and choose Table To Text from the submenu. In the Convert Table To Text dialog box, click the Paragraph Marks option to have the contents of each cell separated by a paragraph mark when converted into text, and click OK. If you don't like the result, click the Undo button on the Standard toolbar. Click in the table, open the Convert Table To Text dialog box again, and click the Tabs option to have the contents of each cell in a row separated by a tab, and to have each row separated by a paragraph mark. If you still don't like the result and you want to change the text back into a table, select the text, point to Convert on the Table menu, and choose Text To Table from the submenu. In the Convert Text To Table dialog box, specify the table options you want, and click OK.

Aligning a Table

A table is usually positioned with the same alignment as the accompanying text. However, you might want to set a table off a bit by changing its horizontal position—indenting or centering it, for example. By using Word's alignment settings instead of moving the table manually, you'll ensure that the settings will remain in effect even if you change the margins or any other page-layout settings.

Set the Alignment

1 Right-click anywhere in the table, and choose Table Properties from the shortcut menu.

2 On the Table tab of the Table Properties dialog box, click an alignment.

TRY THIS: Create two tables, one smaller than the other. Drag the smaller table and place it on top of the larger table. Note that the smaller table has become "nested" inside the larger table. Right-click in the nested table, choose Table Properties from the shortcut menu, and, on the Table tab of the Table Properties dialog box, click an alignment for the table. Click OK. Note that the alignment of the nested table is relative to the cell in which it's nested. Now click the Undo button to return the tables to their original state.

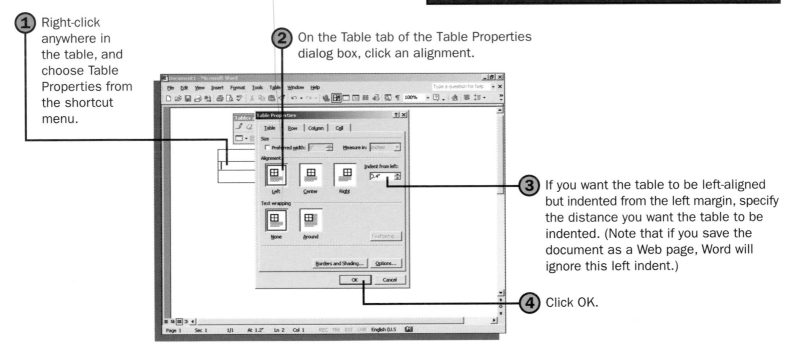

3 If you want the table to be left-aligned but indented from the left margin, specify the distance you want the table to be indented. (Note that if you save the document as a Web page, Word will ignore this left indent.)

4 Click OK.

SEE ALSO: For information about setting text to wrap around a table, see "Moving a Table" on the facing page.

Moving a Table

If you're not happy about the position of a table, you can easily move it into a better location. When you drag a table, you can position it both horizontally and vertically on the page, just as you can position a picture on the page. When you move the table horizontally, you're also setting it to have text wrapping, so, if there's room, any text can wrap around all four sides of the table.

Move the Table

1 Switch to Print Layout view or Web Layout view if you aren't already in either view.

2 Hold the mouse pointer over the table until the little Move box containing a four-headed arrow appears at the top left of the table.

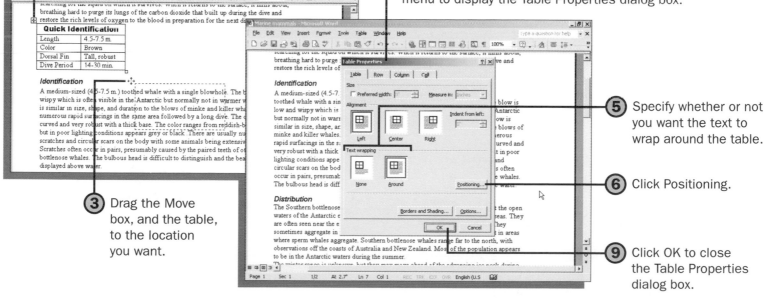

3 Drag the Move box, and the table, to the location you want.

7 Make any changes to the position of the table, and specify how far the table should be from any surrounding text.

8 Click OK.

4 If you can't place the table in the exact location you want, or if the text isn't wrapping in the way you want, right-click the table, and choose Table Properties from the shortcut menu to display the Table Properties dialog box.

5 Specify whether or not you want the text to wrap around the table.

6 Click Positioning.

9 Click OK to close the Table Properties dialog box.

Creating a Bulleted or Numbered List

A great way to clearly present information is to put it in a numbered or bulleted list. Not only does Word add numbers or bullets to your list, with consistent spacing between the number or bullet and the text, but it keeps track of your list so that if you move an item within a numbered list, Word will renumber the list to keep the items in the correct order.

Create a List

TRY THIS: Create a list. When you've entered the last item, press Enter twice.

TIP: Sometimes, between the items in a numbered list, you need to insert unnumbered paragraphs that aren't part of the list. You can control whether the numbering of the items in the part of the list that follows the unnumbered paragraphs should continue the numbering from the previous item or restart the numbering. To do so, right-click the paragraph following the unnumbered paragraph, and click either Restart Numbering or Continue Numbering.

SEE ALSO: For information about using AutoFormat to create a bulleted or numbered list, see "Formatting as You Compose" on page 36.

For information about changing the look of a list, see "Customizing a List" on page 120.

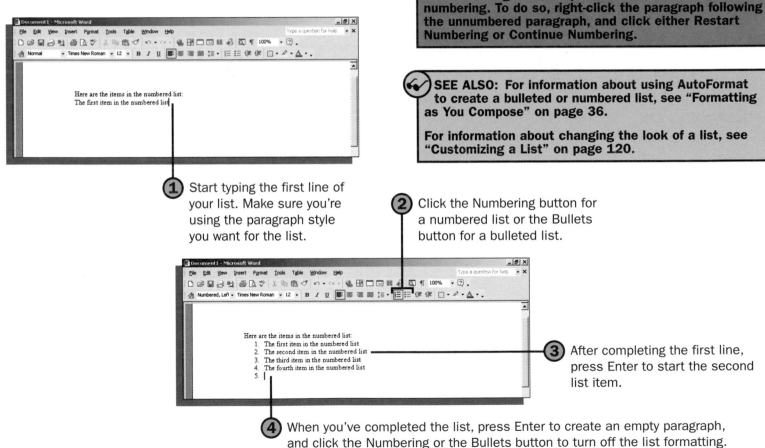

(1) Start typing the first line of your list. Make sure you're using the paragraph style you want for the list.

(2) Click the Numbering button for a numbered list or the Bullets button for a bulleted list.

(3) After completing the first line, press Enter to start the second list item.

(4) When you've completed the list, press Enter to create an empty paragraph, and click the Numbering or the Bullets button to turn off the list formatting.

Creating a Multilevel List

Sometimes a regular list just doesn't do the job for you. If you want a list within a list, or if you need to classify the relationship of items by listing them under specific categories, you can quickly and easily create a multilevel list.

Create a Multilevel List

(1) Start typing the first line of your list, and click either the Numbering or the Bullets button on the Formatting toolbar to format the type of list you want.

(2) At the beginning of the paragraph that you want to start the next level of the list, press Tab. Type the item, and press Enter. Continue entering the items that belong in this level of the list. To return to the previous level of the list, press Shift+Tab.

(3) If you don't like a sublevel's indent, point to the number or the bullet, and drag it to where you want the indent. All the items in the list at that level will move to the new indent.

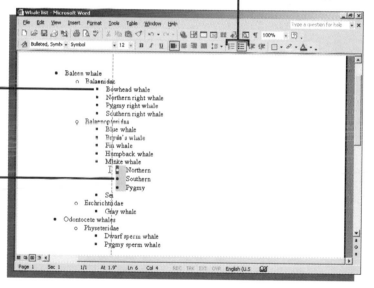

! TIP: If you use multilevel bulleted or numbered lists frequently, consider creating paragraph styles or modifying the existing List styles for each level of the list. That way, you'll be able to make the list look exactly the way you want by simply applying the style.

! TIP: You can create a list with as many as nine levels. If you need more than nine levels, you might want to reconsider your organizational structure!

Customizing a List

If you don't like the type of bullets or the numbering format you've chosen for your list, you can easily change either.

Change the Bullets or the Numbering Format

② Double-click a bullet or a number in your list to display the Bullets And Numbering dialog box. If you want to change a bullet or a numbering format in a sublevel of a multilevel list, double-click the bullet or the number in that sublevel.

① Create your list, using second- or third-level entries if you want.

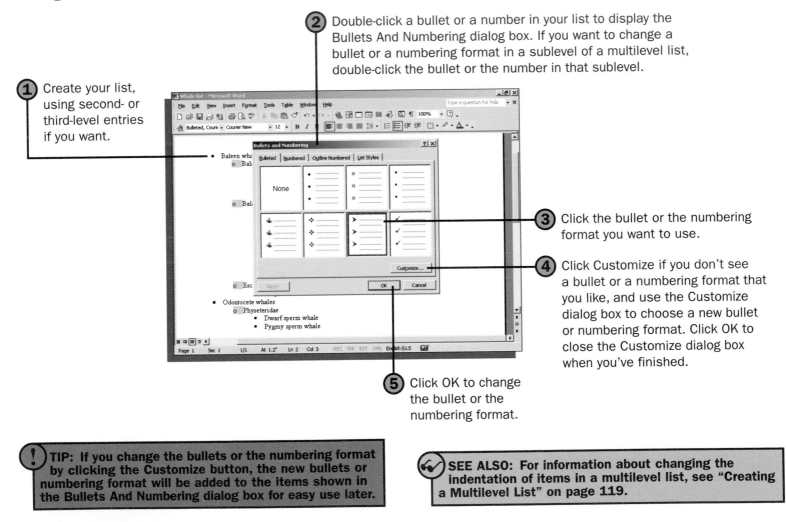

③ Click the bullet or the numbering format you want to use.

④ Click Customize if you don't see a bullet or a numbering format that you like, and use the Customize dialog box to choose a new bullet or numbering format. Click OK to close the Customize dialog box when you've finished.

⑤ Click OK to change the bullet or the numbering format.

> **TIP:** If you change the bullets or the numbering format by clicking the Customize button, the new bullets or numbering format will be added to the items shown in the Bullets And Numbering dialog box for easy use later.

> **SEE ALSO:** For information about changing the indentation of items in a multilevel list, see "Creating a Multilevel List" on page 119.

Designing a List ⊘ NEW FEATURE

You're not limited to the choices Word gives you for bullets or numbers in a list. By designing your own list style, you can create exactly the type of list you want. Once you've defined the style, you simply apply it your to list.

Create a New List Style

> **TIP: A list style doesn't replace a paragraph style.** Use a paragraph style to define the formatting of the text, the paragraph spacing, and so on. Then apply the list style you've designed to define the way the bullets or the numbering will be added to the paragraph.

(1) Click the Styles And Formatting button on the Formatting toolbar to open the Styles And Formatting task pane. Click the New Style button.

(2) Type a name for the style.

(3) Click List.

(4) Specify whether you want a bulleted or a numbered list.

(5) Use the tools to specify the font, font size, and any other formatting for the bullets or numbers in the list.

(6) Click the bullet style or the numbering format you want to use for this level.

(7) Click a different level, and repeat steps 5 and 6. Repeat for each level.

(9) Click OK. Apply the style to your list just as you'd apply any other style.

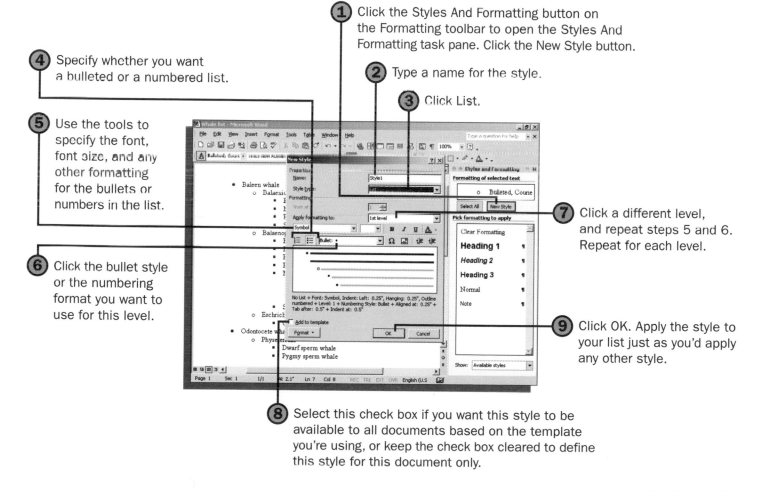

(8) Select this check box if you want this style to be available to all documents based on the template you're using, or keep the check box cleared to define this style for this document only.

Organizing Your Information

Tables and lists are invaluable tools for presenting information briefly and clearly, and you can make them even more useful by organizing them as efficiently as possible. If you have a table or a list that you want to rearrange so that it's presented in alphabetic or numeric order, all you need to do is tell Word to sort it for you.

Sort a Table

① With the insertion point anywhere in the table, choose Sort from the Table menu to display the Sort dialog box.

③ Specify which column to use to sort the table, the type of content in the column, and whether you want the information to be sorted in ascending or in descending order.

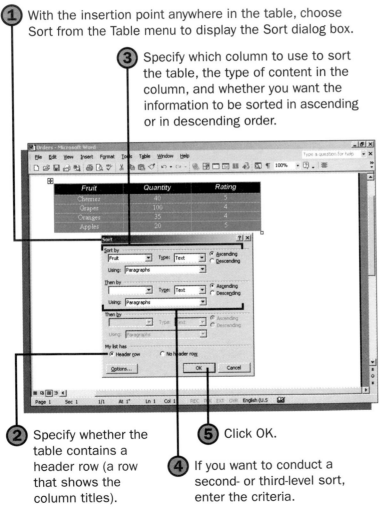

② Specify whether the table contains a header row (a row that shows the column titles).

⑤ Click OK.

④ If you want to conduct a second- or third-level sort, enter the criteria.

Sort a List

② Choose Sort from the Table menu to display the Sort Text dialog box.

③ Specify whether to sort by paragraphs, the type of information that's in the list, and whether you want the information to be sorted in ascending or in descending order.

① Select the entire list.

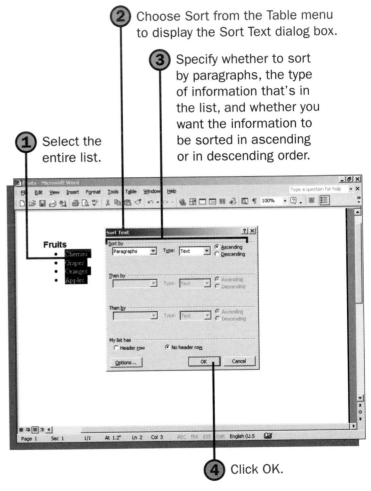

④ Click OK.

9

Adding Pictures and Drawings

Putting pictures or drawings into your documents is one of the most exciting and satisfying ways to use today's technology. In the not-too-distant past, combining text and graphics images—whether those images were drawings, photographs, or clip art—was an expensive and time-consuming proposition. You had to gather up all the separate pieces—your typed text and all the graphics images you were planning to use—and take them to a typographer. Type shops were the only businesses able to afford the technology that could combine text, pictures, and other elements. Now, using the power of Microsoft Word 2002, you can create these complex documents with very little effort or time, and the results can be quite spectacular!

As you might expect, Word gives you the ability to do much more than just plop those pictures into your documents. You can modify your pictures by changing their size or cropping out the parts you don't want. You can make changes to the brightness or contrast of a picture and can even change a color photograph into a grayscale one. You can place a border around a picture to give it a nice "finished" look, and, for a really professional touch, you can wrap text around your pictures in various configurations.

It's easy and fun to play around with the different effects you can create. Try it—if you don't like the results, just click the Reset Picture button to retrieve the unspoiled original, and start again.

Inserting Clip Art

When you're looking for just the right piece of clip art to illustrate your story, you can hunt through different categories or conduct a search using keywords. When you add a picture to a document, the picture becomes part of the document.

Find and Insert Clip Art

SEE ALSO: For information about installing the Clip Organizer if it isn't already installed, see "Adding or Removing Components" on page 222.

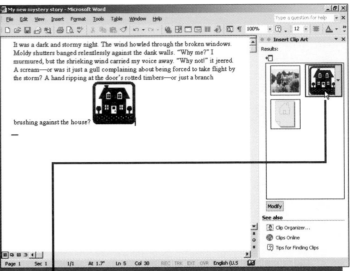

(1) Click in your document where you want to place the clip art.

(2) Point to Picture on the Insert menu, and choose Clip Art from the submenu. If the Add Clips To Organizer dialog box appears, click the Later button.

(7) Click to insert the picture into your document. Add any other clip art you want, and close the Insert Clip Art task pane when you've finished.

(3) In the Insert Clip Art task pane, type the keyword or keywords that describe the type of picture you want.

(4) In the list, click the clip-art collection you want. To select all the categories in the collection, double-click the check box for the collection. To select only certain categories, expand the list under the collection, and select the check box for each category you want to look through.

(5) Specify the type of clip you want.

(6) Click Search to view the items that match your criteria.

Inserting a Picture

You can add different types of picture files to a single document—photographs and drawings, for example, as well as pieces of clip art—provided the pictures are in one of the many different file formats Word can use.

Insert a Picture

1 Click in your document where you want to insert the picture.

2 Point to Picture on the Insert menu, and choose From File from the submenu.

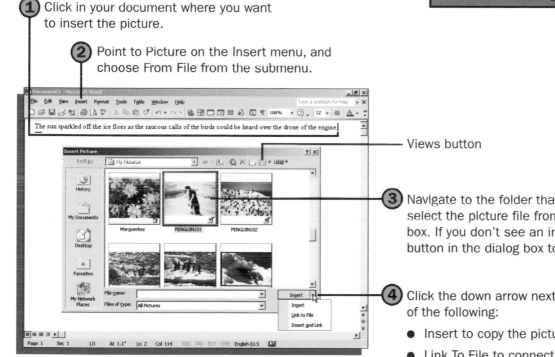

Views button

3 Navigate to the folder that contains the picture you want, and select the picture file from the list in the Insert Picture dialog box. If you don't see an image of the picture, use the Views button in the dialog box to switch to Preview or Thumbnails view.

4 Click the down arrow next to the Insert button, and click one of the following:

- Insert to copy the picture and store it in the Word document.

- Link To File to connect to the picture file without increasing the file size of your Word document. The source picture file must be available for the picture to be displayed.

- Insert And Link to copy the picture, store it in the Word document, and update the picture automatically whenever the source picture file changes.

> **TIP:** Although you can insert a picture directly from a scanner or camera using the From Scanner Or Camera command on the Picture submenu of the Insert menu, you'll usually get better results using a scanner, a camera, or an image-editing program to create the file. Then, if necessary, you can edit the picture before you insert the file into your document.

> **SEE ALSO:** For information about inserting pictures that you cataloged using the Clip Organizer, see "Inserting Clip Art" on the facing page.
>
> For information about modifying a picture or its placement, see "Editing a Picture" on page 126.

Editing a Picture

After you've placed a picture in your document, you can make substantial modifications to the picture to make it look exactly the way you want. The key to your editing capabilities is the Picture toolbar.

Modify the Color

(2) Click the Color button, and choose one of the following to specify how you want the image to appear:

- Automatic to use the original color
- Grayscale to use shades of gray instead of color
- Black & White to use only those two colors
- Washout to create a faint image

(3) Click to adjust the contrast in the picture.

(4) Click to adjust the brightness of the picture.

(1) Click the picture to select it and to display the Picture toolbar if it isn't already displayed.

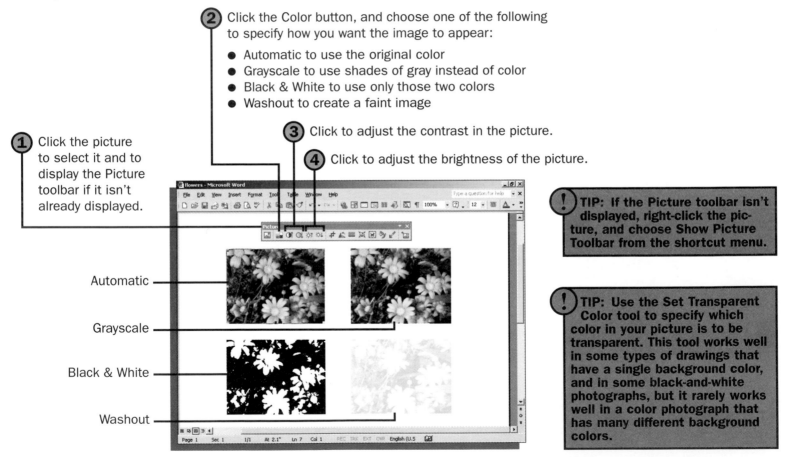

Automatic

Grayscale

Black & White

Washout

TIP: If the Picture toolbar isn't displayed, right-click the picture, and choose Show Picture Toolbar from the shortcut menu.

TIP: Use the Set Transparent Color tool to specify which color in your picture is to be transparent. This tool works well in some types of drawings that have a single background color, and in some black-and-white photographs, but it rarely works well in a color photograph that has many different background colors.

Resize the Picture

(1) Click the picture to select it.

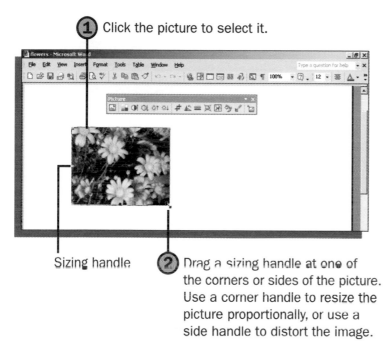

Sizing handle

(2) Drag a sizing handle at one of the corners or sides of the picture. Use a corner handle to resize the picture proportionally, or use a side handle to distort the image.

> (!) **TIP:** When you crop a picture, the cropped part isn't deleted unless you tell Word to delete it. To restore the cropped part of the picture, use the cropping tool to drag the picture border outward to reveal the entire picture.

> (✓) **SEE ALSO:** For information about permanently deleting the cropped portion of a picture, see "Reducing the File Size of a Picture" on page 134.

Crop the Picture

(1) Click the picture to select it and to display the Picture toolbar if it isn't already displayed.

(2) Click the Crop button to use the cropping tool.

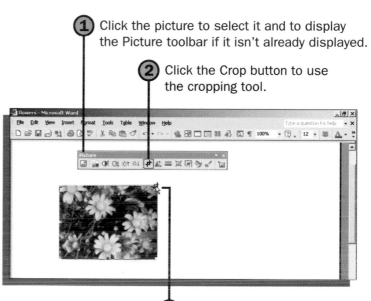

(3) Place the cropping pointer over a sizing handle at one of the corners or sides of the picture, and drag the pointer inward to crop the picture. Click outside the picture to turn off the cropping tool.

> (🖱) **TRY THIS:** With the picture selected, click the Format Picture button on the Picture toolbar. On the Size tab, set a specific height, width, or scaling. On the Picture tab, set the cropping, color, and brightness. Close the dialog box when you've finished. Note the precision of the changes you can make to the picture using the Format Picture dialog box.

Positioning a Picture

When you position a picture in a document, you usually place the picture in line with the regular text so that the picture aligns just like a single text character—albeit a very large one. By changing the text wrapping, you can change the way the picture is positioned in the document.

Set the Text Wrapping

TRY THIS: Choose Options from the Tools menu, and, in the Insert/Paste Pictures As list on the Edit tab, specify the type of text wrapping you'll want to use for most of the pictures you'll be inserting. Click OK. Now you won't need to change the text-wrapping option each time you insert a picture.

(1) Click the picture to select it and to display the Picture toolbar if it isn't already displayed.

(2) Click the Text Wrapping button, and specify the text-wrapping option you want.

(3) Drag the picture to determine its position in the paragraph and the way you want the text to wrap around it.

In Line With Text

Square

Behind Text

In Front Of Text

SEE ALSO: For information about arranging pictures, drawings, and text labels, see "Combining Text and Graphics" on page 143.

Rotate the Picture ⊕ NEW FEATURE

(1) Click the picture to select it and to display the Picture toolbar if it isn't already displayed.

(2) Click the Rotate Left button to rotate the picture 90 degrees. Continue clicking the button to rotate the picture at 90-degree increments.

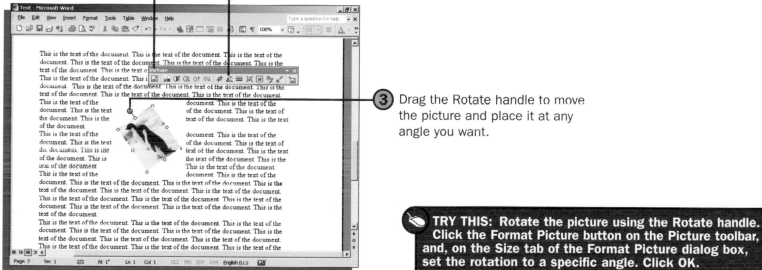

(3) Drag the Rotate handle to move the picture and place it at any angle you want.

TRY THIS: Rotate the picture using the Rotate handle. Click the Format Picture button on the Picture toolbar, and, on the Size tab of the Format Picture dialog box, set the rotation to a specific angle. Click OK.

TIP: You can't rotate a picture with the Rotate handle until Word has changed the picture into an *object*. Word does this automatically when you set the picture for text wrapping or when you click the Rotate Left button on the Picture toolbar.

SEE ALSO: For information about methods of arranging pictures and other items on the page, see "Positioning Items on the Page" on page 144.

For information about changing the way text wraps around a picture, see "Customizing Text Wrapping" on page 146.

Creating a Drawing ⊛ NEW FEATURE

For those of us who aren't great artists, Word's drawing tools provide a quick and easy way to create a variety of professional-looking drawings directly on the page. For an extremely complex drawing, you'll probably want to use a drawing program and then insert the picture, but try using Word's tools first. As artistically challenged individuals, we were really astonished at some of the lively effects we created.

Draw a Shape

1 Click the Drawing button on the Standard toolbar to display the Drawing toolbar if it isn't already displayed.

3 On the Drawing Canvas that appears, drag the mouse to create the shape in the dimensions you want. Hold down the Shift key while dragging to draw the shape without distortion.

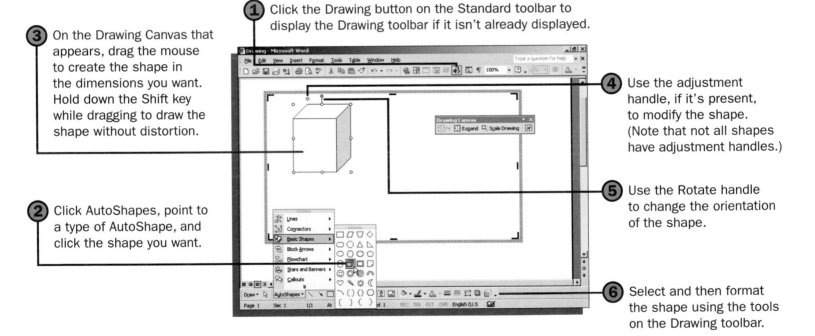

4 Use the adjustment handle, if it's present, to modify the shape. (Note that not all shapes have adjustment handles.)

5 Use the Rotate handle to change the orientation of the shape.

2 Click AutoShapes, point to a type of AutoShape, and click the shape you want.

6 Select and then format the shape using the tools on the Drawing toolbar.

SEE ALSO: For information about the Handwriting tools, see "Writing Text by Hand" on page 198.

Combine Drawings

SEE ALSO: For information about formatting a drawing, see "Formatting a Drawing" on page 133.

For information about including text with AutoShapes and adding labels to pictures set for text wrapping, see "Combining Text and Graphics" on page 143.

(6) Drag the drawing to the location you want.

(7) Click outside the Drawing Canvas to return to your normal text.

(1) Create and format any additional AutoShapes you want. Drag the objects (the drawings) to arrange them. Right-click an object, choose Order from the shortcut menu, and change the *stacking order* of the objects. Continue rearranging the objects until they're in the desired form.

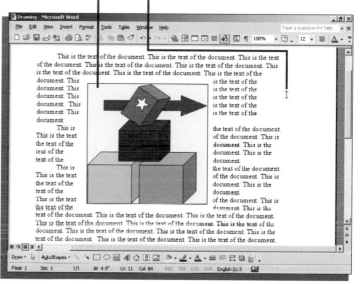

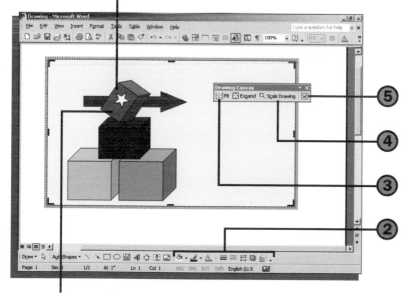

(5) Click Text Wrapping, and specify how you want the drawing positioned in relationship to the text.

(4) If you want to scale the entire drawing, click Scale Drawing, and drag the sizing handles on the canvas to scale it.

(3) When all the elements are arranged to your liking, click Fit to shrink the Drawing Canvas to fit the drawing.

(2) If you want to format the background or the border of the Drawing Canvas, click inside the canvas so that no drawing element is selected, and then use the tools on the Drawing toolbar to add a color fill, a line border, or a shadow or 3-D effect.

The stacking order of the objects is set so that the star is on top of the box, and the box is on top of the arrow.

Adding a Border to a Picture

You've inserted a picture into a document, but the picture's slightly jagged edges make for an unprofessional look that you're not happy with. You can easily create a nice "finished" look by placing a border around the picture. The way you insert the border, however, depends on how Word deals with a picture, and this is usually determined by whether the picture has been set for text wrapping or has been rotated. Fortunately, you don't need to figure this out—Word will display the correct dialog box for you.

Add a Border

1 With the picture selected, choose Borders And Shading from the Format menu. Which dialog box appears depends on whether or not you've set the picture for text wrapping.

The Borders dialog box appears if the picture isn't set for text wrapping. Use the Borders tab to specify the type of border you want and its line style, color, and width. Click OK when you've finished.

TIP: The process of adding borders to items isn't for pictures only. You'll see different dialog boxes depending on the way Word handles the different settings for items such as inserted Microsoft Excel charts, clip art, and a variety of other inserted objects.

TRY THIS: Set a picture for text wrapping, and add a border. Click the Shadow Style button on the Drawing toolbar, and add a shadow. If the entire shadow doesn't show up, use the cropping tool to drag the edges of the picture out to create some white space around the picture so that there's room for the shadow.

The Format Picture dialog box appears if the picture is set for text wrapping. Use the Colors And Lines tab to set the line color, style, pattern, and weight (thickness). Click OK to create the border.

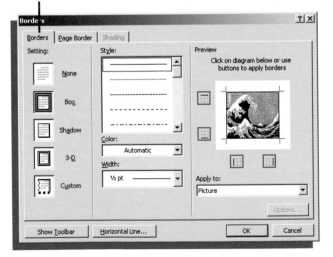

Formatting a Drawing

Just as you can format text to enhance or emphasize the information you're presenting, you can format a drawing to improve the way it looks or to subtly accent parts of it. To format a drawing, you use the Drawing toolbar.

> **TIP:** You can use many of the methods described here to format a picture or a piece of clip art.

Format the Drawing

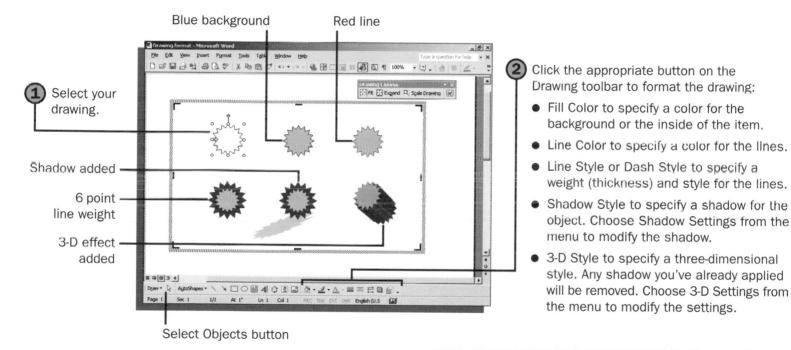

Blue background

Red line

1 Select your drawing.

Shadow added

6 point line weight

3-D effect added

Select Objects button

2 Click the appropriate button on the Drawing toolbar to format the drawing:

- Fill Color to specify a color for the background or the inside of the item.
- Line Color to specify a color for the lines.
- Line Style or Dash Style to specify a weight (thickness) and style for the lines.
- Shadow Style to specify a shadow for the object. Choose Shadow Settings from the menu to modify the shadow.
- 3-D Style to specify a three-dimensional style. Any shadow you've already applied will be removed. Choose 3-D Settings from the menu to modify the settings.

> **SEE ALSO:** For information about drawing a shape and working with the Drawing Canvas, see "Creating a Drawing" on page 130.
>
> For information about adding text to an AutoShape, see "Creating a Pull Quote" on page 149 and "Flowing Text Between Text Boxes and AutoShapes" on page 155.

> **TRY THIS:** Insert and format an AutoShape. Insert and format a second AutoShape. Drag one of the drawings and place it on top of the other. Click the Select Objects button on the Drawing toolbar, and drag a rectangle to encompass both drawings so that both become selected. Right-click in the selection, point to Grouping on the shortcut menu, and choose Group from the submenu. Use the formatting tools. Note that all the formatting applies to both objects.

Reducing the File Size of a Picture ⊕ NEW FEATURE

Pictures are wonderful additions to your documents, but they can make a document's file size so large that it becomes unwieldy. Fortunately, you can drastically reduce the file size of a picture by compressing it, by reducing its resolution, and by deleting from the file any part of the picture that was cropped out on the screen.

Reduce the File Size

① Select the picture or pictures to be compressed. If you want to compress all the pictures in your document, you need to select only one picture.

② Click the Compress Pictures button.

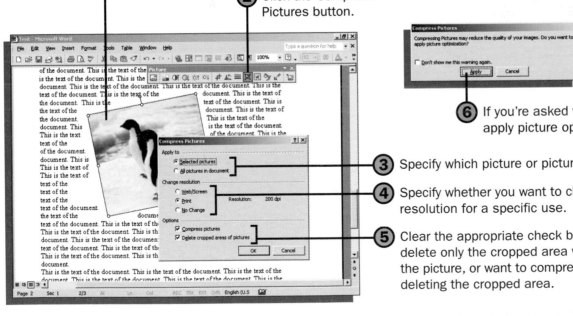

③ Specify which picture or pictures you want to compress.

④ Specify whether you want to change the picture resolution for a specific use.

⑤ Clear the appropriate check box if you want to delete only the cropped area without compressing the picture, or want to compress the picture without deleting the cropped area.

⑥ If you're asked whether you want to apply picture optimization, click Apply.

> **TRY THIS:** Insert a picture into a document, and then save and close the document. Click the Open button on the Standard toolbar, and locate the document. Use Details view to note the document's file size. Open the document, select the picture, compress it, and change its resolution. Save and close the document. Use the Open dialog box again, note the file size, and open the document again. Observe how the file size has changed, and see whether you can notice any difference in the quality of the picture.

> **TIP:** To select multiple pictures, hold down the Ctrl key as you click each picture.

10 Desktop Publishing

Desktop publishing requires neither a desktop (a kitchen table or a lap will do) nor a publisher. Desktop publishing is simply a collection of tools and techniques that let you design and lay out pages so that they look the way you want.

Microsoft Word 2002 provides many of the features you'll find in most commercial desktop publishing programs, so, unless you need to do really specialized tasks, you can use Word to accomplish the most frequently used publishing techniques. For example, you can create illustrations with callouts; add sidebars, pull quotes, dropped capital letters, and borders; write text sideways; and twist text into fantastic shapes using WordArt. If you've ever tried to create and print a small booklet, you know what a nightmare it can be to figure out how to print and then fold the sheets of paper so that your booklet's pages end up in the correct numerical order. Well, no more nightmares! You can leave it to Word to figure out those complexities for you.

One of the critical aspects of desktop publishing is the need to position items exactly where you want them on the page. In Word, when you set an item for text wrapping, you release that item from its usual bonds—that is, it no longer has to stay in line with everything else on the page. Instead, you can move the item wherever you want, and you can even put it in front of or behind the text of your document. A great way to position text is to place it in its own text box or in a text box that's part of an AutoShape. Text boxes give you the freedom to put text inside a "speech balloon" or to *flow* text between columns on different pages.

Flowing Text into Columns

You can flow text into multiple columns on a page, like the columns in a newspaper or magazine. By dividing a page into separate sections, you can even vary the number of columns in each section of the page.

Change the Number of Columns

① Without worrying about the layout just yet, add the content to your document. Make sure the page orientation and the margins are set correctly for the document.

② Click the Show/Hide ¶ button on the Standard toolbar if it isn't already turned on.

SEE ALSO: For information about changing the layout of existing text, see "Changing Page Orientation Within a Document" on page 89.

For information about changing the margins within a document, see "Changing Margins Within a Document" on page 90.

TIP: Word automatically equalizes the length of the text in multiple columns unless you insert a manual column break.

④ Click the Columns button on the Standard toolbar, specify the number of columns you want, and click. Word makes the selected text into a separate section by inserting Continuous section breaks before and after the selected text.

⑥ Choose Columns from the Format menu to display the Columns dialog box.

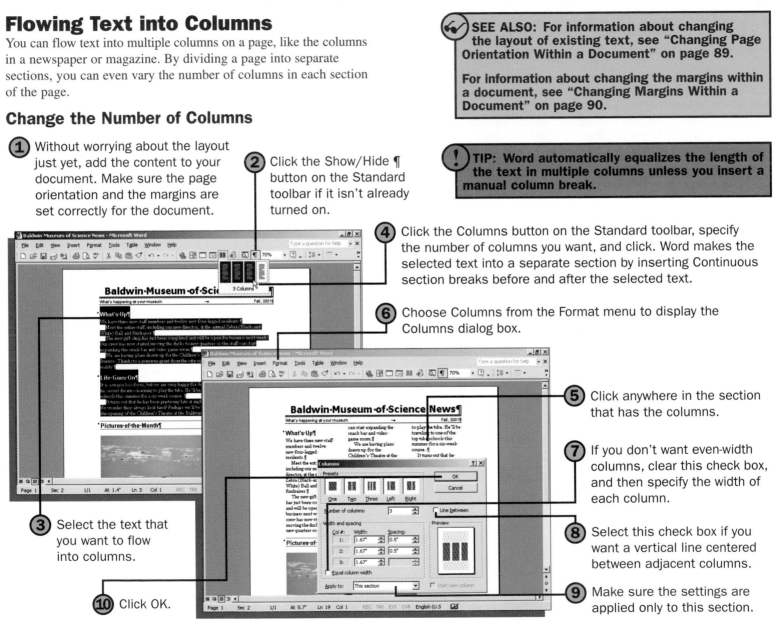

③ Select the text that you want to flow into columns.

⑤ Click anywhere in the section that has the columns.

⑦ If you don't want even-width columns, clear this check box, and then specify the width of each column.

⑧ Select this check box if you want a vertical line centered between adjacent columns.

⑨ Make sure the settings are applied only to this section.

⑩ Click OK.

Creating a Side-by-Side Layout

A side-by-side layout is often used to present an item—a picture, a title, or a topic, for example—in one paragraph, along with a description or an explanation of the item in the adjoining paragraph.

It's easy to create this type of layout using a Word table. With a table, the contents of the two paragraphs are always side by side, regardless of their size or category.

Create the Layout

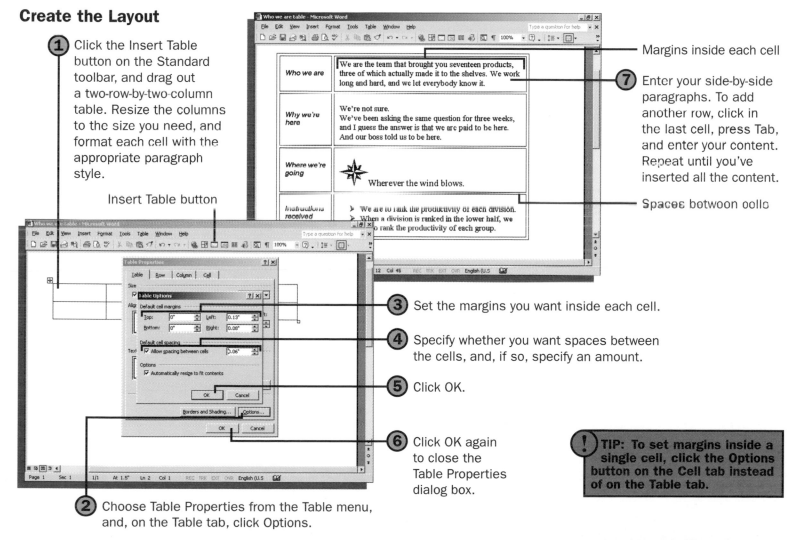

(1) Click the Insert Table button on the Standard toolbar, and drag out a two-row-by-two-column table. Resize the columns to the size you need, and format each cell with the appropriate paragraph style.

Insert Table button

Margins inside each cell

(7) Enter your side-by-side paragraphs. To add another row, click in the last cell, press Tab, and enter your content. Repeat until you've inserted all the content.

Spaces between cells

(3) Set the margins you want inside each cell.

(4) Specify whether you want spaces between the cells, and, if so, specify an amount.

(5) Click OK.

(6) Click OK again to close the Table Properties dialog box.

(2) Choose Table Properties from the Table menu, and, on the Table tab, click Options.

> **! TIP: To set margins inside a single cell, click the Options button on the Cell tab instead of on the Table tab.**

Placing a Line Border Around a Page

You can add a very nice finishing touch to a page by placing a border around it. Word provides a wide variety of easily applied, customizable line styles.

Create a Line Border

(1) Choose Borders And Shading from the Format menu, and click the Page Border tab of the Borders And Shading dialog box.

(2) Click the type of border you want.

(3) Specify a line style, color, and width.

SEE ALSO: For information about placing a border around a paragraph, see "Adding a Border or Shading to a Paragraph" on page 140.

TRY THIS: Insert a page border. Click a button to remove the border from one side. Specify a different line style, width, or color, and click the same border button. Repeat to modify the other sides to create a custom border.

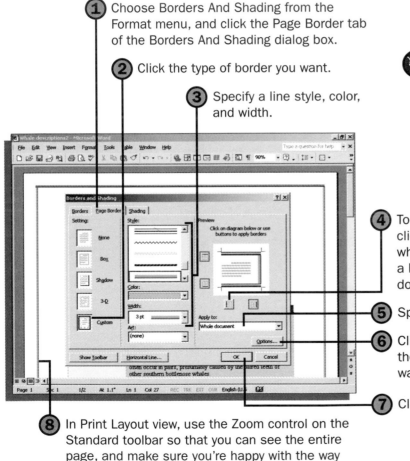

(4) To remove an existing border from one side of the page, click the border button that represents the side of the page whose border you want to remove. To add a border, click a border button that represents a side of the page that doesn't have a border.

(5) Specify the part of the document that will have this border.

(6) Click Options to change the distance of the border from the edge of the page or the text, and to specify whether you want the running heads to be surrounded by this border.

(7) Click OK.

(8) In Print Layout view, use the Zoom control on the Standard toolbar so that you can see the entire page, and make sure you're happy with the way the border looks.

Placing an Art Border Around a Page

You can go beyond line borders and add one of Word's attractive and fanciful art borders around a page. How about a border of cupcakes or ice-cream cones for a party invitation, palm trees for a travel brochure, or ladybugs for an environmental newsletter?

Playing with the different looks you can create with this huge collection of art borders is almost irresistible, and it's so easy and satisfying to do!

Create an Art Border

① Choose Borders And Shading from the Format menu, and click the Page Border tab.

② Click the Box setting.

③ Specify the art you want to use for your border.

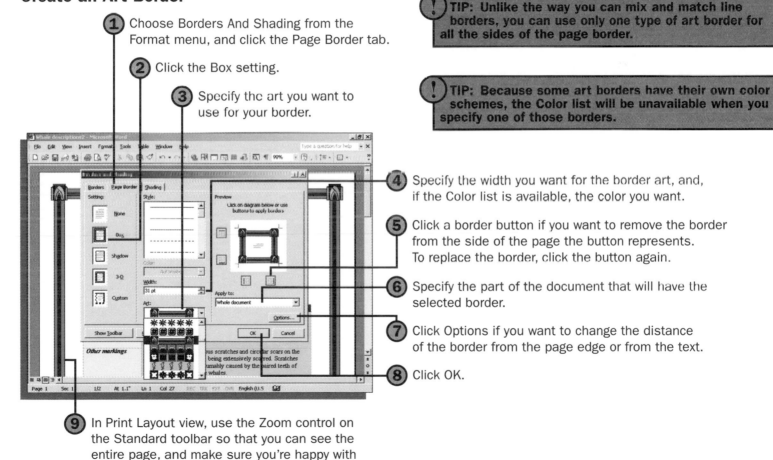

④ Specify the width you want for the border art, and, if the Color list is available, the color you want.

⑤ Click a border button if you want to remove the border from the side of the page the button represents. To replace the border, click the button again.

⑥ Specify the part of the document that will have the selected border.

⑦ Click Options if you want to change the distance of the border from the page edge or from the text.

⑧ Click OK.

⑨ In Print Layout view, use the Zoom control on the Standard toolbar so that you can see the entire page, and make sure you're happy with the way the border looks.

Adding a Border or Shading to a Paragraph

A great way to separate a paragraph from its surrounding text, or to highlight specific information, is to surround the paragraph with a border and/or to add shading to the paragraph.

TRY THIS: Select a word or a sentence, but don't select a whole paragraph. Open the Borders And Shading dialog box, add a border and some shading, and, in the Apply To box, specify Text. Click OK.

Add a Border

(1) With the insertion point in the paragraph that is to have the border, choose Borders And Shading from the Format menu, and click the Borders tab if it isn't already displayed.

(2) Click the type of border you want.

(3) Specify a line style, color, and width.

(4) Click a border button if you want to remove the border from the side of the page the button represents. To replace the border, click the button again.

(5) Specify Paragraph.

(6) Click Options if you want to change the distance of the border from the text.

Add Shading

(1) Click the Shading tab.

(2) Click the color you want.

(3) Specify Paragraph.

(4) Click OK.

(5) Adjust the paragraph indents and the line spacing to make the paragraph stand out exactly as you want it to.

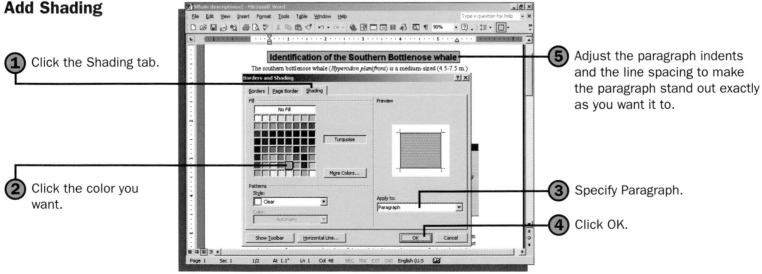

Adjusting the Spacing Between Characters

Sometimes you'll need to squeeze a little more text into a line; at other times you'll want to spread the text out to fill up a line. Perhaps you want to create a special look in a heading by condensing or expanding the text. You can achieve all these effects by adjusting the widths of characters and the spaces between characters and words.

Adjust the Spacing

1 Select the text whose spacing you want to adjust.

2 Choose Font from the Format menu, and click the Character Spacing tab.

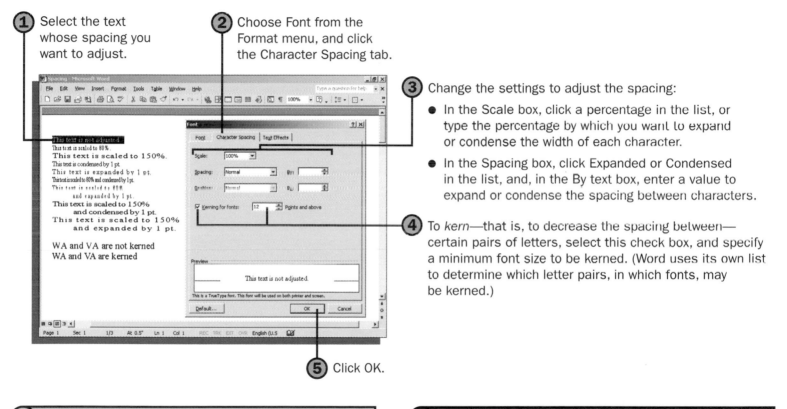

3 Change the settings to adjust the spacing:

- In the Scale box, click a percentage in the list, or type the percentage by which you want to expand or condense the width of each character.

- In the Spacing box, click Expanded or Condensed in the list, and, in the By text box, enter a value to expand or condense the spacing between characters.

4 To kern—that is, to decrease the spacing between—certain pairs of letters, select this check box, and specify a minimum font size to be kerned. (Word uses its own list to determine which letter pairs, in which fonts, may be kerned.)

5 Click OK.

SEE ALSO: For information about adjusting the character spacing in WordArt, see "Creating Stylized Text" on page 150

CAUTION: As a side effect of your increasing or decreasing the character spacing, Word also adjusts the spacing between words.

Creating an Inline Heading

Many document designs use *inline* headings—that is, the first sentence (or part of the first sentence) of a paragraph is formatted as a bold or an italic subheading. An inline heading is also called a *run-in* heading because, unlike more prominent headings, it doesn't have its own separate paragraph but is run in with the paragraph text. Just as you create a main heading with a paragraph style, you create an inline heading with a character style. By using a character style, you assure yourself that the formatting of all inline headings will be consistent throughout your document.

Create the Inline Heading

1 Type your paragraph, including the text for the heading. Use the appropriate paragraph style, but don't worry about the formatting of the heading.

2 Select the text that will be the inline heading, and format it as you want.

> **! TIP:** Depending on your formatting choices, an inline heading can make your paragraph's line spacing inconsistent. If you want all the lines in the paragraph to have the same vertical spacing, choose Paragraph from the Format menu, and set the Line Spacing to At Least and the At value to the same size as that of the inline heading's font.

3 Click the Styles And Formatting button on the Formatting toolbar to display the Styles And Formatting task pane if it isn't already open.

4 Click New Style.

5 In the New Style dialog box, name the style.

6 Specify Character in the Style Type list.

7 Select this check box to save the style to your template.

8 Click OK. The next time you need an inline heading, select the text and apply the character style you just defined.

> **✓ SEE ALSO:** For information about creating a character style, see "Creating Your Own Styles" on page 42.

Combining Text and Graphics ⊘ NEW FEATURE

Many types of publications, from textbooks to great works of literature, contain illustrations—pictures, diagrams, charts, and so on—together with text labels, including *callouts* (such as those you see throughout this book) that label the entire graphic or describe specific parts of it. By assembling the different parts of your graphic on Word's Drawing Canvas, you can build a composite graphic that you can then incorporate as a single unit into your document.

> **TRY THIS:** Create and copy an object such as a Microsoft Excel chart, click the Drawing Canvas, and then use the Paste Special command on the Edit menu to insert the chart as a picture. Now add callouts to identify specific points of interest, and add a text box that contains descriptive text to label the illustration. By including the label on the Drawing Canvas, the label will stay with the illustration even if you change the text wrapping around the illustration.

Combine the Parts

① Point to Picture on the Insert menu, and choose New Drawing from the submenu to start a new, blank Drawing Canvas.

② With the Drawing Canvas selected, use the Insert menu to insert your picture. Format the picture and position it on the Drawing Canvas so that there's enough room around the picture to add your callouts.

③ Use the Line tool or the Arrow tool on the Drawing toolbar to create a callout rule from the picture to the area where you want to place the callout.

Smooth surfaces indicate that the iceberg has flipped over.

The calm water is starting to freeze.

Text Box button

⑦ Click the Text Wrapping button, and specify the way you want the main body of your text to wrap around the entire picture and its callouts.

⑥ When you've finished, click Fit to reduce the size of the Drawing Canvas so that it neatly accommodates the picture and its callouts.

⑤ Repeat steps 3 and 4 to add any other callouts. If you want, add a text box at the top or bottom of the graphic, and insert text to label the entire illustration.

④ Click the Text Box button, and insert a text box that's large enough to contain your text. Type and format the text. If you don't want a rule around the text, select the text box, choose Text Box from the Format menu, and, on the Color And Lines tab, set the Line Color to No Line. Click OK. Use the sizing handles on the text box to make the text box just fit the text.

> **TIP:** When you insert a diagram, it uses its own type of Drawing Canvas. Use that canvas to add callouts or other text.

Positioning Items on the Page

One of the most important aspects of desktop publishing is the ability it provides to position the various graphics elements exactly where you want them. Word provides a *grid* to help you place the items with great precision. You can display the grid, change its dimensions, and specify how you want items to align to the grid.

Use the Grid

(1) Point to Toolbars on the View menu, and choose Drawing from the submenu to display the Drawing toolbar if it isn't already displayed. Switch to Print Layout view if you're not already in that view. Click the Draw button, and choose Grid.

(2) Select this check box if it isn't already selected so that the items will align to the layout grid.

(8) Drag the item near to where you want it to align. It will snap to the closest gridlines.

TRY THIS: Display the grid. Point to Picture on the Insert menu, and choose New Drawing from the submenu. Draw your AutoShapes on the Drawing Canvas, using the grid on the Drawing Canvas. Click Fit on the Drawing Canvas toolbar, and specify the text wrapping you want. Now use the grid on the page (instead of the grid on the Drawing Canvas) to position the Drawing Canvas.

TIP: Don't forget to turn off the grid display when you've finished aligning your items. The grid can be very distracting when you're working on normal text.

(3) Set the dimensions for the grid.

(4) If you want the grid's boundaries to be different from the document's margins, clear this check box, and specify the margins you want for the grid.

(5) Select this check box to see the grid on the screen.

(6) Select this check box to include vertical gridlines, and specify the interval for the display of vertical and horizontal gridlines.

(7) Click OK to display the grid.

Fine-Tune the Alignment

(1) Click to select the item you want to move.

(2) Click the Draw button on the Drawing toolbar, point to Nudge on the menu, and drag the little bar at the top of the submenu into your document to create a floating toolbar.

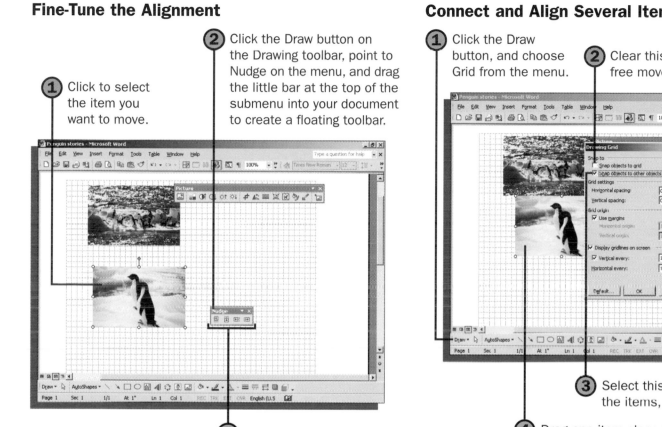

(3) Click a Nudge button to move the item one gridline at a time. Continue using the Nudge buttons until you've positioned the item where you want it. Close the toolbar when you've finished.

> **TIP:** To specify a precisely measured position for an item, choose Format Picture (or Format AutoShape, or whatever type of item it is) from the Edit menu, and, on the Layout tab, click the Advanced button.

Connect and Align Several Items

(1) Click the Draw button, and choose Grid from the menu.

(2) Clear this check box to allow free movement of the items.

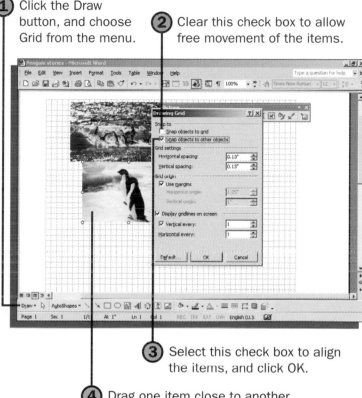

(3) Select this check box to align the items, and click OK.

(4) Drag one item close to another to align the items as desired.

> **TRY THIS:** Draw a couple of AutoShapes. Select the Snap Objects To Grid check box in the Drawing Grid dialog box, and click OK. Display the Nudge toolbar. Slowly resize one item, and note that its size jumps one grid increment at a time. Click a Nudge button and note that the item moves by one grid increment at a time. Go back to the Drawing Grid dialog box, and clear the Snap Objects To Grid check box. Resize and then nudge the item. Note how it behaves this time.

Customizing Text Wrapping

Wrapping text around an item can add another level of polish to the professional look of your document. However, using one of the standard text-wrapping configurations doesn't always produce the desired effect. As you might expect, you can customize the way Word wraps the text.

Create a Customized Word Wrap

TRY THIS: Set an item with Behind Text wrapping, and move the item so that the text runs over it. Now try to select the item. No luck? Click the Select Objects tool (the button that displays a pointer) on the Drawing toolbar, and draw a selection rectangle to surround the item. Now you can move the item or change its text wrapping.

(1) Right-click the item to be wrapped, and choose Format Picture (or Format Object, Drawing Canvas, or whatever type of item it is) from the shortcut menu. On the Layout tab, click Advanced to display the Advanced Layout dialog box.

(2) On the Text Wrapping tab, click the type of wrap you want.

(3) Specify which side or sides of the item you want the text wrap applied to.

(4) Specify the minimum spacing between the item and the text.

(5) Click OK.

(6) Click OK.

TIP: When you're using the Drawing Canvas, set the text wrapping for the Drawing Canvas itself, not for the individual items on the Drawing Canvas.

Change the Wrapping Shape

 Click to select the item to be wrapped if it isn't already selected.

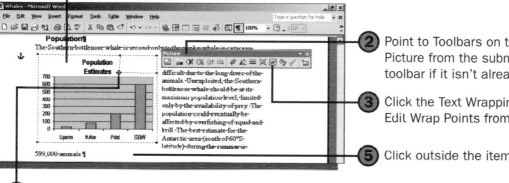

② Point to Toolbars on the View menu, and choose Picture from the submenu to display the Picture toolbar if it isn't already displayed.

③ Click the Text Wrapping button, and choose Edit Wrap Points from the menu.

⑤ Click outside the item to deselect it.

④ Drag a wrapping point to change the wrapping outline. Continue moving wrapping points, or drag the line to create a new wrapping point.

Wrap Part of an Item

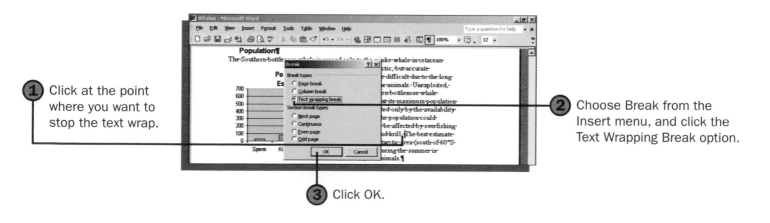

① Click at the point where you want to stop the text wrap.

② Choose Break from the Insert menu, and click the Text Wrapping Break option.

③ Click OK.

Creating a Dropped Capital Letter

A *drop cap,* sometimes called a *fancy first letter,* adds style and interest to a document and attracts the reader's eye to the page. Drop caps are typically used at the beginning of chapters or sections, as in this book.

Create a Drop Cap

① Click at the right of the first letter of your paragraph.

② Choose Drop Cap from the Format menu to display the Drop Cap dialog box.

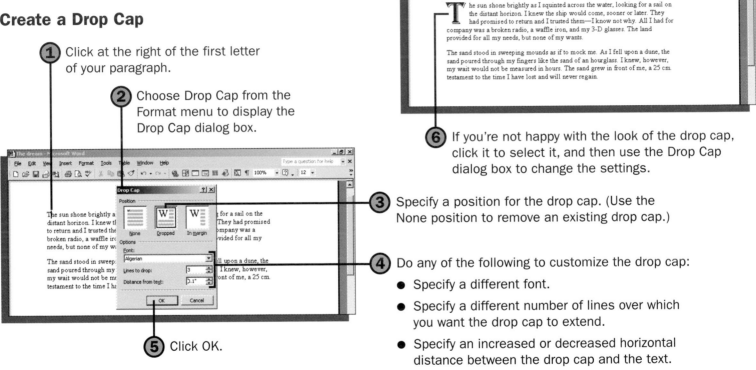

⑤ Click OK.

⑥ If you're not happy with the look of the drop cap, click it to select it, and then use the Drop Cap dialog box to change the settings.

③ Specify a position for the drop cap. (Use the None position to remove an existing drop cap.)

④ Do any of the following to customize the drop cap:

- Specify a different font.
- Specify a different number of lines over which you want the drop cap to extend.
- Specify an increased or decreased horizontal distance between the drop cap and the text.

TRY THIS: You don't have to restrict the drop-cap effect to one solitary letter. Try selecting several letters, or even an entire word, and then apply a drop-cap style.

TIP: A drop cap is created as a separate paragraph, using a frame, so you can add borders and shading to it as you can to any paragraph.

Creating a Pull Quote

A *pull quote* is a short piece of text, extracted from your document, that calls your reader's attention to the content of the page and adds visual interest. You'll want to set the pull quote off from the main text of the document by surrounding it with some white (or colored) space in the shape of your choice. To do so, you'll need to create a drawing without using the Drawing Canvas.

Create the Pull Quote

(1) Select and copy the text you want to use for the pull quote.

> **SEE ALSO:** For information about placing an object relative to a paragraph or to the page, see "Positioning Items on the Page" on page 144.

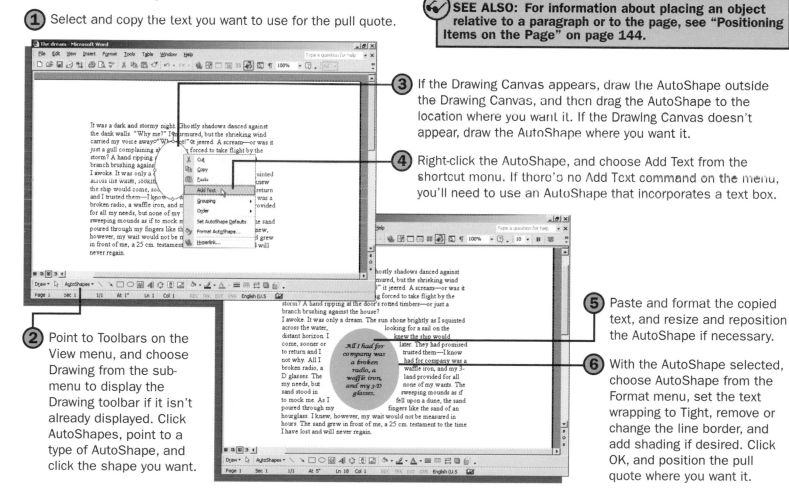

(2) Point to Toolbars on the View menu, and choose Drawing from the submenu to display the Drawing toolbar if it isn't already displayed. Click AutoShapes, point to a type of AutoShape, and click the shape you want.

(3) If the Drawing Canvas appears, draw the AutoShape outside the Drawing Canvas, and then drag the AutoShape to the location where you want it. If the Drawing Canvas doesn't appear, draw the AutoShape where you want it.

(4) Right-click the AutoShape, and choose Add Text from the shortcut menu. If there's no Add Text command on the menu, you'll need to use an AutoShape that incorporates a text box.

(5) Paste and format the copied text, and resize and reposition the AutoShape if necessary.

(6) With the AutoShape selected, choose AutoShape from the Format menu, set the text wrapping to Tight, remove or change the line border, and add shading if desired. Click OK, and position the pull quote where you want it.

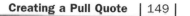

Creating Stylized Text

You can achieve some spectacular effects by creating text as art. Word uses an accessory program called WordArt that lets you twist your text into weird and wonderful shapes and three-dimensional configurations, and then inserts the result into your document as an object. WordArt might look a bit jagged and rough on your computer screen, but the edges smooth out when it's printed, and the results can be dazzling. Try it. But heed our warning—it's highly addictive!

Create Some WordArt

① Point to Picture on the Insert menu, and choose WordArt from the submenu to display the WordArt Gallery dialog box.

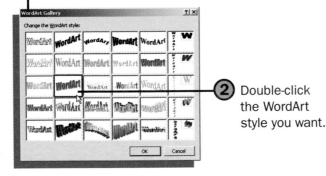

② Double-click the WordArt style you want.

 TIP: To transform some existing text into WordArt, select the text before you click the Insert WordArt button on the WordArt toolbar.

TRY THIS: Type the text for your WordArt in the Edit WordArt Text dialog box, and click OK. Double-click the WordArt to open the Edit WordArt dialog box again, and make any changes you want to the text, the font, the font size, or the emphasis. Click OK. Click the WordArt Gallery button on the WordArt toolbar to display the WordArt Gallery dialog box again. Click a different WordArt style, and click OK. You'll see how easy it is to change the entire setup of the WordArt you just created.

③ In the Edit WordArt Text dialog box, specify a font, a font size, and any character emphasis you want. The same formatting will apply to all the text in this piece of WordArt.

④ Type your text. (Note that WordArt text doesn't wrap automatically; you have to press Enter to start a new line.)

⑤ Click OK.

Fine-Tune the Result

(1) Click the WordArt to select it.

(2) Use the sizing handles to change the size of the art.

TRY THIS: Create some WordArt, and then use the WordArt toolbar to change the shape, color, and rotation of the text. Use the 3-D button on the Drawing toolbar to apply a three-dimensional effect. Click 3-D Settings on the 3-D button, and use the 3-D toolbar to change the tilt, lighting, and 3-D angle. Amazing, isn't it? And so much fun!

TIP: To change the colors of dual-colored or multi-colored WordArt, click the Format WordArt button on the WordArt toolbar, and use the Fill Effects item in the Color list on the Colors And Lines tab of the Format WordArt dialog box.

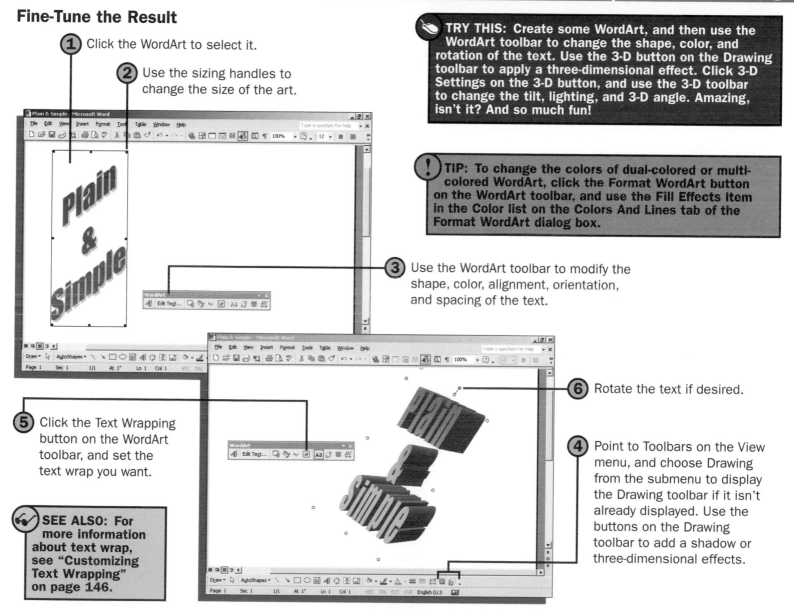

(3) Use the WordArt toolbar to modify the shape, color, alignment, orientation, and spacing of the text.

(5) Click the Text Wrapping button on the WordArt toolbar, and set the text wrap you want.

(6) Rotate the text if desired.

(4) Point to Toolbars on the View menu, and choose Drawing from the submenu to display the Drawing toolbar if it isn't already displayed. Use the buttons on the Drawing toolbar to add a shadow or three-dimensional effects.

SEE ALSO: For more information about text wrap, see "Customizing Text Wrapping" on page 146.

Creating Margin Notes

A popular design choice for many documents is to create wide outside margins and then use them to place notes—cross-references or tips, for example—that are separate from the flow of the document's main content.

SEE ALSO: For information about creating a style, see "Creating Your Own Styles" on page 42.

For information about changing the width of the margins, see "Changing Margins Within a Document" on page 90.

Create a Layout

1 Choose Page Setup from the File menu, and, on the Margins tab, click Mirror Margins in the Multiple Pages list.

TIP: If you'll be printing on only one side of the page—that is, if the document isn't set up for mirror margins—create a wide left or right margin, and position the frame on the left or right side of the page.

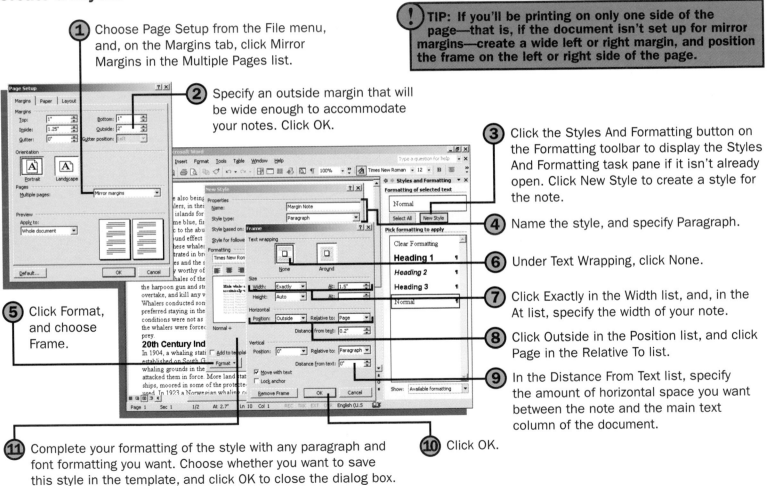

2 Specify an outside margin that will be wide enough to accommodate your notes. Click OK.

3 Click the Styles And Formatting button on the Formatting toolbar to display the Styles And Formatting task pane if it isn't already open. Click New Style to create a style for the note.

4 Name the style, and specify Paragraph.

5 Click Format, and choose Frame.

6 Under Text Wrapping, click None.

7 Click Exactly in the Width list, and, in the At list, specify the width of your note.

8 Click Outside in the Position list, and click Page in the Relative To list.

9 In the Distance From Text list, specify the amount of horizontal space you want between the note and the main text column of the document.

10 Click OK.

11 Complete your formatting of the style with any paragraph and font formatting you want. Choose whether you want to save this style in the template, and click OK to close the dialog box.

Create a Margin Note

1 Click in the paragraph that you want to use as a margin note. If there isn't any existing text you want to use, type new text in a blank paragraph.

! TIP: To make a margin note more noticeable, you can format the style with a border or shading.

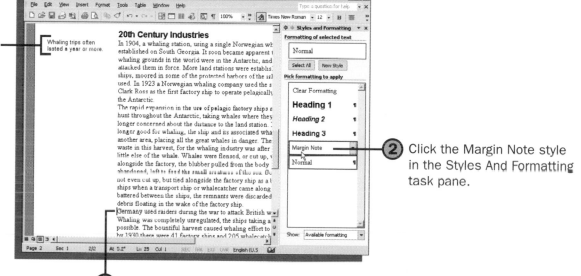

Margin notes are located in the wide outside margin (the left margin on even-numbered pages and the right margin on odd-numbered pages).

2 Click the Margin Note style in the Styles And Formatting task pane.

3 Continue working through your document, clicking in each paragraph that you want to use as a margin note, and then clicking the Margin Note style.

TRY THIS: Click the Show/Hide ¶ button if it isn't already turned on, and click the margin note. You'll see a little anchor at the beginning of the paragraph to which the margin note is anchored. Add a blank paragraph before this paragraph, and note that the margin note moves when the paragraph moves.

! TIP: To move a margin note into a different area of the document, select the margin note, including its frame, and cut it (press Ctrl+X). Then paste it (press Ctrl+V) at the beginning of the paragraph that it's to be associated with.

Writing Text Sideways

Although the bulk of the text in your documents is written horizontally across the page, you might occasionally want to create a special effect by including some sideways, or vertically aligned, text. You can do this quickly and easily in Word by placing the text in a text box and then rotating the text so that it looks the way you want.

Create a Text Box

1 Choose Text Box from the Insert menu.

2 If the Drawing Canvas appears, click outside it to replace the Drawing Canvas with a text box. If no Drawing Canvas appears, drag out a text box. Use the sizing handles to create a text box with the dimensions you want.

5 Click the Change Text Direction button on the Text Box toolbar. Click the button again if you want the text to run in a different direction.

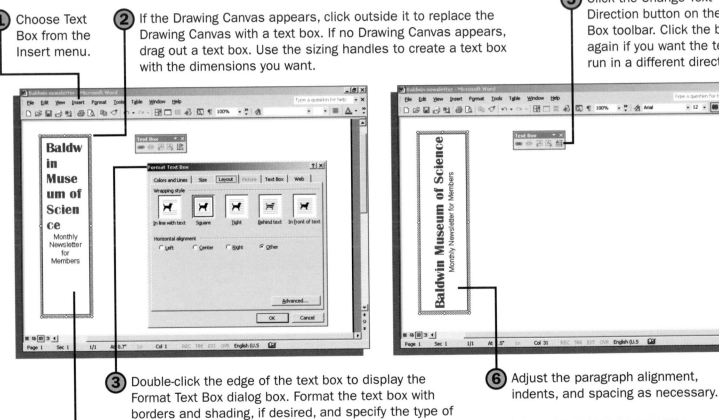

3 Double-click the edge of the text box to display the Format Text Box dialog box. Format the text box with borders and shading, if desired, and specify the type of text wrapping you want. Click OK when you've finished.

4 Type or paste your text in the text box, and format the text as desired.

6 Adjust the paragraph alignment, indents, and spacing as necessary.

! TIP: You can also write text sideways in a table cell, and in many different directions using WordArt.

Flowing Text Between Text Boxes and AutoShapes

You can create text that flows from one location to another by placing the text in a text box (or in the text box of an AutoShape) and linking that text box to a second one. As you edit the text, it ebbs and flows between the text boxes. This feature is very useful when you're working with items such as sidebars that often continue on another page, or with a series of AutoShapes each of which contains some text.

Flow the Text

(1) Point to Toolbars on the View menu, choose Drawing from the submenu to display the Drawing toolbar, and create a text box or an AutoShape. Format the item as desired. If you're using an AutoShape, right-click it, and choose Add Text from the shortcut menu to activate the text box. (If the Add Text command doesn't appear, use an AutoShape that includes a text box.)

(2) Create a second text box or AutoShape, and format it as desired. If it's an AutoShape, right-click it, and choose Add Text from the shortcut menu.

(7) Type or paste your text into the first linked item. Format the text, set the alignment, and modify the size of each text box or AutoShape to control how much text appears in each item. If necessary, add extra paragraphs to force the text to flow into the next text box.

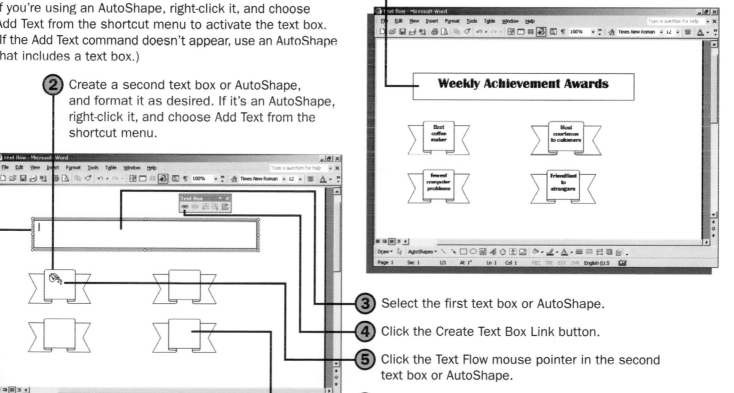

(3) Select the first text box or AutoShape.

(4) Click the Create Text Box Link button.

(5) Click the Text Flow mouse pointer in the second text box or AutoShape.

(6) Repeat steps 2 through 5 for any other text boxes or AutoShapes that you want to be linked.

Creating a Booklet ⊕ NEW FEATURE

Figuring out the logistics of creating a folded booklet so that the pages appear in the correct order is really a major challenge. Chances are that if you tried it once, you probably don't *ever* want to do it again! Well, if you want a nice little surprise, give it another try—but *this* time let Word figure out which page goes where. Word will arrange the pages in the correct order, and all you have to do is print, fold, and staple the perfect little booklet.

> **! TIP:** When you print a booklet, the pages aren't printed in numerical order—that is, page 1 isn't next to page 2—but are printed in an order that puts the pages in sequence after the booklet has been folded. To print two consecutive pages on a single sheet of paper, specify 2 Pages Per Sheet instead of Book Fold in the Multiple Pages list in the Page Setup dialog box.

Create a Booklet

① Choose Page Setup from the File menu, and click the Margins tab if it isn't already displayed.

> **SEE ALSO:** For information about manual duplex printing, see "Printing on Both Sides of the Paper" on page 94.

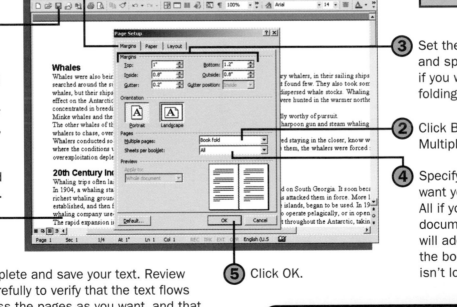

⑦ Print the booklet. Word expects the pages to be printed on both sides of the paper, so either use duplex printing, or use a copier to create a two-sided document. Fold and staple your booklet.

③ Set the margins for the booklet, and specify a gutter measurement if you want extra room for the folding and stapling.

② Click Book Fold in the Multiple Pages list.

④ Specify how many pages you want your booklet to contain. Click All if you want to print the entire document in one booklet. Word will add blank pages to the end of the booklet if your document's text isn't long enough to fill the booklet.

⑥ Complete and save your text. Review it carefully to verify that the text flows across the pages as you want, and that you've specified the correct number of pages for your finished booklet.

⑤ Click OK.

> **✋ CAUTION:** If you specify fewer pages in the Sheets Per Booklet list than are in your document, Word will create one booklet with the number of pages you specify and additional booklets for the remaining pages.

11 Working with Others

Although printed documents are still an important part of most offices, many companies, from giant corporations to mom-and-pop operations, are doing business on line. Working on a network reduces the time and clutter spent on paperwork and lets you share documents and files on line so that you can interact productively with other people.

Microsoft Word 2002 makes it a snap to create online documents that contain active *hyperlinks*, or jumps, that move you from place to place within a document or to designated spots in other documents. Working on line simplifies collaboration with your coworkers, whether they're down the hallway or halfway around the world. You can circulate or route a document for comments or editing and then review the returned document and accept or reject the proposed changes. With Microsoft SharePoint Team Services available on your intranet or through an Internet service provider, you and your team can post messages to discuss a document without changing its content, or you can insert your comments directly into the document. And, if everyone in your group works on the same types of documents, you can all use the same templates so that all the documents produced in the group have the same appearance.

Whether you call it the Internet, the intranet, or the Web, and whether you use it for business or pleasure, the Web is probably already a part of your life. In this section, you'll see how easy it is to use the Web Page Wizard to create Web pages from scratch, or to convert existing Word documents into Web pages, and then put the resulting pages into your own Web site.

Creating an Online Document

An effective online Word document can fully utilize the benefits of being on line—that is, using *hyperlinks* to other parts of the current document or to other documents, and including other documents or files as icons—to make it as easy as possible for readers to quickly obtain the information they want.

Create the Document

1 Create your document, format and proofread it, and save it with a descriptive name.

2 Select the text that you want to turn into a link to other information. Click the Insert Hyperlink button on the Standard toolbar, and use the Insert Hyperlink dialog box to link to another document or to a different part of this document.

✋ CAUTION: If your online document includes hyperlinks to other documents, make sure that the recipients of your document have access to the linked files. If you're uncertain about this, include the original documents, and display them as icons.

! TIP: You can include any type of file as an icon: a video, a sound clip, a Microsoft Excel file, and so on. The readers of your document, however, must have the proper programs installed on their computers to be able to open these files.

👁 SEE ALSO: For information about inserting hyperlinks, see "Using Hyperlinks" on page 160.

For information about adding special formatting for online documents, see "Formatting an Online Document" on page 162.

3 To insert an entire file as an icon, choose Object from the Insert menu.

4 On the Create From File tab of the Object dialog box, click Browse, locate the file, and click Insert.

5 Select this check box.

6 Click Change Icon.

8 Click OK in the Object dialog box. Set the text wrapping for the icon if desired.

7 Type a caption for the icon, and click OK.

Protect the Document

① Choose Options from the Tools menu, and click the Security tab of the Options dialog box.

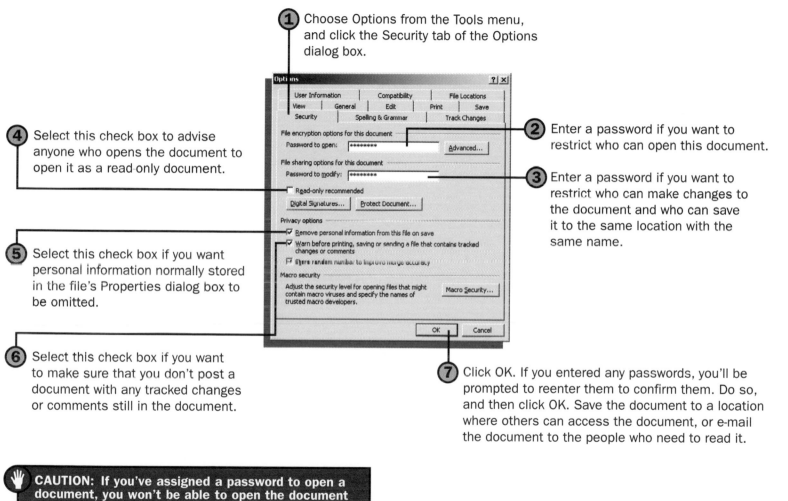

④ Select this check box to advise anyone who opens the document to open it as a read-only document.

② Enter a password if you want to restrict who can open this document.

③ Enter a password if you want to restrict who can make changes to the document and who can save it to the same location with the same name.

⑤ Select this check box if you want personal information normally stored in the file's Properties dialog box to be omitted.

⑥ Select this check box if you want to make sure that you don't post a document with any tracked changes or comments still in the document.

⑦ Click OK. If you entered any passwords, you'll be prompted to reenter them to confirm them. Do so, and then click OK. Save the document to a location where others can access the document, or e-mail the document to the people who need to read it.

> **CAUTION:** If you've assigned a password to open a document, you won't be able to open the document if you forget the password! To avoid locking yourself out of a vital document, either write down the password in a secure place or keep a copy of the document, without password protection, in a secure location.

Using Hyperlinks

A hyperlink, often called a *link* or a *jump,* creates a connection to different parts of your document, to other Word documents, or to other types of files in an online document.

Link to an Item in Your Document

(1) Type or select the text you want to use as a hyperlink.

(2) Click the Insert Hyperlink button on the Standard toolbar.

(3) Click Place In This Document to see the headings and bookmarks that are contained in the document.

(4) Click the heading or bookmark you want to link to.

(5) Click ScreenTip, type a short description of the link, and click OK.

(6) Click OK.

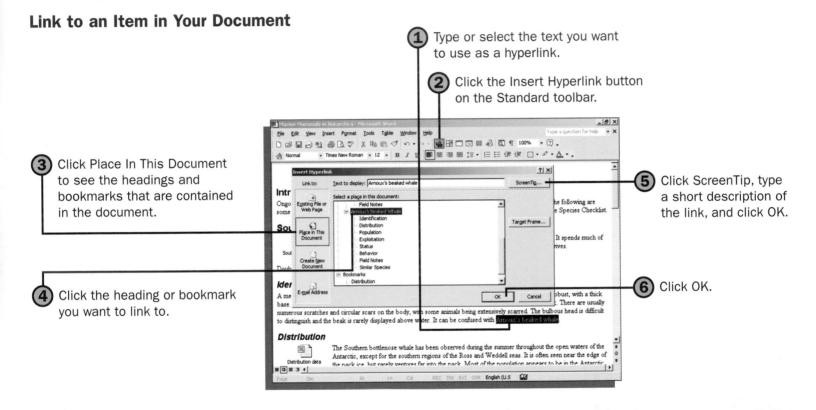

SEE ALSO: For information about creating hyperlinks in a table of contents, see "Creating a Table of Contents" on page 91.

For information about creating a bookmark, see "Bookmark a Page Range" on page 93.

TRY THIS: Right-click any toolbar, and choose Web from the shortcut menu to display the Web toolbar. Create a few hyperlinks to different parts of your document. Hold down the Ctrl key and click a link. Now click the Back button on the Web toolbar to return to your original location.

Link to a Different Document

① Type and select the text you want to use as a hyperlink.

② Click the Insert Hyperlink button on the Standard toolbar.

⑤ Use the Browse tools to move to the correct folder if the file is in a different folder.

③ Click Existing File Or Web Page.

④ Click a category to locate the file you want to link to:

- Current Folder for a file in your default document folder, or to locate a file in another folder on your computer or network
- Browsed Pages for Web pages you've visited
- Recent Files for files you've used recently

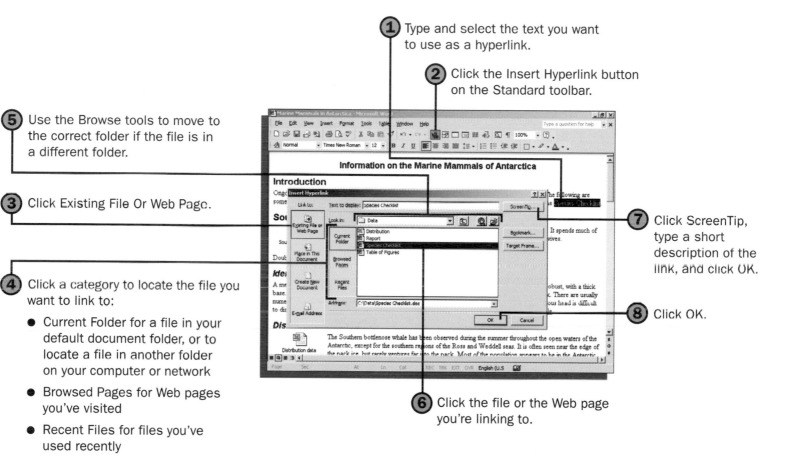

⑦ Click ScreenTip, type a short description of the link, and click OK.

⑧ Click OK.

⑥ Click the file or the Web page you're linking to.

TIP: Unless you enter some descriptive text in the ScreenTip dialog box, the ScreenTip will display the entire path and file name of the document, which can be rather unsightly.

NEW FEATURE: By default, you must hold down the Ctrl key and click a hyperlink to use the link. Requiring the use of the Ctrl key to follow a hyperlink prevents unintended jumps and simplifies selecting a hyperlink for editing. If you prefer to follow a hyperlink without using the Ctrl key, choose Options from the Tools menu, and, on the Edit tab of the Options dialog box, clear the check box for using the Ctrl key.

Formatting an Online Document

You can use all the standard formatting techniques to full advantage in an online document—special fonts, colored text, borders, and so on—but Word also provides some special formatting features that you can use to create the type of attention-getting design elements that are so critical for holding your reader's attention in an online document.

Use a Theme

1 Switch to Web Layout view.

2 In the document you want to use on line, choose Theme from the Format menu.

TRY THIS: If you don't see a theme you like, you can build one of your own. To add a background color, point to Background on the Format menu, and click a color. For an even wider variety of choices, click Fill Effects, and create a background with a pattern, shading, or even a picture. To create your own picture bullets, choose Bullets And Numbering from the Format menu, and, on the Bulleted tab, click the Customize button, and then click the Picture button. To define your own horizontal line, choose Borders And Shading from the Format menu, and, on the Borders tab, click the Horizontal Line button. You can also change the styles for headings and hyperlinks.

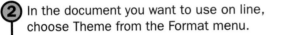

3 Click a theme.

4 Select the check boxes for the options you want to include in the theme:

- Vivid Colors to use more intense colors in the theme

- Active Graphics to include animated graphics, such as motion clips from the Clip Gallery—but be aware that the graphics are active only when they're viewed in a Web browser

- Background Image to include an image as the background

5 Click OK.

Add Text Effects

1 Select the text to which you want to add effects.

2 Choose Font from the Format menu.

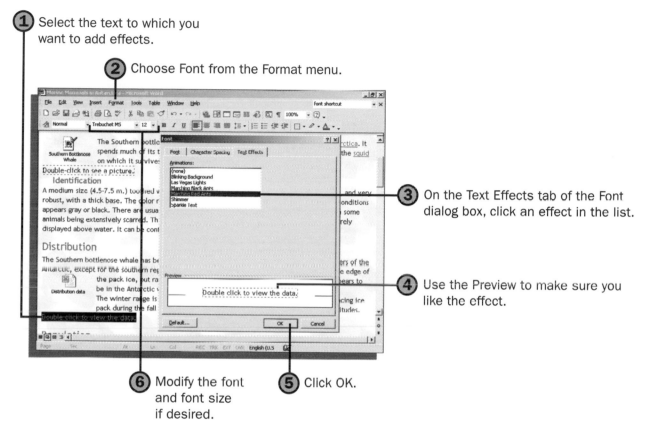

3 On the Text Effects tab of the Font dialog box, click an effect in the list.

4 Use the Preview to make sure you like the effect.

6 Modify the font and font size if desired.

5 Click OK.

CAUTION: Themes and backgrounds are visible only when they're viewed in Web Layout view, but text effects are visible in all views. However, because Web Layout view isn't widely used, it's a good idea to preview your document to see how it looks in the other views.

TIP: The font formatting you use in a standard document can produce dramatic effects in an online document, especially font colors and text effects such as Embossed or Shadow that you add from the Font tab of the Font dialog box.

Converting a Document into a Web Page

You can save your Word document in Web format for one
of two reasons: to add it to a Web site, or to give it increased
compatibility—that is, so that others can read the document
using a Web browser instead of needing access to Word. When
you save your document, you have several options to choose
among for your specific needs.

Save a Document as a Web Page

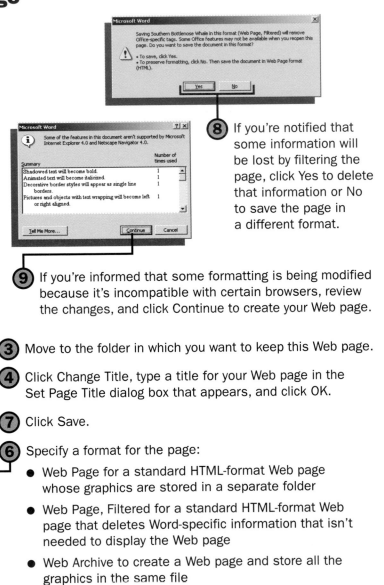

(1) Create your document, proofread it, and
save it as a normal Word document.

(2) Choose Save As Web Page from the File
menu to display the Save As dialog box.

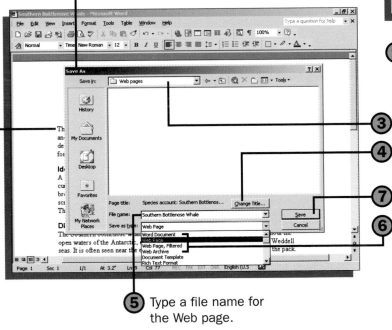

(5) Type a file name for
the Web page.

(8) If you're notified that
some information will
be lost by filtering the
page, click Yes to delete
that information or No
to save the page in
a different format.

(9) If you're informed that some formatting is being modified
because it's incompatible with certain browsers, review
the changes, and click Continue to create your Web page.

(3) Move to the folder in which you want to keep this Web page.

(4) Click Change Title, type a title for your Web page in the
Set Page Title dialog box that appears, and click OK.

(7) Click Save.

(6) Specify a format for the page:

- Web Page for a standard HTML-format Web page
  whose graphics are stored in a separate folder

- Web Page, Filtered for a standard HTML-format Web
  page that deletes Word-specific information that isn't
  needed to display the Web page

- Web Archive to create a Web page and store all the
  graphics in the same file

Creating a Web Page

Word provides a variety of Web page templates. Each template provides the basic layout for a Web page, including placeholder text and hyperlinks that you can replace or modify as you create your own Web page.

Use a Template

SEE ALSO: For information about applying a theme or a background, see "Formatting an Online Document" on page 162.

For information about the various ways you can save a Web page, see "Converting a Document into a Web Page" on the facing page.

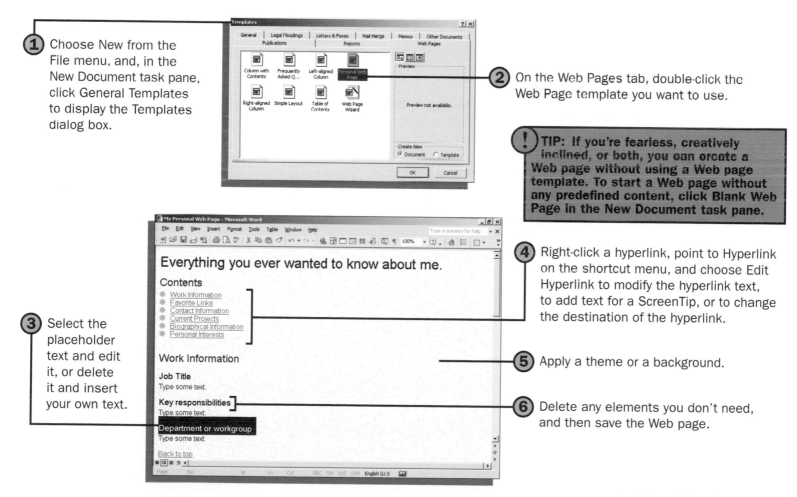

1 Choose New from the File menu, and, in the New Document task pane, click General Templates to display the Templates dialog box.

2 On the Web Pages tab, double-click the Web Page template you want to use.

TIP: If you're fearless, creatively inclined, or both, you can create a Web page without using a Web page template. To start a Web page without any predefined content, click Blank Web Page in the New Document task pane.

3 Select the placeholder text and edit it, or delete it and insert your own text.

4 Right-click a hyperlink, point to Hyperlink on the shortcut menu, and choose Edit Hyperlink to modify the hyperlink text, to add text for a ScreenTip, or to change the destination of the hyperlink.

5 Apply a theme or a background.

6 Delete any elements you don't need, and then save the Web page.

Creating a Web Site

The Web Page Wizard is designed to help you set up your entire Web site—its location, the *navigation frames,* and all the pages in the site, including any that you create using the Web Page templates.

Use the Web Page Wizard

(1) Choose New from the File menu, click General Templates in the New Document task pane, and, on the Web Pages tab, double-click Web Page Wizard to start the wizard.

(2) Step through the wizard, specifying the following design elements for the Web site:

- The name and location of the site
- The type of navigation frame or other navigation method
- The pages (blank, from a template, or existing) that are to be included and the order in which they're listed
- Any theme used in your formatting

(3) Click Finish, and wait while Word creates and saves the pages and frames.

(4) Edit the pages as desired to complete the information, and then save the pages to create your Web site.

> **!** **TIP:** The wizard can create a site that uses frames to divide up a page. Each frame contains a separate document. In the Web site shown on this page, there's a table-of-contents document in the left frame and a personal Web page in the right frame. Use the Frame toolbar to add, remove, or modify a frame.

Saving a Document to the Internet ⊕ NEW FEATURE

If you sometimes need access to your documents from different computers but you aren't always connected to a network, you can save your documents to a special storage area of The Microsoft Network (MSN). With access to the Internet, and with the proper Microsoft *Passport,* you can download or save any documents you want.

> **! TIP:** Although you don't need to be a member of MSN to use the storage area, you do need to have a Microsoft Passport. To obtain a Passport, click the link in the Sign In With Microsoft Passport dialog box, or sign up for a Hotmail account.

Save Your Document

1 Connect to the Internet if you're not already connected.

2 Choose Save As from the File menu to display the Save As dialog box.

> **TRY THIS:** In the Open dialog box, right-click a file that's stored on your MSN Web site, and choose Properties from the shortcut menu. Drag over the Web address next to Location, and press Ctrl+C to copy it. In Internet Explorer, click In the Address Bar, press Ctrl+V to paste the address, and press Enter. You can now manage your storage site in Internet Explorer.

3 Click My Network Places in the Save In list.

4 Double-click My Web Sites On MSN.

5 If prompted, sign in with your Passport.

6 Move to the folder in which you want to save the file, and click Save. Wait for the file to be transferred.

7 To retrieve a document, choose Open from the File menu, repeat steps 3 through 5, locate the file, and click Open.

Sharing Documents with SharePoint ⊕ NEW FEATURE

Microsoft SharePoint Team Services is a Web service that's part
of Microsoft Office 2002. If SharePoint is available on your intranet
or through an Internet service provider, and you're a member of the
SharePoint Team Web site, you can use the service to share your
documents with others.

NEW FEATURE: SharePoint Team Services is a Web-based team-management tool. Contact the SharePoint administrator and/or review the Help files for some ideas about how to use the full power of SharePoint. It can also be fully customized, so what you see will probably look a bit different from what we show here. A more powerful SharePoint server, the SharePoint Portal Service, provides even more features for document control.

Save or Open a Document

1 Choose Save As from the File menu to
save a document, or choose Open to open
a document from the SharePoint site.

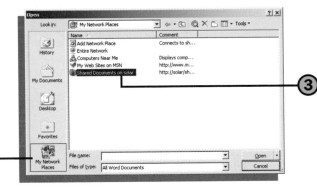

2 Click My Network
Places (or Web Folders,
depending on your
operating system) in
the list.

3 Double-click the icon for the Internet or intranet
location of the shared files on SharePoint. If you
don't see a shortcut to the SharePoint site,
use the Add Network Place or Add Web Folder
item to create a shortcut to the Web address
(the URL) that was provided to you by the ISP.

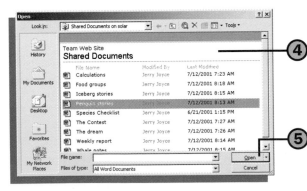

4 Browse the site to find the correct
location for the document.

TIP: If necessary, use the Views button in the Save As or in the Open dialog box to switch to the view that you're most familiar with.

5 Type a name for the document. Click Save
to save the document, or click the document
to select it, and then click Open to open it.

Working Simultaneously on a Document

When a document is available to others on a network or on the SharePoint Team Web site, there's always the possibility that more than one person will want to work on the same document at the same time. To avoid the confusion and problems that often result from simultaneous editing by different people, Word provides a document-management service.

Work on an Open Document

1 Open the document from the shared folder or Web site.

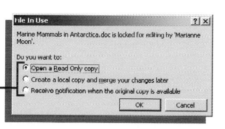

2 Specify the way you want to work with the document:

- Open A Read-Only Copy to review the document without saving any changes

- Create A Local Copy... to copy the contents to a new document and later merge the new document with the original document

- Receive Notification... to open the document as read-only and to receive a message when the document has been closed by another user so that you can edit it

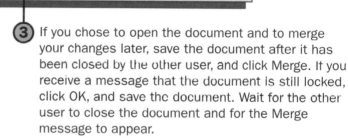

3 If you chose to open the document and to merge your changes later, save the document after it has been closed by the other user, and click Merge. If you receive a message that the document is still locked, click OK, and save the document. Wait for the other user to close the document and for the Merge message to appear.

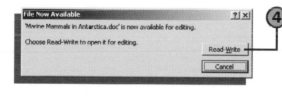

4 If you chose to receive a notice that the document was available, click Read-Write in the File Now Available dialog box when it appears so that you can open and edit the document.

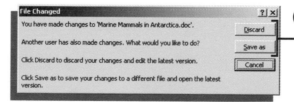

5 If the File Changed dialog box appears, click Discard to discard any changes you made to the read-only document and to open the original document for editing, or click Save As to save the document with your changes using a different file name.

SEE ALSO: For information about working with merged documents and tracked changes, see "Sending a Document Out for Review" on page 172.

TIP: If you make changes to a read-only document, save it using a different file name or in a different location from that of the original document.

Discussing a Document On Line ⊕ NEW FEATURE

With SharePoint Team Services available on your intranet or
through an Internet service provider, you and your team can post
messages to discuss a document without changing its content, or
you can insert your comments directly into the document.

Discuss a Document

(1) In the document you want to discuss, point to
Online Collaboration on the Tools menu, and
choose Web Discussions from the submenu.

(2) Click the button for the type
of discussion you want to use:

- To add a discussion item directly
to the document, click where
you want the item, and then
click the Insert Discussion In
The Document button.

- To add an item to the general
discussion without modifying the
contents of the document, click
the Insert Discussion About The
Document button.

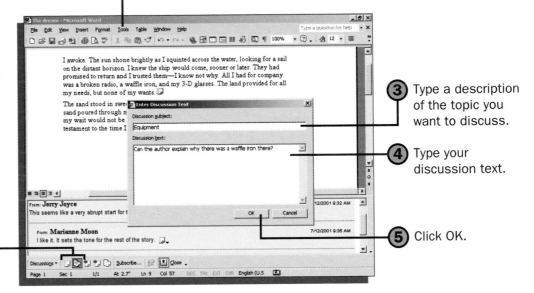

(3) Type a description
of the topic you
want to discuss.

(4) Type your
discussion text.

(5) Click OK.

❗ **TIP:** If the document under discussion isn't located
on a SharePoint Team Web site, you'll need to specify
a discussion server the first time you try to insert a
discussion into the document. To specify a discussion
server, click the Discussions button, and choose
Discussion Options from the menu.

Review the Discussions

(1) Click a discussion icon to see the specific inline discussion about this part of the document.

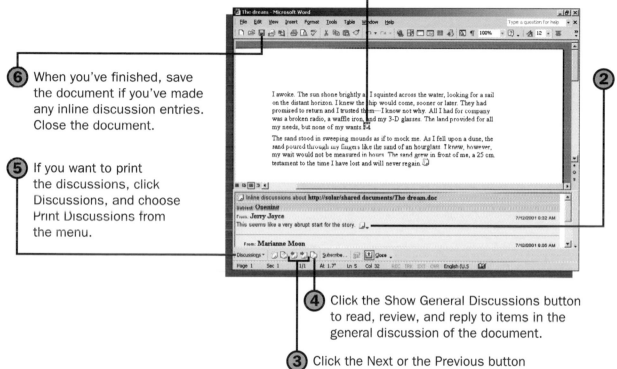

(6) When you've finished, save the document if you've made any inline discussion entries. Close the document.

(5) If you want to print the discussions, click Discussions, and choose Print Discussions from the menu.

(2) Click a discussion icon in the discussion pane, and choose Reply from the menu that appears to allow you to add an item to this discussion topic. Type your message in the Enter Discussion Text dialog box that appears, and click OK.

(4) Click the Show General Discussions button to read, review, and reply to items in the general discussion of the document.

(3) Click the Next or the Previous button to locate other inline discussions.

CAUTION: Don't rename the document or save it to another location after you've made your discussion entries. If you do, you'll lose the discussions.

TIP: Click the Subscribe button to receive an e-mail notification whenever someone else changes the file.

Sending a Document Out for Review

When you need to have a document reviewed, you have a couple of choices: you can e-mail the document to all the reviewers at once and have their changes and comments added to the document, or you can route the document to individual reviewers in a specific sequence.

Send the Document to All Reviewers

(1) With the document completed and saved, point to Send To on the File menu, and choose Mail Recipient (For Review) from the submenu.

(2) Address the mail message to the reviewers.

(3) Click Send. If you don't have Microsoft Outlook set to send messages immediately, switch to Outlook and send the message.

NEW FEATURE: When you send a document out for review, Word turns on the Track Changes feature so that reviewers' changes are marked and tracked.

Route a Document for Review

(1) With the document completed and saved, point to Send To on the File menu, and choose Routing Recipient from the submenu to open the Routing Slip dialog box.

(2) Click Address, and add the recipients' names from your Contacts list.

(8) Click Route to send the document immediately.

(3) Click the Move arrows to change the order of the recipients.

(4) Type a subject line or accept the proposed text.

(5) Type a message if you want one to be included with the document.

(7) Select the check boxes for your other routing options.

(6) Specify that you want the document to be routed sequentially.

Assemble the Reviews

 1 Save the returned document in a different folder or with a different name from that of the original document.

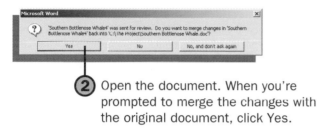

2 Open the document. When you're prompted to merge the changes with the original document, click Yes.

! TIP: If the document was routed sequentially, and if you made no changes to the original document while it was being routed, there's no need to merge the returned document with the original document. All the comments and changes are contained in the returned document.

✋ CAUTION: Documents that you receive from other people can contain computer viruses. Always save and then scan a document with a virus-checking program before you open the document.

3 Review the document with the merged changes. Repeat steps 1 and 2 to incorporate the returned reviews from other reviewers.

SEE ALSO: For information about editing documents that have been returned to you after reviewing, see "Reviewing Reviews" on page 175.

For information about manually combining the reviews, see "Combining Reviews" on page 177.

Reviewing a Document

When you're asked to review a document, Word marks your changes and comments so that they can be noted and either accepted or deleted at a later time. You can use the special tools on the Reviewing toolbar to help you review the document.

Review the Document

(1) Open the document to be reviewed, and switch to Print Layout view if you aren't already in that view. If the Reviewing toolbar isn't displayed, right-click any toolbar, and choose Reviewing from the shortcut menu.

(2) Specify Final Showing Markup.

(3) Edit the text. Note that inserted text is underlined and that deleted text is contained in a balloon in the margin.

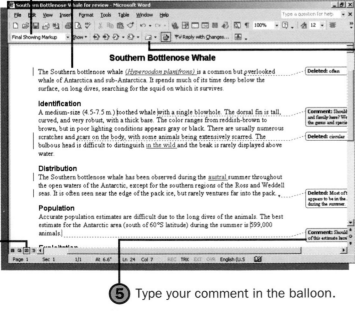

(5) Type your comment in the balloon.

> **! TIP: In Normal view, all your changes are marked in the document, and the descriptions and comments are displayed in the Reviewing pane at the bottom of the window.**

(6) Switch views to see how the document will look with your changes included, to see how it looked before your changes, and to see your changes marked on the original.

(7) Save the document. If there's a Reply With Changes button on the Reviewing toolbar, click the button to mail the document back to the person who sent it to you.

(4) Select the text you want to comment on, and click the New Comment button to insert a new comment.

(8) If there's no Reply With Changes button, close the document. If you're prompted to send the document to the next person on the routing slip, click Yes to mail the document to the next recipient. Otherwise, create a mail message to the person who sent the document out for review, and include the document as an attachment.

Reviewing Reviews

When a document that you sent out for review has been returned to you, you can easily review the comments and changes that have been added by the reviewers. As you review, you can add new comments or delete inappropriate ones, and you can accept or reject the changes that were made by the reviewers.

Review the Document

(1) Open the document to be reviewed, and switch to Print Layout view if you aren't already in that view. If the Reviewing toolbar isn't displayed, right-click any toolbar, and choose Reviewing from the shortcut menu.

(2) Specify Final Showing Markup if it isn't already displayed.

(4) Click Show, and select the check boxes for the items you want displayed. Click Show again, point to Reviewers, and select which reviewers' changes and/or comments you want to see.

NEW FEATURE: When you're reviewing a document in Print Layout view or Web Layout view, you can view the document in four different ways: Original, in which all the changes are hidden; Original Showing Markup, which is the same as Original except that the proposed changes are visible; Final, in which the text appears as though all the changes have been accepted; and Final Showing Markup, which is the same as Final except that all the proposed changes are visible.

SEE ALSO: For information about sending a document out for review, see "Sending a Document Out for Review" on page 172.

(3) If the document is set for tracking changes, click the Track Changes button to turn off the tracking so that the changes you make will be incorporated into the document.

(7) If you routed the document for review using the Send To Mail Recipient (For Review) command and you don't want to incorporate any more returned reviews and changes into this document, click End Review. Save and close the document.

(5) Click the appropriate reviewing button:

- Previous to review a change or comment that was skipped
- Next to review the next change
- Accept Change to incorporate the change into your document
- Reject Change/Delete Comment to restore the original version or to delete a comment

(6) If you want to see how a change will affect the document, switch to Final to see how the document will read if the change is accepted. Switch to Original to see how the document will read if the change is rejected. Switch back to Final Showing Markup, and accept or reject the change.

Comparing Documents

If you've ever stared at two or more copies of a document and wondered which one contains the correct updated information, or if other people have edited a document without using the Track Changes feature, don't despair! Word is ready to come to your rescue. Provided you have the original document and the revised document, Word can mark all the changes for your review so that you can compare the revised document with the original.

Compare Two Documents

① Open the revised document.

② Choose Compare And Merge Documents from the Tools menu to open the Compare And Merge Documents dialog box.

③ Select the original document.

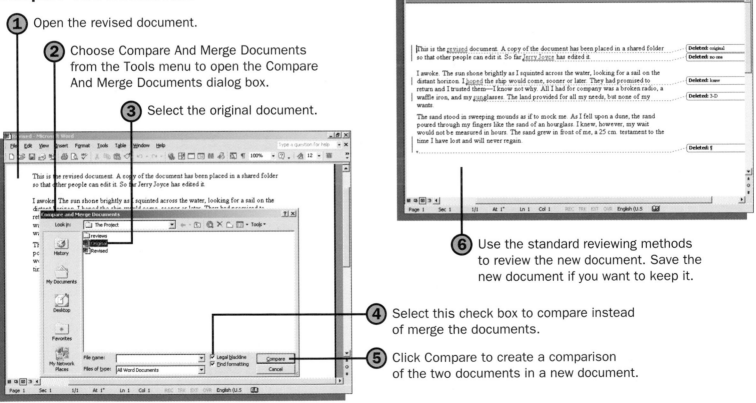

> **SEE ALSO:** For information about reviewing a document that has tracked changes, see "Reviewing Reviews" on page 175.

⑥ Use the standard reviewing methods to review the new document. Save the new document if you want to keep it.

④ Select this check box to compare instead of merge the documents.

⑤ Click Compare to create a comparison of the two documents in a new document.

Combining Reviews

If you sent a document out for review without using the Send To Mail Recipient (For Review) command, you'll probably end up with several separate reviewed and/or edited copies of the document. However, provided the reviewers used the Track Changes feature, you can combine all their changes and comments by merging the separate documents into one document to easily create a final version.

> **TIP:** When you use the Send To Mail Recipient (For Review) command, the returned documents can be merged automatically with the original document. However, if you receive a late review that you want to incorporate after you've clicked the End Review button on the Reviewing toolbar, you'll need to use the procedure on this page to incorporate those additional changes.

Merge the Documents

(1) Open the original document, and choose Compare And Merge Documents from the Tools menu to open the Compare And Merge Documents dialog box.

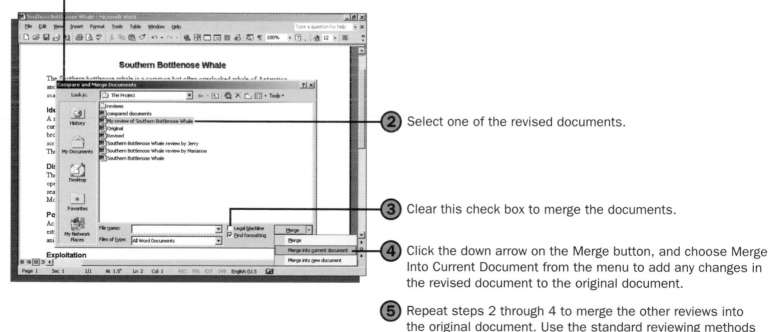

(2) Select one of the revised documents.

(3) Clear this check box to merge the documents.

(4) Click the down arrow on the Merge button, and choose Merge Into Current Document from the menu to add any changes in the revised document to the original document.

(5) Repeat steps 2 through 4 to merge the other reviews into the original document. Use the standard reviewing methods to review the changes to the document.

Controlling What Can Be Reviewed

When you have a document available for review—in a shared folder, for example—you can control what people can and can't do to the document in their reviews.

SEE ALSO: For information about preventing any changes to the document, see "Creating an Online Document" on page 158.

Set the Access

(1) Open the document that's going to be reviewed, and choose Protect Document from the Tools menu to open the Protect Document dialog box.

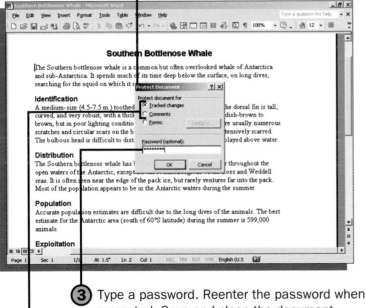

(3) Type a password. Reenter the password when prompted. Save and close the document.

(2) Specify the option you want:

- Tracked Changes to allow a reviewer to add comments and make edits using Tracked Changes
- Comments to allow a reviewer to add comments but not to make any editing changes

Edit the Document

(1) When you're ready to edit a document to which other people have made changes, open the protected document.

(2) Choose Unprotect Document from the Tools menu to open the Unprotect Document dialog box.

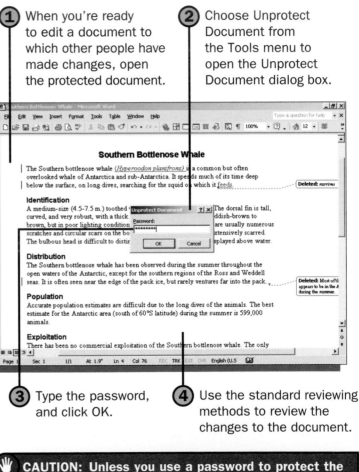

(3) Type the password, and click OK.

(4) Use the standard reviewing methods to review the changes to the document.

CAUTION: Unless you use a password to protect the document, anyone who has access to it can simply turn off the protection and modify the document.

Highlighting Text

When you're reviewing a document on line, you can highlight text in a variety of colors to call attention to certain information. Then, when you're looking through the document at a later date, you can use the Find command to locate every instance of highlighted text. It's so much faster than having to scroll through the entire document searching for the material yourself.

> **TIP:** If you don't select text, clicking the Highlight button turns the mouse pointer into a highlighter— just drag over the text to highlight it. Press Esc, or click the Highlight button again to turn it off.

Highlight Text

(1) Select the text you want to highlight.

(2) Do any of the following:

- Click the Highlight button to use the selected highlight color.
- Click the down arrow next to the Highlight button, and click a highlight color.
- Click the down arrow next to the Highlight button, and click None to remove an existing highlight from the selected text.

Find Highlighted Text

(1) Choose Find from the Edit menu, and, on the Find tab, click the More button in the Find dialog box to display the full dialog box. (Note that the More button becomes the Less button.)

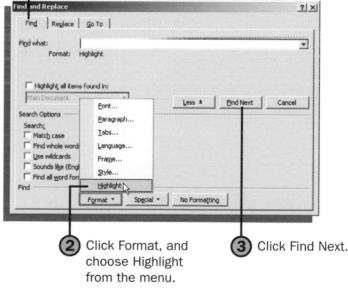

(2) Click Format, and choose Highlight from the menu.

(3) Click Find Next.

Sharing Templates

If your computer is part of a network and everyone in your group works on the same types of documents, you can all use the same templates so that all the documents produced in the group have the same general appearance. And if a template needs to be updated, only the shared template needs to be replaced.

Share the Templates

① Create a Templates folder on a computer that's accessible to everyone in your group. Create subfolders in the Templates folder to classify the template types, and place the templates to be shared in the folders.

> **① TIP:** If you want to be certain that only the administrator of the folder can modify a workgroup template, set the access in the Templates folder to Read Only. To protect some templates from change while allowing others to be modified, set full access for the shared folders, and save the templates to be protected as Read Only. Check the Windows Help system for information on how to do this.

④ In the Modify Location dialog box that appears, locate the Templates folder.

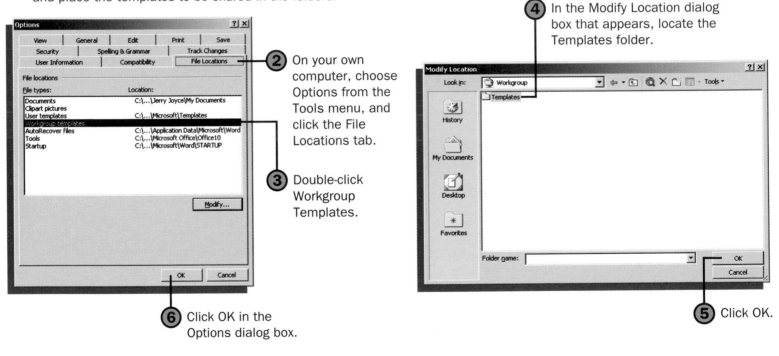

② On your own computer, choose Options from the Tools menu, and click the File Locations tab.

③ Double-click Workgroup Templates.

⑥ Click OK in the Options dialog box.

⑤ Click OK.

12 Alternative Ways to Add Content

We had a lot of fun when we wrote this section of the book—we played with the new features in Microsoft Word 2002 and revisited the tried-and-true "golden oldies." We hope you'll be as intrigued as we are by the innovative, imaginative, and timesaving features that take you and your computer to a new level of usefulness and efficiency.

Among the tried-and-true features are AutoText and AutoCorrect. You can save as AutoText all the frequently used and/or difficult-to-type long words or phrases that regularly cause you trouble. Then all you have to do is type the first few letters, and Word inserts the entire word or phrase into your document for you. AutoCorrect works its own magic in a similar way by correcting common misspellings as you type.

Among Word's new features are smart tags, which you use to obtain additional information about various items in your documents, and Actions buttons, which allow you to take certain actions relevant to the items they're associated with. Another new feature is Word's ability to translate just a few words or an entire document into another language. *È meravigliosa! C'est magnifique!*

Another bit of wizardry is a Microsoft Office feature that lets you scan a printed document (or a fax that you've received on your computer) and convert the text into a Word file. And then there's Word's speech-recognition feature. You dictate the text, and Word types it. You tell Word how you want a document formatted, and Word obeys you. What could be better? And we haven't even mentioned the Handwriting feature or the On-Screen Keyboard, so read on…

Inserting Frequently Used Text

If you type the same words or phrases repeatedly, you can save yourself a lot of time (especially if you use long technical terms or difficult names) by saving those words or phrases as AutoText. You assign the AutoText a short name—a nickname of sorts, with at least four letters—and when you type the nickname, or just the first few letters of it, Word's *AutoComplete* feature inserts the

word or phrase into your document. And AutoText isn't limited to text; the information can be anything you can put into a document—pictures, tables, even fields. Word comes already equipped with numerous AutoText entries for some of the most common types of information.

Store the Information

1 In your document, select all the information you want to include in the AutoText entry.

2 Point to AutoText on the Insert menu, and choose New from the submenu.

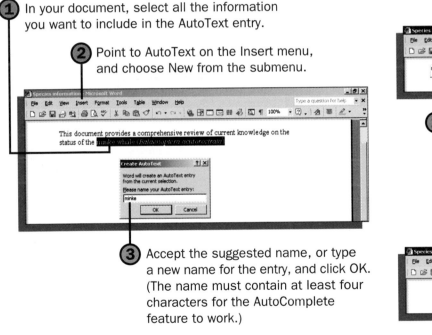

3 Accept the suggested name, or type a new name for the entry, and click OK. (The name must contain at least four characters for the AutoComplete feature to work.)

> **!** **TIP: If the AutoComplete tip never appears, choose AutoCorrect Options from the Tools menu. On the AutoText tab, select the Show AutoComplete Suggestions check box, and click OK.**

Insert the Information

1 Start typing the AutoText name.

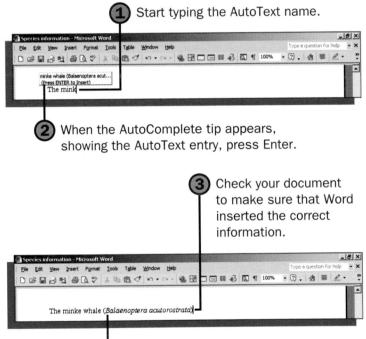

2 When the AutoComplete tip appears, showing the AutoText entry, press Enter.

3 Check your document to make sure that Word inserted the correct information.

Word inserts the complete AutoText entry.

Find and Insert an AutoText Entry

① Point to AutoText on the Insert menu.

② Point to the appropriate category on the submenu.

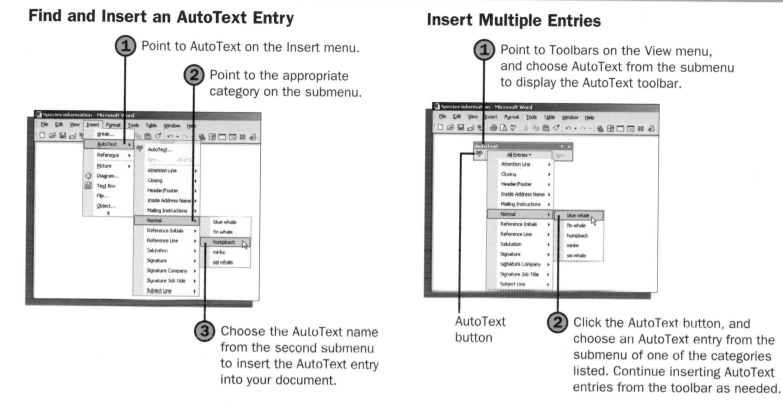

③ Choose the AutoText name from the second submenu to insert the AutoText entry into your document.

Insert Multiple Entries

① Point to Toolbars on the View menu, and choose AutoText from the submenu to display the AutoText toolbar.

AutoText button

② Click the AutoText button, and choose an AutoText entry from the submenu of one of the categories listed. Continue inserting AutoText entries from the toolbar as needed.

> **TIP:** To store an AutoText entry in an open template other than the Normal template, choose AutoCorrect Options from the Tools menu, and, on the AutoText tab, specify the template. Type a name for the AutoText entry, and click Add. You can also use the AutoCorrect dialog box to delete AutoText entries you no longer need. Click OK when you've finished.

> **TRY THIS:** Type sund and press Enter to insert the AutoComplete suggestion "Sunday." This is just one example from Word's long list of built-in AutoText entries that frequently show up as AutoComplete entries.

Correcting Text Automatically

Word provides an exceptionally useful feature called AutoCorrect that you can use to correct the common misspellings of certain words. You can also customize the AutoCorrect feature to include your own common repetitive typing errors and misspellings, and you can make AutoCorrect work even harder for you by defining special AutoCorrect entries.

Add Your Own Misspellings

1 Right-click one of your own common misspellings, point to AutoCorrect on the shortcut menu, and choose the correct spelling from the list of suggestions.

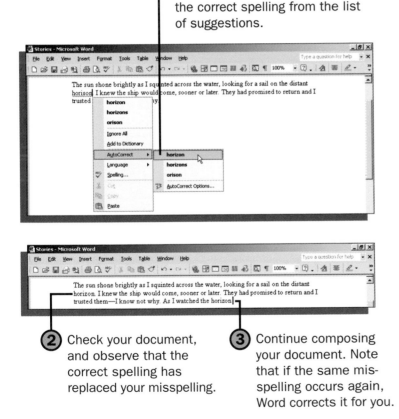

2 Check your document, and observe that the correct spelling has replaced your misspelling.

3 Continue composing your document. Note that if the same misspelling occurs again, Word corrects it for you.

Add Other Entries

1 Choose AutoCorrect Options from the Tools menu.

2 With the Replace Text As You Type check box selected on the AutoCorrect tab, enter the abbreviated or incorrect text that you'll type.

3 Type the text that you want to replace the text you typed.

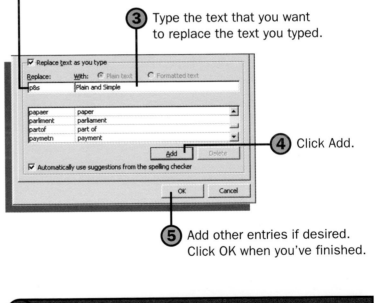

4 Click Add.

5 Add other entries if desired. Click OK when you've finished.

> **TRY THIS: Choose Symbol from the Insert menu.**
> **Select the Yen symbol (¥), and click AutoCorrect. In the Replace box in the AutoCorrect dialog box, type (yn) (include the parentheses), and click OK. Now type (yn) and a space to see the magic of AutoCorrect.**

Control the Corrections

(1) Choose AutoCorrect Options from the Tools menu, and click the AutoCorrect tab of the AutoCorrect dialog box.

(2) Select this check box to have AutoCorrect changes marked with an Actions button in your document so that you can reverse the changes if you want.

(3) Select or clear check boxes to specify the items you want Word to correct.

(4) Select this check box to have Word replace any item in the list with its correction.

(5) Select this check box to have a mis-spelling automatically replaced with a correction from the spelling dictionary, provided the correction is unambiguous.

(6) Click Exceptions to specify when a word that would normally start with a capital letter is *not* to be capitalized (for example, after the apparent end of a sentence or after a specified word or abbreviation), when two capitalized letters in a row are not to be corrected, and any other exceptions you want to add.

(7) Click OK.

NEW FEATURE: AutoCorrect remembers when you don't want it to change items such as the capitalization of the first letter in a sentence, or two initial capital letters. However, if you do want it to make these changes on a case-by-case basis, you have two choices. You can use the Backspace key to remove the correction and can then retype the text the way you want it (but for this to work, the Automatically Add Words To List check box must be selected in the AutoCorrect Exceptions dialog box), or you can click the Actions button for the correction and use the menu to prevent Word from making these corrections.

SEE ALSO: For information about using Actions buttons to reverse an automatic change, see "Formatting as You Compose" on pages 36–37.

Using Smart Tags ⊕ NEW FEATURE

Word provides many different types of smart tags and continually creates new ones. Despite their differences, smart tags have a common structure, so you can easily figure out how to manage and use them. Basically, Word searches through your document for recognizable text (names, phone numbers, stock symbols, and so on) and, when it finds that text, attaches a smart tag to it. You use the smart tag to obtain additional information about an item or to perform some type of action.

Manage the Tags

② Select this check box to use smart tags, if it isn't already selected.

① Choose AutoCorrect Options from the Tools menu, and click the Smart Tags tab of the AutoCorrect dialog box.

③ Select the check boxes for the smart tags you want to use, and clear the check boxes for those you don't want to use.

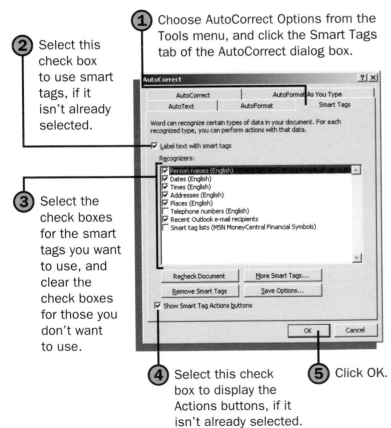

④ Select this check box to display the Actions buttons, if it isn't already selected.

⑤ Click OK.

> **TIP:** Note the difference between smart tags and Actions buttons. A smart tag identifies a certain type of text. An Actions button lists the actions you can perform. Some Actions buttons, such as the AutoCorrect and Paste Options buttons, aren't associated with smart tags.

Use the Tags

① Look through your document for text with the purplish-red dotted underline that indicates a smart tag.

② Point to the text and click the Actions button that appears.

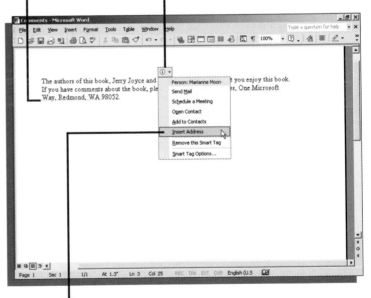

③ Click the action you want to take. The actions listed depend on the type of data represented by the text (an address or a name, for example) and the type of smart tag being used.

Having Word Insert Information for You

To include in a document some information that might change—the number of words, for example, or the number of the current section of the document—you can insert a *field*. A field is a bit of code that's used to insert some information or to execute a task automatically. Word often inserts fields automatically when you use

elements such as captions, cross-references, dates, page numbers, and tables of contents. However, you have more choices and more options for customizing the way a field works when you insert it directly—and there are, in fact, some fields that can be used *only* when you've inserted them directly.

Insert a Field

1 Click in the document where you want the field to appear, and choose Field from the Insert menu to display the Field dialog box.

2 Click a category in the list, or click All to browse through all the field names.

3 Click a field name.

4 Specify any information or select an available option to customize and format the field result. The Field Properties list varies depending on the field name you selected.

5 Select or clear check boxes or select available options for the results you want. Not all fields provide options, and the options that are provided vary by field.

7 Click OK.

6 Select this check box if you want any direct formatting of the field result to be preserved when the field is updated. Clear the check box if you want the field result to always use the paragraph formatting.

NEW FEATURE: The Field dialog box is designed to help you insert a field without worrying about the syntax used in the field code. If you prefer working directly with the field code, as in previous versions of Word, click Field Codes in the Field dialog box.

TIP: Fields are usually updated when you open or print a document.

Translating Foreign-Language Text ● NEW FEATURE

You can translate a word or a common phrase into or from another language by using one of the language dictionaries installed on your computer. When you work in the Translate task pane, you can translate several words, or you can obtain additional resources either to translate in languages for which you don't have dictionaries or to translate large sections of text, including entire documents.

Translate a Word

(1) Select a word, right-click it, and choose Translate from the shortcut menu.

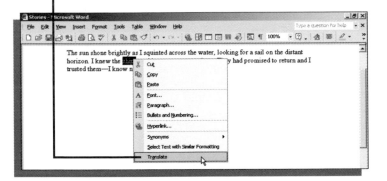

NEW FEATURE: Word provides two translation resources. If the dictionary for the language you want to translate to or from is installed on your computer, Word uses that dictionary to translate a word or phrase. To translate in a language whose dictionary you don't have installed, or to translate large amounts of text, Word can link you directly to a translation service on the Web. Because these Web services aren't part of Office and aren't provided by Microsoft, each service will work a bit differently.

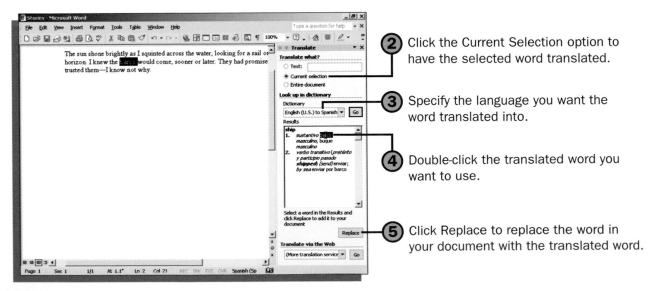

(2) Click the Current Selection option to have the selected word translated.

(3) Specify the language you want the word translated into.

(4) Double-click the translated word you want to use.

(5) Click Replace to replace the word in your document with the translated word.

Translate More Text

(1) Connect to the Internet if you aren't already connected.

(2) Specify what you want to have translated.

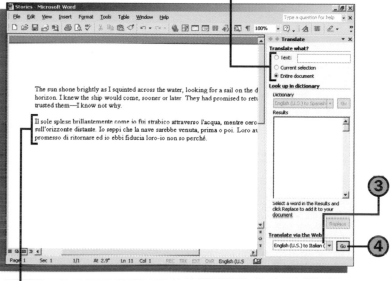

(!) **TIP:** If there aren't any translation services shown in the Translate Via The Web box, you'll need to install them. To do so, click More Translation Services in the Translate Via The Web box, click Go, and select to download the Web translation services you want to install.

(3) Specify the language you want the text translated into.

(4) Click Go. Wait for the Web page of the translation service to open and to translate the document. Copy the translated text.

(5) Paste the translated text where you want it. If you're translating an entire page, open a new document, and paste the translation into it.

(👆) **CAUTION:** Don't assume that the computer translation will be absolutely accurate, especially if you've used any idiomatic or colloquial language. If possible, ask a native speaker of the language to proofread the translation to make sure that it doesn't contain any potentially embarrassing or politically incorrect wording.

(👓) **SEE ALSO:** For more information about working with text in different languages, see "Proofing in Another Language" on page 208.

Scanning Text ● NEW FEATURE

If you need to edit a printed document and you don't have access to its electronic file, you don't need to retype the document. You can simply scan it, and then let Office convert the printed text into a Word file.

! **TIP: Some scanners won't work properly unless you use them with their own software. If your scanner doesn't work with Document Scanning, use its own software to scan the document as a TIF file, and then follow the procedure for scanning a fax.**

Scan a Text Document

① With the document in the scanner, and with the scanner turned on and properly configured for your computer, point to Programs and then to Microsoft Office Tools on the Windows Start menu, and choose Microsoft Office Document Scanning from the submenu.

② Specify the type of scanning you want.

③ Select the check boxes for the options you want.

⑤ Click Scan. If any dialog boxes specific to your scanner appear, complete the information necessary to start the scan.

④ If you have more than one scanner, or if you're not sure whether the scanner you're using is set up properly, click Scanner. Specify the scanner you're using, and test it. Click OK when you've finished.

⑥ Wait for the document to be analyzed.

⑦ Specify how much of the scanned text you want to be converted into a Word document:

● To convert part of a page, drag the mouse to select that part of the text in the right pane.

● To convert one page or several pages of a multiple-page document, select the page or pages in the left pane. Hold down the Ctrl key and click to select multiple pages.

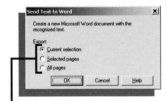

⑨ Click the appropriate option, and click OK. Wait for the document to be created in Word.

⑧ Click the Send Text To Word button to start the conversion process.

SEE ALSO: For information about converting a fax file into an editable Word document, see "Converting a Fax into a Word Document" on the facing page.

Converting a Fax into a Word Document ● NEW FEATURE

When you receive a fax on your computer, you'll notice that
the fax is saved as a picture in the TIF file format rather than
as a Word document. If you want to edit the contents of the fax,
you can use one of the Office tools to read the fax and convert
it into a Word document.

Convert the Fax

② Click the Open
button, and open
your fax document.

① Point to Programs and then to Office Tools on the
Windows Start menu, and choose Microsoft Office
Document Imaging from the submenu.

③ If you want to convert
one page or several
pages of a multiple-
page fax, select the
page or pages in
the left pane of the
window. Hold down
the Ctrl key and click
to select multiple
pages.

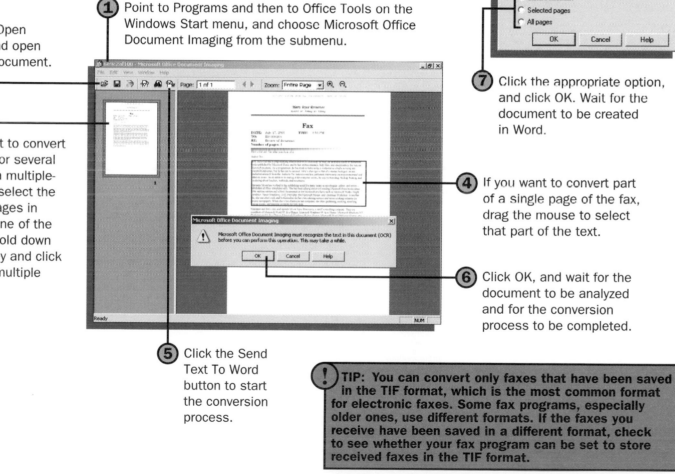

⑦ Click the appropriate option,
and click OK. Wait for the
document to be created
in Word.

④ If you want to convert part
of a single page of the fax,
drag the mouse to select
that part of the text.

⑥ Click OK, and wait for the
document to be analyzed
and for the conversion
process to be completed.

⑤ Click the Send
Text To Word
button to start
the conversion
process.

> **TIP:** You can convert only faxes that have been saved
> in the TIF format, which is the most common format
> for electronic faxes. Some fax programs, especially
> older ones, use different formats. If the faxes you
> receive have been saved in a different format, check
> to see whether your fax program can be set to store
> received faxes in the TIF format.

Dictating Your Text ⊕ NEW FEATURE

Wouldn't it be great if you could abandon your keyboard and just tell Word what to type in your document? Although the new speech-recognition capabilities of Word might not enable you to send your keyboard and mouse into a dusty and forgotten retirement just yet, you can substantially reduce the amount of typing you need to do by dictating your text to Word.

Dictate Your Text

① Choose Speech from the Tools menu to display the Language Bar if it isn't already displayed. If the Speech feature hasn't been installed, follow the directions on the screen to install it, set up your microphone, and go through the training exercises (see facing page).

Language Bar

④ When you've finished dictating, click Microphone, or say **microphone**, to turn off the speech-recognition feature.

✋ **CAUTION:** You need the proper equipment for successful dictation. If your system doesn't have at least a 400 MHz processor and 128 MB of memory, you won't be able to install Speech capabilities. You also need a good microphone for your dictation to be effective.

🖱 **TRY THIS:** There are many more phrases you can use, and alternatives to the ones listed here. Create a new document and experiment with different phrases, noting which ones work for you. **Try saying** new line, new paragraph, 5551234, 9, force num 9, **and** at sign, and see what happens. **Now say** scratch that **to delete the last thing you dictated. Remember to speak normally, and don't put extra emphasis on single words or short phrases.**

② Click Dictation. If the button isn't displayed, click Microphone first.

③ Speak as you did in the training exercises, pausing only after completing a phrase or sentence. Word will insert the text after a brief pause.

● To insert a punctuation mark, say the name of the mark—for example, say **period**, **comma**, **question mark**, and so on.

● To insert a number, say the number. Word inserts numbers 0 through 20 as numerals, and spells out numbers higher than 20.

● To insert special characters, say the name of the character—for example, say **quote**, **open parenthesis**, **close parenthesis**, **hyphen**, **ampersand**, and so on.

● To start a new paragraph, say **enter**.

Correct the Errors

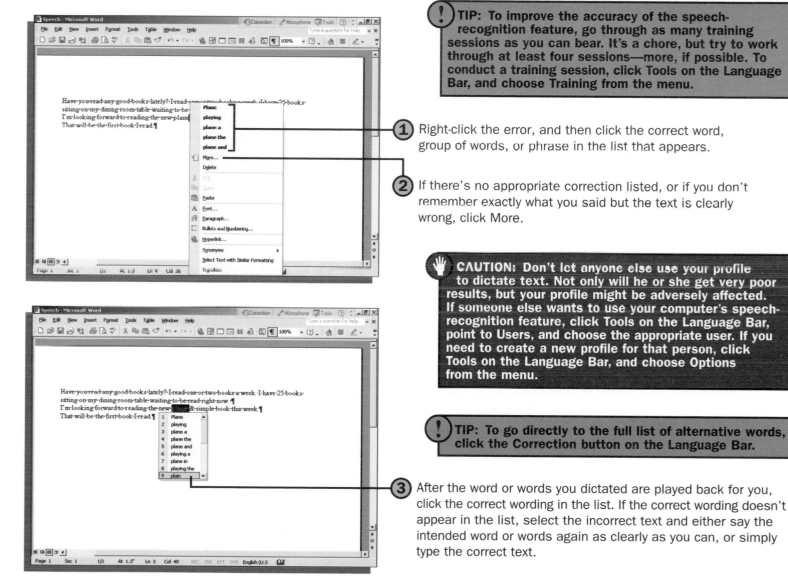

TIP: To improve the accuracy of the speech-recognition feature, go through as many training sessions as you can bear. It's a chore, but try to work through at least four sessions—more, if possible. To conduct a training session, click Tools on the Language Bar, and choose Training from the menu.

(1) Right-click the error, and then click the correct word, group of words, or phrase in the list that appears.

(2) If there's no appropriate correction listed, or if you don't remember exactly what you said but the text is clearly wrong, click More.

CAUTION: Don't let anyone else use your profile to dictate text. Not only will he or she get very poor results, but your profile might be adversely affected. If someone else wants to use your computer's speech-recognition feature, click Tools on the Language Bar, point to Users, and choose the appropriate user. If you need to create a new profile for that person, click Tools on the Language Bar, and choose Options from the menu.

TIP: To go directly to the full list of alternative words, click the Correction button on the Language Bar.

(3) After the word or words you dictated are played back for you, click the correct wording in the list. If the correct wording doesn't appear in the list, select the incorrect text and either say the intended word or words again as clearly as you can, or simply type the correct text.

Dictating Custom Text ⊕ NEW FEATURE

When you dictate text, you might encounter a word that Word just can't get right no matter how many times you repeat it. When this happens, you can either spell the word out or add it to a list of custom words so that Word will recognize it in your future dictation sessions.

> ⚠ **TIP:** If you have a problem with a word that you're pretty sure you'll be using only once, you might find it faster to simply type that word instead of trying to correct it in Dictation mode.

Spell a Word

(1) In Dictation mode, say **spelling mode**. Note that the speech message on the Language Bar confirms that you're switching to Spelling mode.

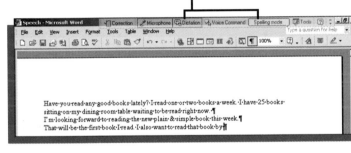

(2) Say each letter of the word without pausing. When you do pause, Word will switch back to Dictation mode.

Add Words from a Document

(1) After you've inserted any unrecognized text and fixed any incorrectly inserted text, turn off the microphone, click the Tools button on the Language Bar, and choose Learn From Document from the menu to open the Learn From Document dialog box.

(2) Click a word and listen to its pronunciation.

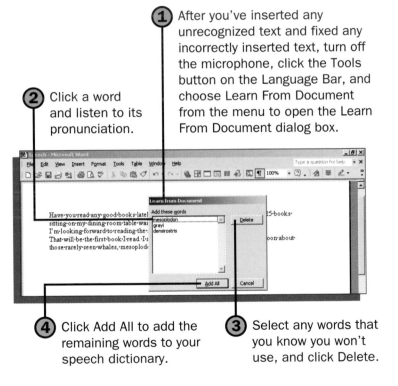

(4) Click Add All to add the remaining words to your speech dictionary.

(3) Select any words that you know you won't use, and click Delete.

Add Unusual Words

(1) Click the Tools button on the Language Bar, and choose Add/Delete Word(s) from the menu to open the Add/Delete Word(s) dialog box.

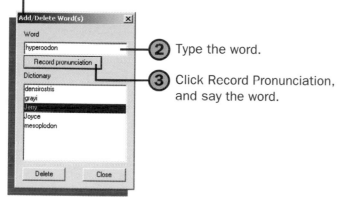

(2) Type the word.

(3) Click Record Pronunciation, and say the word.

Correct the Pronunciation

(1) Select the word in the list, and listen to its pronunciation.

(2) If the pronunciation is incorrect, click Record Pronunciation, and pronounce the word correctly.

(3) Click Close when you've finished.

TRY THIS: Open a document that's a typical example of your work, or a document that you use frequently. Click Options on the Language Bar, and choose Learn From Document from the menu. Wait for Word to examine the document, and, when the Learn From Document dialog box appears, add the words that you want Word to recognize in the future.

CAUTION: Try to restrain yourself from adding too many words. Doing so can slow down voice recognition or can even cause additional errors in recognition. If you rarely use an especially obscure or technical term, consider using Spelling mode to spell the word, entering it manually by typing it, or using the AutoText or AutoComplete feature to insert the word for you.

Telling Word What to Do ⊙ NEW FEATURE

You can be a ruthless dictator and boss Word around unmercifully, provided you have speech recognition installed. When you're in Voice Command mode, you can choose items from menus, dialog boxes, and task panes, and you can move text around in your document and format it, all with voice commands.

Dictate Your Commands

(1) Choose Speech from the Tools menu to display the Language Bar if it isn't already displayed. If the Speech feature hasn't been installed, follow the directions on the screen to install it, set up your microphone, and go through the training exercises.

(3) Say the commands in your normal voice, as you did in the training exercises. Most commands are the names of items on the screen.

- To select text, say the appropriate commands—for example, **select next word**, **select paragraph**, and so on.

- To open a menu, say the menu's name. To choose a command from the menu, say the name of the command. To expand a menu, say **expand**.

- To choose a toolbar button, say the name of the button as it's shown on the button's ScreenTip.

- To choose an item in a list, say the full text of the item.

- To move around the document, say the appropriate commands—for example, **page up**, **page down**, **end**, **back one word**, **go left**, and so on.

- To format text, select the text you want to format, and then say the names of the formatting buttons.

(2) Click Voice Command (or say **voice command**). If the button isn't displayed, click Microphone first.

(4) When you've finished dictating, click Microphone, or say **microphone**, to turn off the speech-recognition feature.

TRY THIS: Switch to Voice Command mode. Say file and then new. When the New Document task pane opens, say blank document. Now type some text, and use the mouse and keyboard to format and edit some of the text. Each time you do some editing, note the corresponding voice command in the Speech Message balloon on the Language Bar. Now use those voice commands to format the rest of your document.

Typing on the Screen ⊕ NEW FEATURE

If the Handwriting feature has been installed on your computer, you can use two different on-screen keyboards—one to enter normal text and the other to enter symbols.

Type Some Text

② Click in your document where you want to enter some text.

① Click Handwriting on the Language Bar, and choose On-Screen Standard Keyboard from the menu.

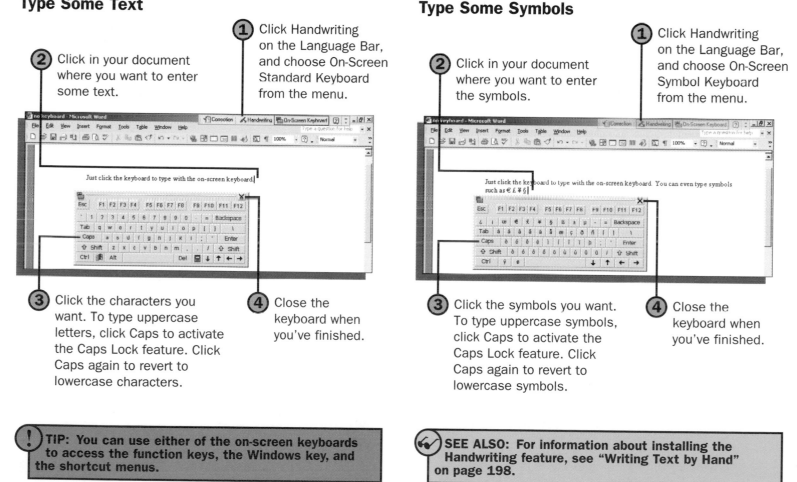

③ Click the characters you want. To type uppercase letters, click Caps to activate the Caps Lock feature. Click Caps again to revert to lowercase characters.

④ Close the keyboard when you've finished.

Type Some Symbols

② Click in your document where you want to enter the symbols.

① Click Handwriting on the Language Bar, and choose On-Screen Symbol Keyboard from the menu.

③ Click the symbols you want. To type uppercase symbols, click Caps to activate the Caps Lock feature. Click Caps again to revert to lowercase symbols.

④ Close the keyboard when you've finished.

> **! TIP:** You can use either of the on-screen keyboards to access the function keys, the Windows key, and the shortcut menus.

> **SEE ALSO:** For information about installing the Handwriting feature, see "Writing Text by Hand" on page 198.

Writing Text by Hand ⊕ NEW FEATURE

If you're tired of typing, or if you simply want to add a little handwriting to your documents to give them that personal touch, Word is ready to do your bidding. You can write by hand using a drawing tablet, a tablet PC, or even your mouse. Word will convert your handwriting into regular text or, if you prefer, will insert your handwriting as is so that your friends and coworkers can behold your exquisite penmanship.

Write Some Text

1 Click Handwriting, and, from the menu that appears, choose the way you want to write your text:

- Writing Pad to use a little window with a baseline to help you write straight
- Write Anywhere to write anywhere in the Word window

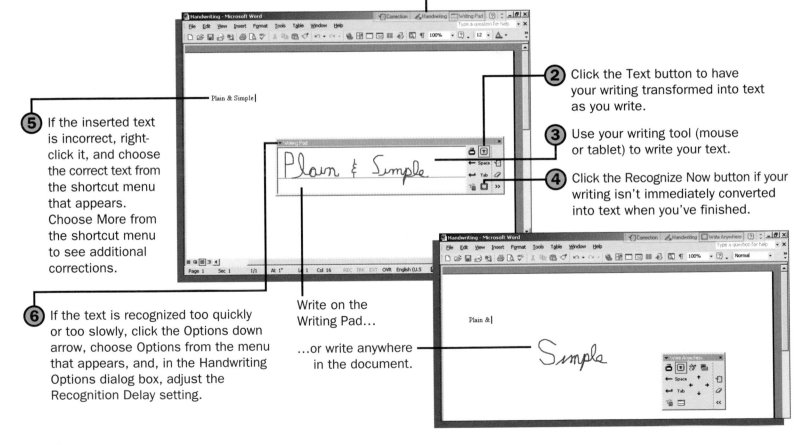

2 Click the Text button to have your writing transformed into text as you write.

3 Use your writing tool (mouse or tablet) to write your text.

4 Click the Recognize Now button if your writing isn't immediately converted into text when you've finished.

5 If the inserted text is incorrect, right-click it, and choose the correct text from the shortcut menu that appears. Choose More from the shortcut menu to see additional corrections.

6 If the text is recognized too quickly or too slowly, click the Options down arrow, choose Options from the menu that appears, and, in the Handwriting Options dialog box, adjust the Recognition Delay setting.

Write on the Writing Pad...

...or write anywhere in the document.

Insert Your Handwriting

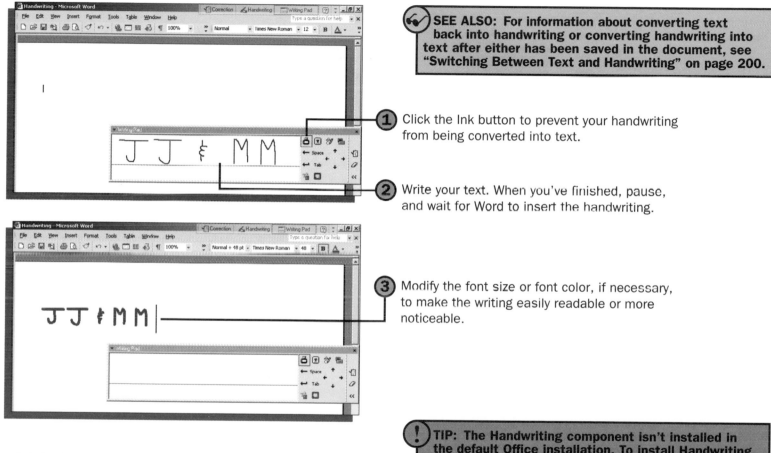

SEE ALSO: For information about converting text back into handwriting or converting handwriting into text after either has been saved in the document, see "Switching Between Text and Handwriting" on page 200.

1 Click the Ink button to prevent your handwriting from being converted into text.

2 Write your text. When you've finished, pause, and wait for Word to insert the handwriting.

3 Modify the font size or font color, if necessary, to make the writing easily readable or more noticeable.

TIP: Handwriting is inserted in line with the text. To format your handwriting with text wrapping, either insert the handwriting into a text box or use a frame to position it.

TIP: The Handwriting component isn't installed in the default Office installation. To install Handwriting, run the Microsoft Office XP Setup program to add or remove components, and, under Office Shared Features, expand the Alternative User Input item to find both the Speech and the Handwriting components. Set the Handwriting item to Run From My Computer.

Switching Between Text and Handwriting ⊕ NEW FEATURE

If you've been writing your text by hand and inserting it into your document as typed text, you can convert it back into handwriting. Likewise, if you inserted your handwriting directly into the document, you can convert that handwriting back into text.

Convert Text into Handwriting

① Click anywhere in the text that's to be converted.

② Click Correction to display the Alternative Words list.

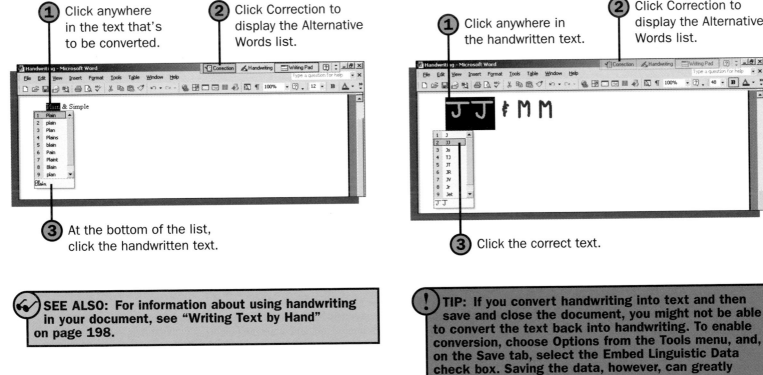

③ At the bottom of the list, click the handwritten text.

> ⟨✓⟩ **SEE ALSO:** For information about using handwriting in your document, see "Writing Text by Hand" on page 198.

Convert Handwriting into Text

① Click anywhere in the handwritten text.

② Click Correction to display the Alternative Words list.

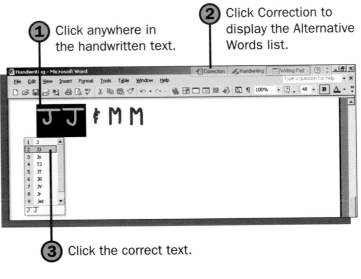

③ Click the correct text.

> ⟨!⟩ **TIP:** If you convert handwriting into text and then save and close the document, you might not be able to convert the text back into handwriting. To enable conversion, choose Options from the Tools menu, and, on the Save tab, select the Embed Linguistic Data check box. Saving the data, however, can greatly increase the file size.

Doodling in Your Document ● NEW FEATURE

If you like the idea of adding little electronic "doodles," or simple drawings, to your document, provided the Handwriting component is installed on your computer, you can create quick line drawings using the Drawing Pad.

> **TIP:** If the Picture toolbar isn't displayed when you select your drawing, right-click the drawing, and choose Show Picture Toolbar from the shortcut menu.

Do Some Doodling

1 Click Handwriting on the Language Bar, and choose Drawing Pad from the menu.

> **NEW FEATURE:** Using the Drawing Pad is a quick way to create and insert a simple line drawing. If you have a good drawing tablet, however, you can create illustrations that go well beyond the scope of doodles.

2 Draw your picture on the Drawing Pad.

3 When you've finished, click the Insert Drawing button to insert the picture.

4 Click the picture to select it.

5 Use the tools on the Picture toolbar to modify the drawing and to set any text wrapping you want.

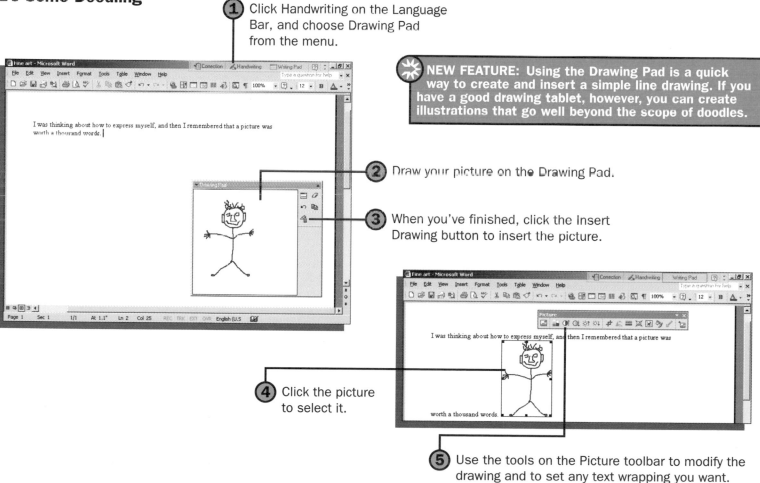

Summarizing a Document

Wouldn't it be nice if you could tell Word to read a document and summarize the important points for you? With AutoSummarize you can do just that—provided you feel that you can trust Word and your computer to decide what the important points are!

Your best bet is to let Word summarize the document, after which you can review the summary to add any missing items or to delete anything that seems superfluous.

Create a Summary

1 Choose AutoSummarize from the Tools menu to open the AutoSummarize dialog box, and specify the type of summary you want. Depending on the length of the document, Word might take a little while to review it.

Click for an online document or to print a summary showing highlighted text.

Click to circulate the summary separately from the document.

Click to include a summary at the beginning of the document. (This is the most common format for printed documents.)

Click for an online document.

4 Point to the split box at the top of the vertical scroll bar. When you see the split-bar mouse pointer (a small horizontal bar with one arrow pointing up and another pointing down), drag it halfway down the window to split the window horizontally in two.

AutoSummarize

Word has examined the document and picked the sentences most relevant to the main theme.

Type of summary

- Highlight key points
- Insert an executive summary or abstract at the top of the document
- Create a new document and put the summary there
- Hide everything but the summary without leaving the original document

Length of summary

Percent of original: 10%

Summary: 353 words in 25 sentences
Original document: 3,526 words in 184 sentences

☑ Update document statistics (click Properties on the File menu)

OK   Cancel

3 Click OK.

2 Specify the length of the summary.

5 Review the summary, and compare it carefully with the contents of the original document. Delete any unnecessary information from the summary, and copy any missing information from the main text into the summary.

Exploitation and regulation - Microsoft Word

File Edit View Insert Format Tools Table Window Help

Summary

Seals

Sealing continued, but the fur-seal population was rapidly disappearing.

Whales

Whales were also being hunted at the same time in the Antarctic. Whaling did have a profound effect on the Antarctic right whale and humpback whale stocks, for these whales were hunted in the warmer northern waters, where they concentrated in breeding areas.

The other whales of the Antarctic were soon to feel the pressure of whaling as the harpoon gun and steam whaling ship enabled the whalers to chase, overtake, and kill any whale in the ocean. Whaling was completely unregulated, the ships taking as many whales as possible. Over eighty percent of the whales being caught worldwide were being

Whales

Whales were also being hunted at the same time in the Antarctic. Eighteenth century whalers, in their sailing ships and long boats, searched around the subAntarctic islands for their prized prey, the right whale, but found few. They also took some blue, fin, and sperm whales, but their ships were no threat in the Antarctic to the abundant and widely dispersed whale stocks. Whaling did have a profound effect on the Antarctic right whale and humpback whale stocks, for these whales were hunted in the warmer northern waters, where they concentrated in breeding areas.

The other whales of the Antarctic were soon to feel the pressure of whaling as the

Page 3   Sec 1   3/9   At   Ln   Col   REC TRK EXT OVR English (U.S

13 Reviewing Your Document

✻ NEW FEATURE

✻ NEW FEATURE

We all know that glaring errors in a document—spelling mistakes, bad grammar, and so on—can seriously compromise the credibility of your presentation. Microsoft Word 2002 provides a variety of tools to help you make your publication inviting to look at, easy to read, and error free.

When you use Word's proofing tools, you can be confident that your document won't contain any misspelled words or grammatical errors. You can even tailor the levels of spelling and grammar checking Word uses so that they're appropriate for certain types of documents—for example, you can have Word point out gender-specific words, collo-quialisms, jargon, and so on. When your tired brain can't come up with that elusive perfect word, you can trust Word's synonym finder or the Thesaurus to find it for you. And, if you use foreign words or phrases in your writing, Word's multilingual abilities can ensure that you don't make any embarrassing *faux pas*.

Of course, the appearance of your layout is every bit as important as your document's contents. Here again, Word provides all the tools you need to check and refine the look of your publication. You can ensure, for example, that your reader never finds a heading at the bottom of a page and the relevant text on the next page! If you've used a variety of different styles, you can unify your document's appearance quickly and easily by applying consistent formatting to each design element. And before you print your work, you can double-check all the details in Print Preview.

Reviewing Your Grammar and Spelling

Reviewing a long document can be a tedious and time-consuming chore when you have to scroll through the document to find each spelling and grammar error or inconsistency and then correct those errors one at a time. Word can speed up the process for you by finding and marking each error and suggesting some changes, which you can either use or ignore. If you later decide that you shouldn't have ignored certain errors, just tell Word to review the document again.

Find and Fix Problems

1 With your document open, click the Spelling And Grammar button on the Standard toolbar to display the Spelling And Grammar dialog box, and look at the first problem Word has marked.

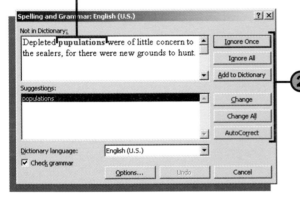

2 If the problem is a spelling error, select the correct spelling, if shown, and click the appropriate button.

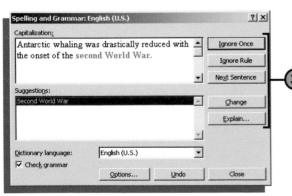

3 If the problem is a grammatical error, select the correct grammar, if shown, and click the appropriate button.

4 If the suggestions don't include an appropriate replacement, type your own correction. It will replace the highlighted error in the upper part of the dialog box.

5 Click Change, and continue reviewing the document.

> **SEE ALSO:** For information about correcting errors one at a time, see "Correcting Your Spelling and Grammar" on page 18.

Recheck the Document

1 Choose Options from the Tools menu, and click the Spelling & Grammar tab of the Options dialog box.

TRY THIS: Look at the Spelling And Grammar Status icon on the status bar. A red "X" on the icon indicates that there are marked errors in your document. Double-click the icon to move to the first error, and note the suggestions on the shortcut menu. Fix the error, and double-click the icon again. Continue moving through the document until you see a red check mark on the icon, indicating that there are no outstanding errors.

2 Click Recheck Document. Word will recheck the document and will mark the corrections you told it to ignore in your previous review.

5 Review the document, and decide which suggested corrections you want to use this time.

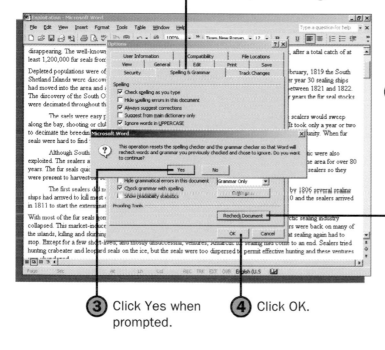

3 Click Yes when prompted.

4 Click OK.

Controlling What's Checked

Depending on the type of document you're working on, you might need to tailor the levels of spelling and grammar checking to make them appropriate for that type of document. You can control what types of checking Word does, and you can even specify that certain text not be checked at all.

> **TIP:** When you add words to the dictionary, you're adding them to your personal dictionary. If you've mistakenly added incorrectly spelled words to your dictionary, click the Custom Dictionaries button on the Spelling & Grammar tab to edit the entries in the dictionary. You can also use this button to add other custom dictionaries.

Specify What's to Be Checked

1 Choose Options from the Tools menu, and click the Spelling & Grammar tab of the Options dialog box.

2 Select this check box to have each word checked for spelling as it's typed.

3 Select this check box to hide the red squiggles that mark spelling errors.

4 Select these check boxes if you don't want certain types of words to be checked.

5 Select this check box to have each phrase and sentence checked as it's typed.

6 Select this check box to hide the green squiggles that mark grammatical errors.

7 Select this check box to have your grammar checked whenever a spelling check is conducted.

8 Specify the type of grammar you want Word to check.

9 Click Settings to define the grammar rules you want Word to use to check your document.

10 Click OK to use your new settings.

Specify Text that Isn't to Be Checked

(1) Select the text that you don't want to be checked.

(2) Point to Language on the Tools menu, and choose Set Language from the submenu to display the Language dialog box.

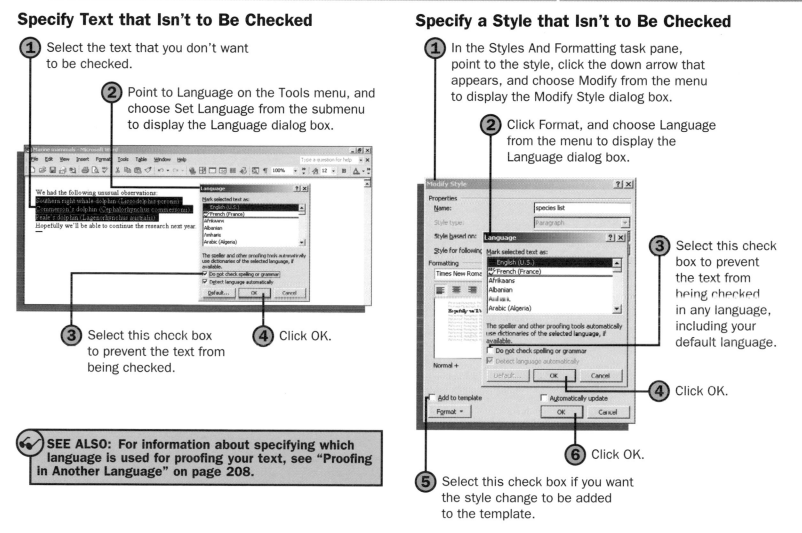

(3) Select this check box to prevent the text from being checked.

(4) Click OK.

> SEE ALSO: For information about specifying which language is used for proofing your text, see "Proofing in Another Language" on page 208.

Specify a Style that Isn't to Be Checked

(1) In the Styles And Formatting task pane, point to the style, click the down arrow that appears, and choose Modify from the menu to display the Modify Style dialog box.

(2) Click Format, and choose Language from the menu to display the Language dialog box.

(3) Select this check box to prevent the text from being checked in any language, including your default language.

(4) Click OK.

(6) Click OK.

(5) Select this check box if you want the style change to be added to the template.

Proofing in Another Language

Word speaks many languages. Using the Microsoft Office language tools, Word can automatically identify which paragraphs are in which language. With the proper dictionaries and spelling and grammar checkers installed, Word can check a multilingual document, using the correct proofing tools for each language. If your document contains only a few scattered words in another language, you can identify those words as being in another language so that they'll be checked correctly. If the proofing tools for a particular language aren't installed, Word won't be able to detect the language. However, if you identify the language to Word, it will skip the text in that language to avoid adding unnecessary spelling and grammar squiggles to the document.

Turn On Office Language Detection

(1) Close Word and any other open Office programs.

(2) On the Start menu, point to Programs and then to Microsoft Office Tools, and choose Microsoft Office XP Language Settings from the submenu to open the Language Settings dialog box.

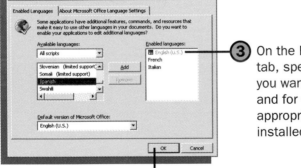

(3) On the Enabled Languages tab, specify the languages you want Word to detect and for which you have the appropriate dictionaries installed.

(4) Click OK. Office and Word will remember the enabled languages for all your Word sessions.

TIP: The language of the text at the insertion point is identified on the status bar.

(5) Start Word, open your document, point to Language on the Tools menu, and choose Set Language from the submenu to display the Language dialog box. Select this check box if it isn't already selected.

(6) Click OK to activate language detection.

Work in Different Languages

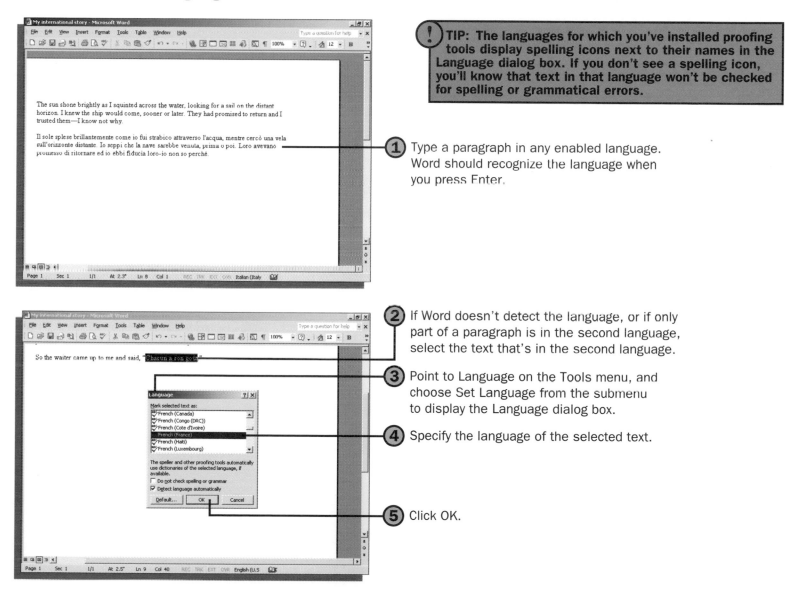

TIP: The languages for which you've installed proofing tools display spelling icons next to their names in the Language dialog box. If you don't see a spelling icon, you'll know that text in that language won't be checked for spelling or grammatical errors.

① Type a paragraph in any enabled language. Word should recognize the language when you press Enter.

② If Word doesn't detect the language, or if only part of a paragraph is in the second language, select the text that's in the second language.

③ Point to Language on the Tools menu, and choose Set Language from the submenu to display the Language dialog box.

④ Specify the language of the selected text.

⑤ Click OK.

Finding Alternative Wording

If you find that you're using the same word repeatedly in one sentence or paragraph (or even too many times in one document), or if a word you've used doesn't express your meaning precisely enough or provide the impact you want, Word can come to your rescue. It will automatically provide you with a wide choice of similar words. If you're still not satisfied, you can use the Thesaurus to browse through a list of related words until you find exactly what you're looking for.

> **TIP:** When you're looking for a synonym for a word that's formatted in another language, Word will search for a synonym in that language, provided you have the appropriate proofing tools and thesaurus installed.

Choose an Alternative Word

(1) Right-click the word you want to replace.

(2) Point to Synonyms on the shortcut menu.

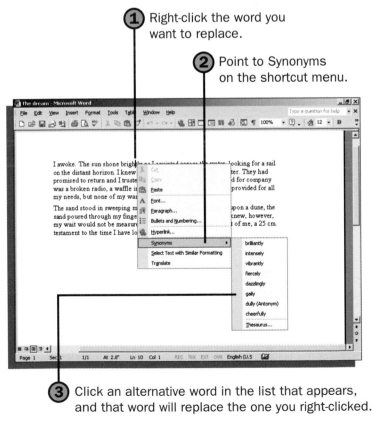

(3) Click an alternative word in the list that appears, and that word will replace the one you right-clicked.

Find Related Words

(1) Right-click the word you want to replace, and choose Thesaurus from the shortcut menu to display the Thesaurus dialog box.

(2) Click one of the listed meanings of the word.

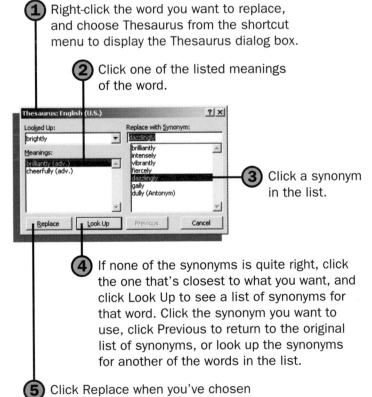

(3) Click a synonym in the list.

(4) If none of the synonyms is quite right, click the one that's closest to what you want, and click Look Up to see a list of synonyms for that word. Click the synonym you want to use, click Previous to return to the original list of synonyms, or look up the synonyms for another of the words in the list.

(5) Click Replace when you've chosen the synonym you want to use.

Improving the Layout with Hyphenation

Sometimes the right edges of left-aligned paragraphs look ragged and uneven. Justified paragraphs can contain big white spaces between words, especially in columnar text. You can easily repair these common problems with automatic hyphenation. Word does the work for you by inserting *optional hyphens* wherever they're needed. An optional hyphen shows up only when a whole word won't fit on a line, so if a hyphenated word moves from the end of a line because of changes in your text, the optional hyphen will disappear.

Set Automatic Hyphenation

(1) Point to Language on the Tools menu, and choose Hyphenation from the submenu to display the Hyphenation dialog box.

(2) Select this check box to use automatic hyphenation.

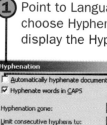

(3) Specify the maximum distance between the end of the last word and the edge of the column.

(4) Specify whether you want to limit the number of consecutive line-end hyphens.

(5) Click OK.

> **SEE ALSO:** For information about other ways to change line breaks (or word, column, or page breaks), see "Fine-Tuning Your Document" on page 212.

Hyphenate Manually

(1) Point to Language on the Tools menu, and choose Hyphenation from the submenu to display the Hyphenation dialog box.

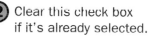

(2) Clear this check box if it's already selected.

(3) Click Manual.

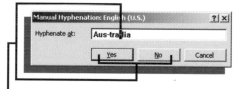

(4) When Word proposes hyphenating a word, do any of the following:

- Click Yes to accept the proposed hyphenation.
- Click No to skip the current word and locate the next candidate for hyphenation.
- Click at another proposed break, and then click Yes to hyphenate at that point.

Fine-Tuning Your Document

After you've composed your document, you can adjust the text flow—especially when a paragraph "breaks" across pages—to improve the look of the document. Word does much of this automatically, but you can make a few adjustments yourself.

Control Widows and Orphans

(1) Switch to Print Layout view if you're not already in that view.

(2) Select the paragraph or paragraphs in which you want to make changes.

(3) Choose Paragraph from the Format menu to display the Paragraph dialog box.

(4) Click the Line And Page Breaks tab.

(5) Select or clear this check box to control the way paragraphs break across a page.

(6) Select this check box if the paragraph is a heading that must always be on the same page as the beginning of the following paragraph.

(7) Select this check box if you never want a paragraph to break across a page.

(8) Click OK.

> **TIP:** There are many definitions of the sad terms "widow" and "orphan" in the publishing world. In Word's world, widows and orphans are single lines that get separated from the paragraph to which they belong and become marooned alone at the top (orphan) or bottom (widow) of a page. Widows and orphans are considered aesthetically undesirable in both worlds.

> **TIP:** To change widow and orphan control throughout a document, change the setting for the paragraph format in the style definition.

> **SEE ALSO:** For information about making style changes, see "Creating Your Own Styles" on pages 42–43.

> **TIP:** Breaking manually means that when you don't like the place where Word automatically ended, or broke, a line (or a word, a column, or a page, for that matter), you can change the break yourself.

Break Lines

Before fine-tuning

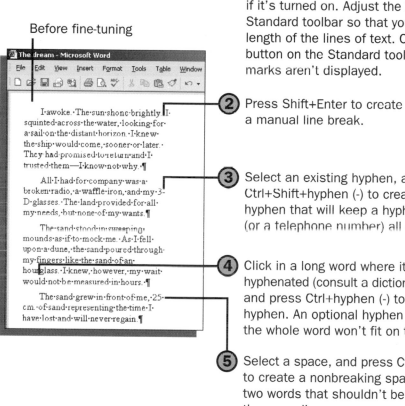

The result after
a little tweaking

(1) Switch to Print Layout view if you're not already in that view, and turn off automatic hyphenation if it's turned on. Adjust the Zoom setting on the Standard toolbar so that you can see the entire length of the lines of text. Click the Show/Hide ¶ button on the Standard toolbar if the paragraph marks aren't displayed.

(2) Press Shift+Enter to create a manual line break.

(3) Select an existing hyphen, and press Ctrl+Shift+hyphen (-) to create a nonbreaking hyphen that will keep a hyphenated word (or a telephone number) all on one line.

(4) Click in a long word where it can be correctly hyphenated (consult a dictionary if you're not sure), and press Ctrl+hyphen (-) to create an optional hyphen. An optional hyphen appears only when the whole word won't fit on the line.

(5) Select a space, and press Ctrl+Shift+Spacebar to create a nonbreaking space that will keep two words that shouldn't be separated on the same line.

(6) Inspect your finished result and determine whether you need to make any adjustments or undo any adjustments you just completed.

CAUTION: Always apply manual page breaks as the very last adjustment you make to a document before you print it. Editing a document after you've applied page breaks can result in an unacceptably short page or an extra blank page. However, if you do need to edit the document after page breaking, use Print Preview to examine the page breaks.

TIP: When you adjust the line breaks manually, try to get the resulting paragraph edges into the shape of a backward letter "C"—that is, try to make the first and last lines of the paragraph shorter than the other lines.

Reviewing Different Versions

During the creation of a long document, you might change the text a dozen times. Each time you save the document, your changes are saved in the current version, and the original text is lost. If you want to refer to the original text, you can save each changed version of the document. When you print the document, you can include information that clarifies which version you're printing.

> **TIP:** Word creates a new version only when you click the Save Now button in the Versions dialog box or, if the Automatically Save A Version check box is selected, when you close the document.

Save a Version

① Choose Versions from the File menu to display the Versions dialog box.

② Select this check box so that Word will save the current version whenever you close the document.

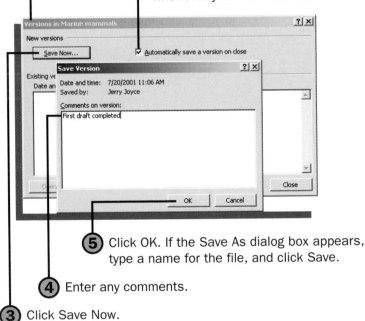

⑤ Click OK. If the Save As dialog box appears, type a name for the file, and click Save.

④ Enter any comments.

③ Click Save Now.

Review a Previous Version

① Choose Versions from the File menu to display the Versions dialog box.

② Double-click the version you want to review.

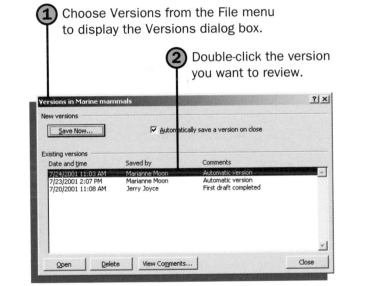

③ Close the document when you've finished your review.

> **TIP:** To quickly open the Versions dialog box after you've saved the first version, double-click the Versions icon on the status bar.

What Happened to My Document?

You worked long and hard on your document. You can't wait to see it. You eagerly retrieve the pages from the printer, and...oh, the horror! How did your masterpiece turn into this ugly mess? We'll try to provide some answers here.

Know Your Printer

Different printers have different capabilities. Some print in color; some print on both sides of the paper; some use the PostScript printer language; some use their own fonts; and some can't print close to the edges of the paper, so you have to set wide margins in your document. Make sure the printer is properly set up on your computer and that you've specified the correct printer in the Print dialog box. If the document is being sent out to a printer that isn't connected to your computer or that isn't accessible on your network, set up the printer to print to a file, and then use the Print dialog box to print to that printer. If you switch printers in the Print dialog box, reexamine your document in both Print Layout view and Print Preview before you print it.

Know Your Fonts

A document you see on the screen is displayed with *screen fonts*. A printed document is created with *printer fonts*. The trick is to get the screen fonts and the printer fonts to match. All TrueType and OpenType fonts have corresponding screen and printer fonts, but some other fonts don't, which means you can't be sure that what you see on the screen is what will be printed. One way to avoid nasty surprises is to use only TrueType fonts. You can identify them by the double "T" next to their names (and note that OpenType fonts are listed as TrueType fonts). If the document isn't going to be printed from your computer, you can include the TrueType fonts in the document by selecting the Embed TrueType Fonts check box on the Save tab of the Options dialog box.

Know What's in Your Document

Items you've forgotten about can affect the final appearance of your document. If you've tracked changes or added comments, click the Next button on the Reviewing toolbar to see whether any such items are still unresolved. If several people have worked on the document and there are several different versions, make sure this is the correct version! For information about versions, see "Reviewing Different Versions" on the facing page. Also check for items such as backgrounds or animated text that won't print correctly.

Print What You Want

Sometimes a document is printed in a strange format or contains information you didn't intend to be printed. Before you print, check your settings. On the Print tab of the Options dialog box, verify that the Draft Output check box is cleared. If you always want information in fields and links to be updated, make sure the Update Fields and Update Links check boxes are selected. Clear those check boxes if you want the information in the printed document to be the same as what's on the screen. It's usually wise to clear the Field Codes and Hidden Text check boxes and to select the Drawing Objects check box. If you select the Document Properties check box, the document properties will be printed with the document. (To view and modify the document properties, choose Properties from the File menu.) Open the Print dialog box, verify that you have the correct printer, and then, in the Print What box, specify exactly what you want printed.

And Finally...

Last but not least, sit down and read the document carefully. All the spelling, grammar, and formatting checkers in the world can't outdo the human brain. Remember, the computer is smart, but you're smarter!

Standardizing the Formatting ● NEW FEATURE

A document can quickly develop a chaotic look when you apply various types of direct formatting to your text. Word provides several tools that can help you keep track of the formatting, that can indicate where small but significant changes to the formatting exist, and that can allow you to quickly change one style or type of formatting to another.

 TIP: To see all your text in Normal view and with the task pane open, choose Options from the Tools menu, and, on the View menu, select the Wrap To Window check box.

Examine the Formatting

① Choose Reveal Formatting from the Format menu to display the Reveal Formatting task pane.

Compare Different Formats

① Click in the text of one of the formats you want to compare.

② Select this check box.

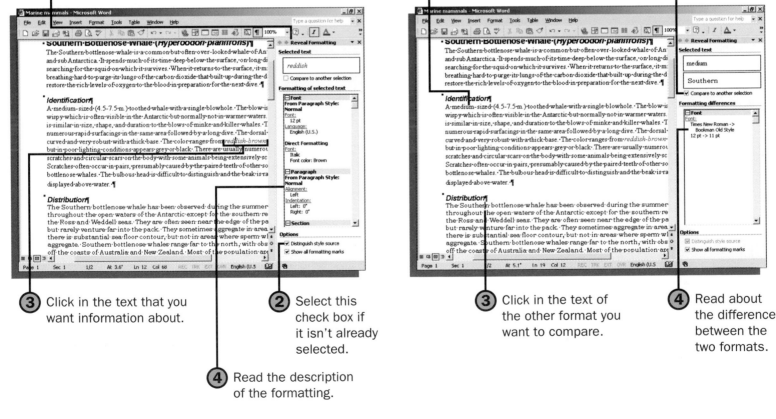

③ Click in the text that you want information about.

② Select this check box if it isn't already selected.

④ Read the description of the formatting.

③ Click in the text of the other format you want to compare.

④ Read about the difference between the two formats.

Find Formatting Inconsistencies

① Choose Tools from the Options menu, and, on the Edit tab, select the Keep Track Of Formatting and the Mark Formatting Inconsistencies check boxes. Click OK.

② Right-click any text that's marked with blue squiggles.

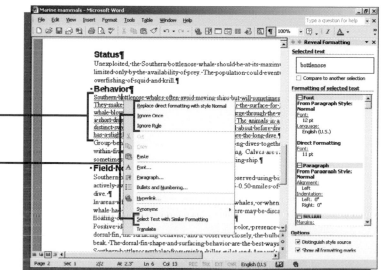

③ Choose the action you want from the shortcut menu:

- The suggested fix to standardize the formatting.

- Ignore Once to keep the existing formatting for this one instance.

- Ignore Rule to keep the existing formatting for all instances in the document.

- Select Text With Similar Formatting— right-click the text again, and choose the suggested fix to standardize the formatting for all instances of this formatting in the document.

TRY THIS: In a blank document, type a short sentence, and press Enter. Copy the paragraph (press Ctrl+C), and paste it (press Ctrl+V) immediately below the first one. Format the second paragraph with a slightly smaller font size. Use the Compare To feature to compare the two paragraphs. (If you don't see blue squiggles under the second paragraph, open the Options dialog box, and, on the Edit tab, select the Mark Formatting Inconsistencies check box. Click OK.) Click in the paragraph that has the blue squiggles, and remove the direct formatting.

Switching Formatting ⊛ NEW FEATURE

A document can wind up with a mishmash of mismatched styles and formatting, especially if you've patched it together using parts of different documents, or if the document in question was created by several authors who each used different formatting. However, you can easily unify an unruly document's incompatible elements by switching them to consistent styles and formatting.

> ⚠ **TIP:** When you replace the formatting of several selected items, the insertion point moves to the last item that was changed. Be sure that you scroll back to resume your review of the document from the first instance of changed formatting.

Switch Formats

② Click in the text whose formatting you want to change.

① Click the Styles And Formatting button on the Formatting toolbar to display the Styles And Formatting task pane if it isn't already open.

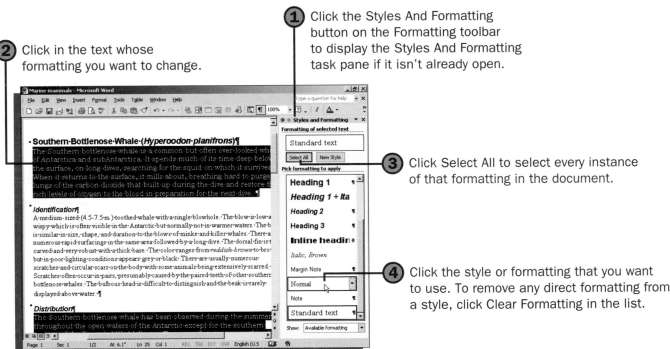

③ Click Select All to select every instance of that formatting in the document.

④ Click the style or formatting that you want to use. To remove any direct formatting from a style, click Clear Formatting in the list.

> ⚠ **TIP:** To remove any direct formatting without changing the style, click Clear Formatting in the Pick Formatting To Apply list.

Double-Checking Your Document

You've spent a huge amount of your time writing and producing the perfect document. You've checked the hyphenation and the line and page breaks; you've searched out widows and orphans; you've repaired inconsistent formatting. You breathe a sigh of relief. But wait! You're not finished yet! Take just a few more minutes and make sure there are no serious flaws that could compromise the presentation of your document—headings at the wrong level, for example, mismatched captions and graphics, incorrectly numbered items, and so on. Check any items that are linked, such as graphics or charts, because updating a field when the document is printed can change the layout. This is also your opportunity to find out in advance whether a linked file is no longer available.

Check the Document

(1) Choose Options from the Tools menu, and, on the View tab of the Options dialog box, specify a measurement (0.7" works well) in the Style Area Width box. Click OK.

(2) Switch to Normal view if you aren't already in that view.

(5) Switch to Print Layout view.

(3) Scroll through your document, checking that each paragraph has the proper style assigned to it. If necessary, apply the correct styles to standardize the document.

(4) Verify that special characters are displayed correctly. For example, make sure that *em dashes* are displayed as single dashes (—) and not as two hyphens (--), that quotation marks are properly formatted as opening (") and closing ("), and that inch (") and foot (') marks aren't formatted as double or single quotation marks.

(6) Scroll through the document, rechecking everything in this view. When you come across a linked graphic or chart, select it, and press F9 to update the field. If you see a field that you don't want to update, click in it, and press Ctrl+Shift+F9 to unlink the field.

(7) Scroll through the document to make sure that items are numbered correctly, that captions are associated with the correct graphics, and so on. Use the Select Browse Object button at the bottom of the vertical scroll bar to review specific types of page elements.

Checking the Layout

No document is complete until you've reviewed its final layout. Before you print the document, check all the details on your screen to see how the finished piece will look when it's printed.

Check the Layout

 1 Click the Print Preview button on the Standard toolbar.

2 Point to the Print button and check the ScreenTip to make sure it identifies the correct printer. If you're going to use a different printer, choose Print from the File menu, specify the correct printer, and click Close.

3 In Print Preview, click the Multiple Pages button, and select the number of pages you want to preview at one time. Review the layout, making sure there are no unexpected blank areas and that any special design elements—facing pages in a bound document, for example—are on the correct pages.

If you need to, you can make whatever last-minute changes are necessary to perfect the layout.

5 Click the One Page button to see a single page. Review the layout of the page to make sure there are no layout errors. Check to make sure the headers and footers are correct, including any page numbers. Click the vertical scroll arrow to display additional pages.

7 Click Close to return to your document, and make any necessary edits. If you do make changes, remember to recheck the layout of the document before you print it.

Magnifier

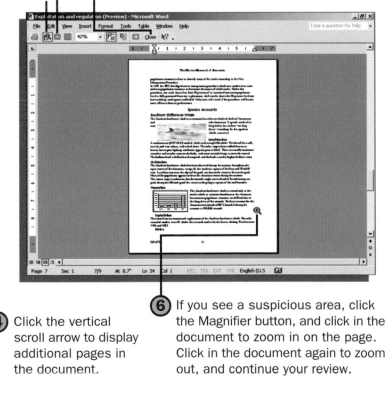

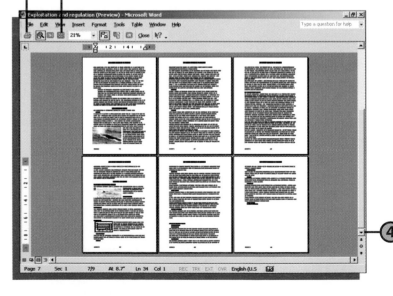

4 Click the vertical scroll arrow to display additional pages in the document.

6 If you see a suspicious area, click the Magnifier button, and click in the document to zoom in on the page. Click in the document again to zoom out, and continue your review.

14

Customizing and Maintaining Word

Throughout this book we've talked about customizing the tools and features provided by Microsoft Word 2002 so that you can streamline your work and tailor Word to meet your specific needs—creating AutoText and AutoCorrect entries to minimize errors, customizing templates to save time, and so on.

Now we'll talk about customizing Word itself—adding components you need or deleting those you never use, and specifying exactly how you want various elements to be displayed, stored, or accessed. For example, you can work in Word using a single window regardless of how many documents are open, or you can use a separate window for each document. If you'd like to see white text on a blue background instead of the same old black-on-white text, you can make it so. You can make significant changes to Word's menus and toolbars too—changing the way they look, moving them into different positions, putting toolbar buttons on menus and putting menu commands on toolbars—in other words, making these items work the way *you* want them to. You can even create your own *macros* (don't be scared—it's easy!) and voice commands.

Of course, you can work productively in Word without changing anything, but if there are aspects of the program you'd like to change, it's good to know that you probably can. One caution: if your computer is part of a network on which company system policies are used, check with the network administrator before you attempt to make any changes. System policies usually set what you can and can't customize, so you'll avoid considerable frustration by being forewarned.

Adding or Removing Components

Word contains such a multitude of components that you probably haven't needed or wanted to install all of them on your computer. You can install additional components on an as-needed basis or remove components that you never use so as to save some hard disk space.

Add or Remove Components

(1) With all your Office programs closed, point to Settings on the Start menu, and, in the Control Panel, double-click Add/Remove Programs. Click the Change Or Remove Programs button (or the Install/Uninstall tab in some systems), click your Office program in the list, and click the Change button (or the Add/Remove button in some systems).

(2) Click the Add Or Remove Features option, and click Next.

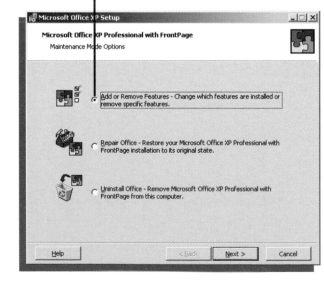

> **TIP:** If a component is set to be installed on first use, Word automatically installs it when you need it, provided you have access to the Microsoft Office or Word CD or the network installation files.

> **TIP:** If you're using Microsoft Windows 2000 or Windows XP, you'll probably need to be logged on as a member of the Administrators group to install additional components. If the program was published over the network for installation, consult with your network administrator before you try to modify the installation.

(3) Click the plus signs to expand the outline of the components until you find the item you want to add or remove.

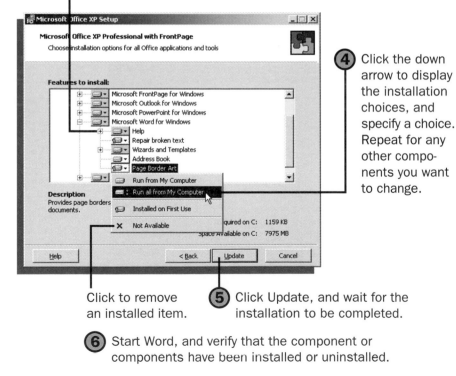

(4) Click the down arrow to display the installation choices, and specify a choice. Repeat for any other components you want to change.

Click to remove an installed item.

(5) Click Update, and wait for the installation to be completed.

(6) Start Word, and verify that the component or components have been installed or uninstalled.

Changing the Way Word Saves Files

If you don't like the locations in which Word proposes to store your documents or to access templates or other tools, you can change those locations and create the organization that works best for you. And if you're working with other people who have different versions of Word, you can save Word in a format that's fully compatible with earlier versions of Word.

> **CAUTION:** If you're working on a network that's set up for "roaming"—meaning that your profile is used regardless of which computer you're using—don't change file locations without first consulting the network administrator.

Change the File Location

1 Choose Options from the Tools menu, and click the File Locations tab of the Options dialog box.

2 Click the item whose location you want to change.

3 Click Modify.

4 Locate and click the folder that you're designating as the new location.

5 Click OK.

6 Set the location for any other file types, and click OK when you've finished.

Change the Format

1 Choose Options from the Tools menu, and click the Save tab of the Options dialog box.

2 Specify the format in which you want to save most of your documents.

3 If you want your documents to be used by others who use earlier versions of Word, select this check box.

4 Specify the earliest version of Word you want to be fully compatible with. Any features that aren't compatible with that version of Word will be disabled in Word 2002.

5 Click OK.

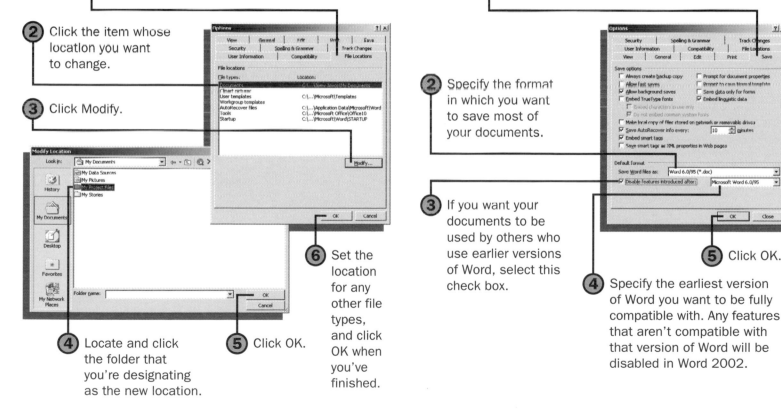

Changing Word's Window

Not too many versions ago, you did your work in Word in a single window (a *multiple-document interface,* or *MDI*), regardless of how many documents were open at one time. You can revert to that style if you'd rather not have a separate window for each document, which is Word's current default. If you want, you can also change the appearance of the window so that it has white text on a blue background.

Work in a Single Window ⊕ NEW FEATURE

1 Choose Options from the Tools menu, and click the View tab of the Options dialog box.

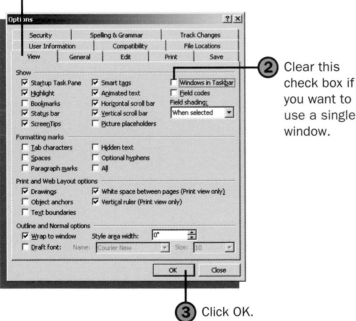

2 Clear this check box if you want to use a single window.

3 Click OK.

 TIP: To switch between open documents when only one document is displayed in the window, use the Window menu to choose the document you want to use.

4 With several documents open, choose Arrange All from the Window menu to view all the documents in a single window. Note, however, that there's only one Word icon on the taskbar.

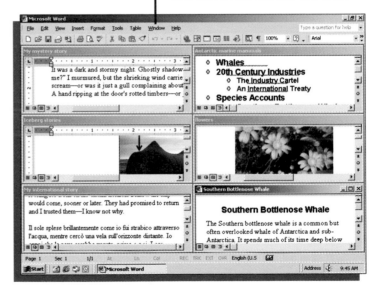

Change the Window's Appearance

(1) Choose Options from the Tools menu, and click the General tab of the Options dialog box.

(2) Select this check box to use "reversed" colors.

(3) Click OK.

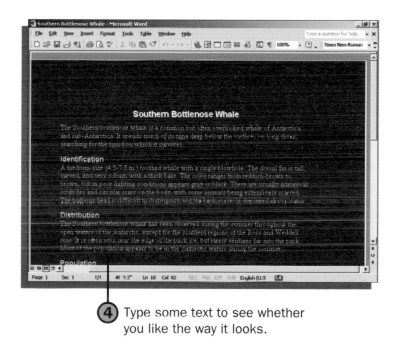

(4) Type some text to see whether you like the way it looks.

> **TIP:** Note that it's only your own version of Word that will display a document with white text on a blue background. If someone opens the document on another computer, it will appear with the usual black text on a white background unless the recipient has set Word to use reversed colors. And if you print a document whose text is reversed, it will print with black text on a white background.

> **CAUTION:** Colored text can disappear into a blue background. Even if you don't normally use any colored text, items such as tracked changes and e-mail messages can contain colors that disappear literally "into the blue."

Keeping Your System Secure

With computer viruses and counterfeit documents commonplace, you can take a few steps to protect yourself. One of the greatest vulnerabilities in Word is for a document to contain a malicious macro. Fortunately, Word can screen out macros from unidentified sources. And to assure other people that any documents you send them are really from you and haven't been altered by anyone else, you can sign them electronically.

> **CAUTION:** By default, Word trusts macros in all installed templates and add-ins, and from anyone whose digital signature is considered safe. If any of these resources has become infected with a virus, click the Trusted Sources tab of the Security dialog box, and clear the Trust All Installed Add-Ins And Templates check box. Remove from the list any sources you don't trust.

Set the Macro Security

(1) Point to Macros on the Tools menu, and choose Security from the submenu to display the Security dialog box.

(2) On the Security Level tab, click one of the following options:

- High to disable all macros except those that have been digitally signed by a trusted source
- Medium if your documents might contain any macros that were created by you or your coworkers and that have not been digitally signed
- Low only if you're certain that all your macros are safe, if you have an updated virus program installed, or if you have problems with your documents and macros when you use either the High or Medium security setting

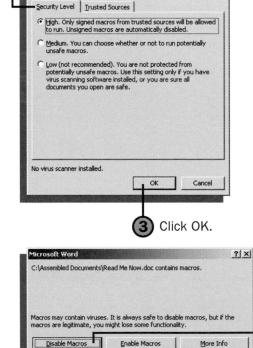

(3) Click OK.

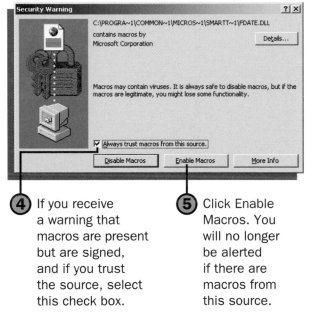

(4) If you receive a warning that macros are present but are signed, and if you trust the source, select this check box.

(5) Click Enable Macros. You will no longer be alerted if there are macros from this source.

(6) If you specified Medium security, and you open a document that contains unsigned macros, click Disable Macros whenever you're uncertain about the source or the security of a document or template. Click Enable Macros if you're sure of the source of the document and feel confident that all the macros are safe.

Digitally Sign a Document ⊕ NEW FEATURE

1 Complete your document, switch to Print Layout view if you're not already in that view, and review the document to make sure it's complete. Save the document.

2 Choose Options from the Tools menu, and click the Security tab of the Options dialog box.

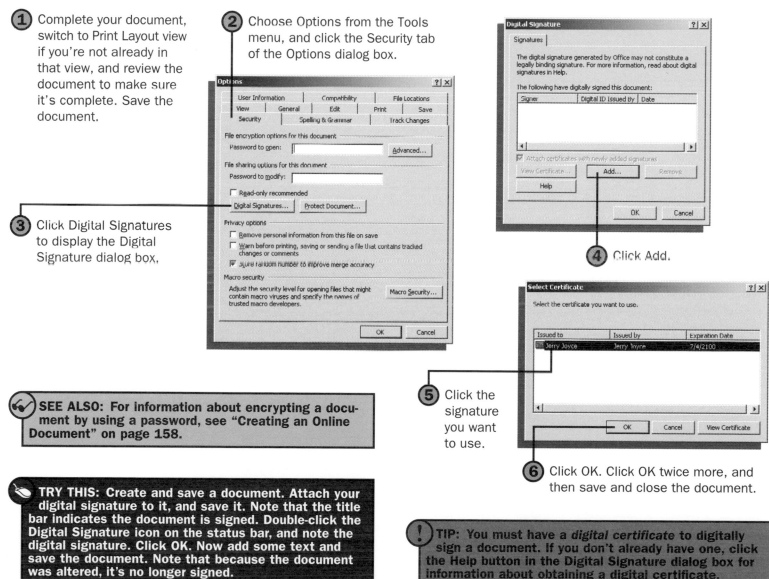

3 Click Digital Signatures to display the Digital Signature dialog box.

4 Click Add.

5 Click the signature you want to use.

6 Click OK. Click OK twice more, and then save and close the document.

SEE ALSO: For information about encrypting a document by using a password, see "Creating an Online Document" on page 158.

TRY THIS: Create and save a document. Attach your digital signature to it, and save it. Note that the title bar indicates the document is signed. Double-click the Digital Signature icon on the status bar, and note the digital signature. Click OK. Now add some text and save the document. Note that because the document was altered, it's no longer signed.

TIP: You must have a *digital certificate* to digitally sign a document. If you don't already have one, click the Help button in the Digital Signature dialog box for information about obtaining a digital certificate.

Managing Toolbars and Menus

Word provides quite a few options that let you manage the way your toolbars and menus are displayed. You can make some really significant changes to these components, so it's a good idea to experiment with them to see which settings are right for your working style. If you make some changes and then decide you don't like them, you can simply reverse them.

Set the Options

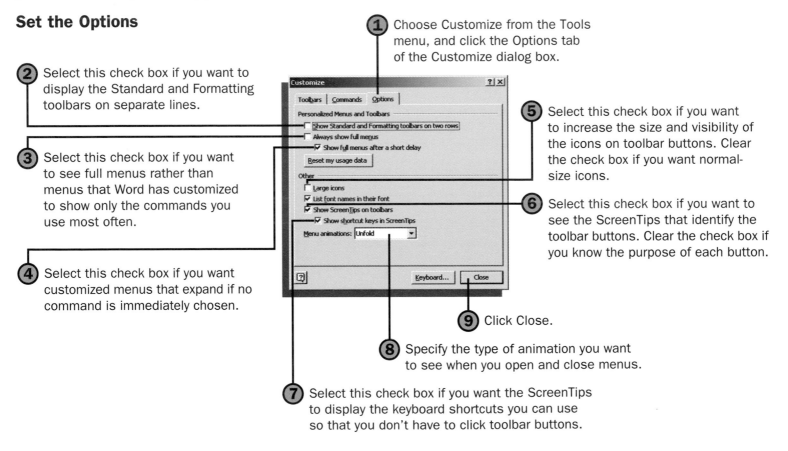

① Choose Customize from the Tools menu, and click the Options tab of the Customize dialog box.

② Select this check box if you want to display the Standard and Formatting toolbars on separate lines.

③ Select this check box if you want to see full menus rather than menus that Word has customized to show only the commands you use most often.

④ Select this check box if you want customized menus that expand if no command is immediately chosen.

⑤ Select this check box if you want to increase the size and visibility of the icons on toolbar buttons. Clear the check box if you want normal-size icons.

⑥ Select this check box if you want to see the ScreenTips that identify the toolbar buttons. Clear the check box if you know the purpose of each button.

⑨ Click Close.

⑧ Specify the type of animation you want to see when you open and close menus.

⑦ Select this check box if you want the ScreenTips to display the keyboard shortcuts you can use so that you don't have to click toolbar buttons.

Rearranging Toolbars

Word has so many toolbars that you'll probably find it necessary to do some toolbar rearrangement. For example, you might want to display three or more toolbars on the same line, or you might want them on different lines stacked one below the other. You might also want to move a toolbar to the side of the window or have it floating in the document.

> **! TIP:** A toolbar is either "docked" or "floating." A docked toolbar resides at one of the four sides of your Word window. A floating toolbar floats over your text in a little window of its own.

Move a Toolbar

(1) Point to a blank part of a toolbar or to the little vertical bar on the toolbar.

(2) Drag a toolbar above or below another docked toolbar to stack the toolbars on separate lines.

(3) Drag a toolbar onto the same line as another toolbar to have both toolbars share the line.

(4) Drag a toolbar to any side of the Word window to dock the toolbar at that side.

(5) Drag a toolbar into the document area to change the toolbar into a floating toolbar.

(6) Double-click the vertical bar at the beginning of a toolbar that shares a line with another toolbar to expand the toolbar as much as possible. Drag the vertical bar to fine-tune how much of the toolbar is visible.

(7) If you can't see all the toolbar buttons, click the double chevrons to see the hidden items.

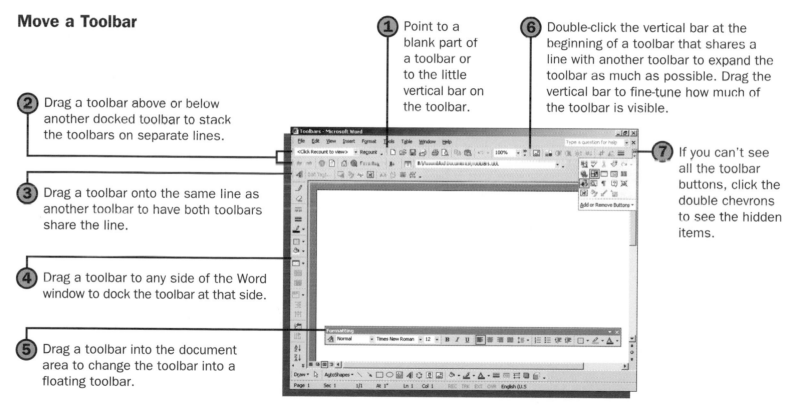

Rearranging Toolbar Buttons and Menus

You don't have to live with the way the toolbar buttons and menus are set up if another arrangement would work more efficiently for you. If you want to move a toolbar button onto a different toolbar or move a menu command onto a different menu, you can easily do so. You can even move toolbar buttons onto menus, and move menu commands onto toolbars.

Move Toolbar Buttons

(1) Choose Customize from the Tools menu, and click the Toolbars tab of the Customize dialog box.

(2) Select the check boxes for the toolbars you want to display and modify.

(3) Click the Commands tab, and specify in which open template or document you want to save the changes you're going to make. (Specify Normal if you want the changes to be available to all documents.)

(4) Drag buttons from one location to another. You can move buttons within one toolbar or among different toolbars.

TRY THIS: In the Customize dialog box, select the check boxes for the toolbars you want to display, and move the buttons you want among the toolbars. On the Toolbars tab, select the check box for one of the toolbars you've modified, and click Reset. In the Reset Toolbar dialog box, specify the same template or document that you specified on the Commands tab. Repeat for any other toolbar you've modified.

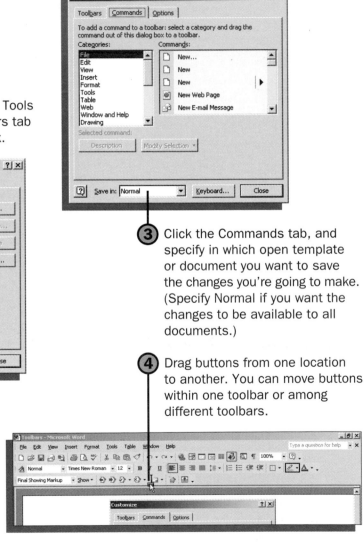

Move Menu Commands

1 With the Customize dialog box still open and the Commands tab displayed, click a menu to open it.

Move Shortcut Menu Commands

1 Click the Toolbars tab of the Customize dialog box, and select this check box.

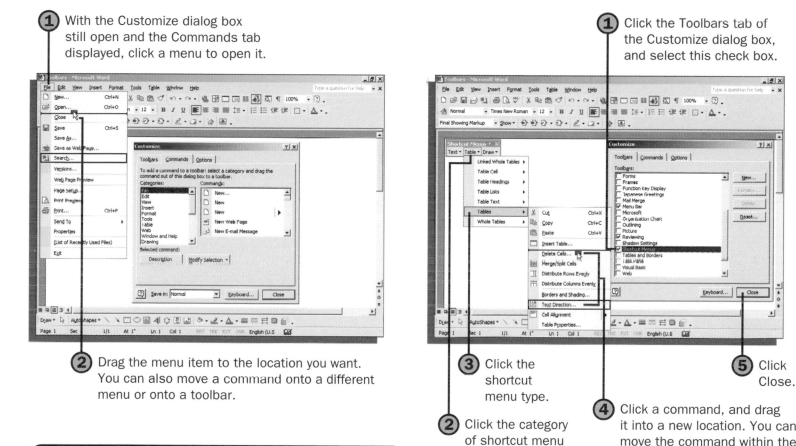

2 Drag the menu item to the location you want. You can also move a command onto a different menu or onto a toolbar.

> **TIP:** To delete a menu item, drag it off the menu. To copy a menu item instead of moving it, hold down the Ctrl key as you drag the item.

3 Click the shortcut menu type.

2 Click the category of shortcut menu on the Shortcut Menus toolbar.

4 Click a command, and drag it into a new location. You can move the command within the shortcut menu or drag it onto another menu.

5 Click Close.

Customizing Toolbars and Menus

You can customize your toolbars and menus by adding or removing buttons and commands to create just the work environment you want.

Add or Remove Toolbar Buttons

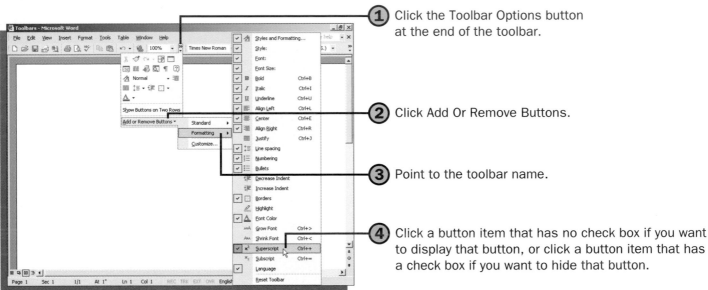

(1) Click the Toolbar Options button at the end of the toolbar.

(2) Click Add Or Remove Buttons.

(3) Point to the toolbar name.

(4) Click a button item that has no check box if you want to display that button, or click a button item that has a check box if you want to hide that button.

SEE ALSO: For information about moving existing toolbar buttons into a different location on the toolbar or onto a different toolbar, see "Rearranging Toolbar Buttons and Menus" on page 230.

TRY THIS: If the Formatting toolbar is sharing a line with another toolbar, click the Toolbar Options button, and choose Show Buttons On Two Rows from the menu to see all the buttons on the Formatting toolbar. Click the Toolbar Options button, and add as many other toolbar buttons as you want to the Formatting toolbar. Choose Customize from the Tools menu to display the Customize dialog box, and then move buttons around on the toolbar and add additional commands to the toolbar. Close the Customize dialog box. Click the Toolbar Options button again, and click Reset Toolbar in the list to restore the Formatting toolbar to its original configuration.

Add Different Items to Toolbars or Menus

(1) With any toolbars that you want to modify displayed in the window, choose Customize from the Tools menu, and click the Commands tab of the Customize dialog box.

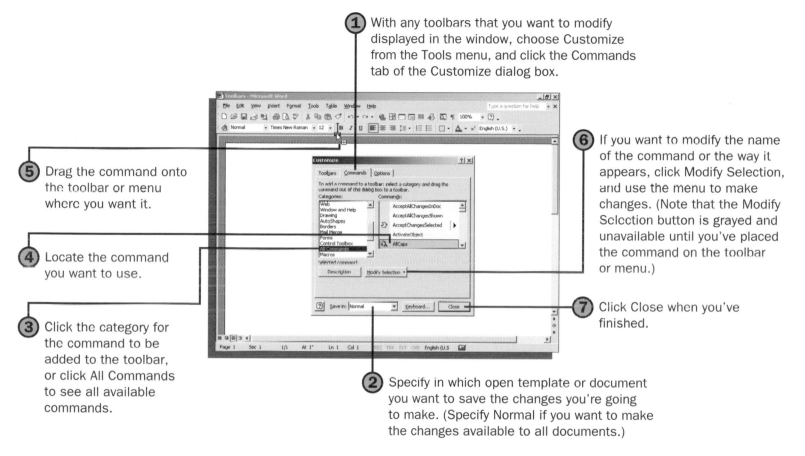

(5) Drag the command onto the toolbar or menu where you want it.

(4) Locate the command you want to use.

(3) Click the category for the command to be added to the toolbar, or click All Commands to see all available commands.

(6) If you want to modify the name of the command or the way it appears, click Modify Selection, and use the menu to make changes. (Note that the Modify Selection button is grayed and unavailable until you've placed the command on the toolbar or menu.)

(7) Click Close when you've finished.

(2) Specify in which open template or document you want to save the changes you're going to make. (Specify Normal if you want to make the changes available to all documents.)

> ! **TIP:** To delete an item from a toolbar or a menu, drag the item off the toolbar or menu (but make sure you don't drag the item onto a different toolbar or menu).

> ! **TIP:** You're not limited to "standard" Word commands. You can include styles, fonts, and macros on a menu or on a toolbar.

Creating Keyboard Shortcuts

It's so much quicker and easier to press a keyboard shortcut for an action you do repeatedly than it is to find a toolbar button or search for a command on a menu to achieve the same result. Many commands already have keyboard shortcuts assigned to them, but you can specify your own assignments—either to make the keyboard shortcut easier to remember or to add keyboard shortcuts to items that don't already have them, including styles, macros, and many of Word's commands.

 TIP: Even if you don't have the time or inclination to assign any new keyboard shortcuts, take a look at the current key assignments. It's a great way to remind yourself of all the things you can do with keyboard shortcuts.

Assign a Keyboard Shortcut

1 Choose Customize from the Tools menu.

5 Locate the command you want to use.

4 Click the category for the command that will have the keyboard shortcut, or click All Commands to see all available commands.

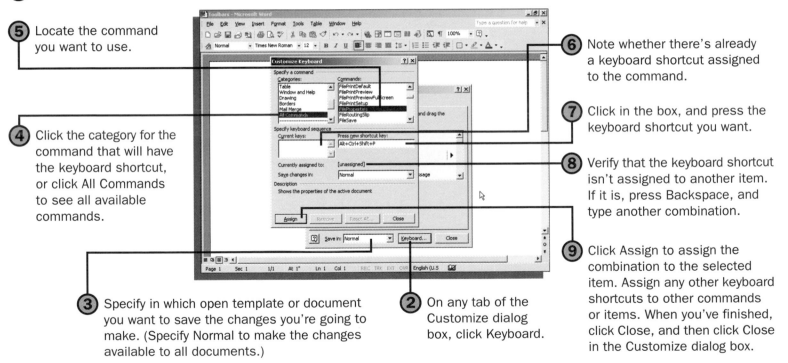

6 Note whether there's already a keyboard shortcut assigned to the command.

7 Click in the box, and press the keyboard shortcut you want.

8 Verify that the keyboard shortcut isn't assigned to another item. If it is, press Backspace, and type another combination.

3 Specify in which open template or document you want to save the changes you're going to make. (Specify Normal to make the changes available to all documents.)

2 On any tab of the Customize dialog box, click Keyboard.

9 Click Assign to assign the combination to the selected item. Assign any other keyboard shortcuts to other commands or items. When you've finished, click Close, and then click Close in the Customize dialog box.

Creating Your Own Voice Commands ⊕ NEW FEATURE

If you're using voice commands to work with your document, and if you find that some of the commands you need aren't available as voice commands, you can either select a command or create a new command, and then place it on a toolbar so that it will be available as a voice command.

> ⚠️ **TIP: The custom voice command will work only when your customized toolbar is displayed.**

Create a Voice Command

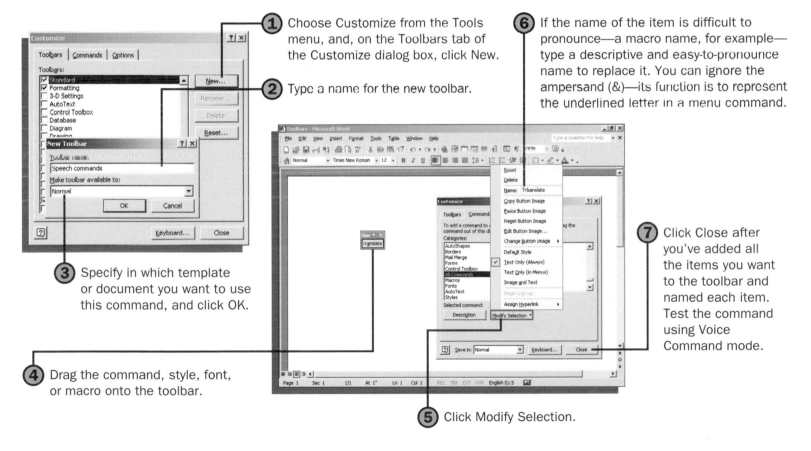

(1) Choose Customize from the Tools menu, and, on the Toolbars tab of the Customize dialog box, click New.

(2) Type a name for the new toolbar.

(3) Specify in which template or document you want to use this command, and click OK.

(4) Drag the command, style, font, or macro onto the toolbar.

(5) Click Modify Selection.

(6) If the name of the item is difficult to pronounce—a macro name, for example—type a descriptive and easy-to-pronounce name to replace it. You can ignore the ampersand (&)—its function is to represent the underlined letter in a menu command.

(7) Click Close after you've added all the items you want to the toolbar and named each item. Test the command using Voice Command mode.

Creating Your Own Commands

If you often find yourself executing the same series of actions over and over again, you can simplify your work and save a lot of time by recording that series of actions to create a *macro*. For example, to repeat the same set of terms in different documents, or to apply special formatting to certain words, you need to record the series of actions only once, using the Find and Replace commands. With the macro stored on a menu or on a toolbar, you can then run the whole series as if it were a single Word command.

Set Up a Macro

① Click in the document where you want to execute the first of the repetitive actions.

⑥ Click OK.

⑤ Type a description so that you'll know what the macro does. The description will appear in the Macro dialog box to remind you of the macro's function.

> **! TIP: A macro name must begin with a letter and can be up to 80 characters long, but it can't contain any spaces or symbols. You can assign the macro to a toolbar button or key combination when you first create it, but you might want to wait to assign it until after the macro is completed and has proven its worth.**

> **✓ SEE ALSO: For information about assigning a macro to a menu or toolbar, see "Customizing Toolbars and Menus" on page 232.**
>
> **For information about using macros in different templates, see "Transferring Styles, AutoText, and Macros" on page 238.**

② Point to Macro on the Tools menu, and choose Record New Macro from the submenu to display the Record Macro dialog box.

③ Type a name for the macro.

④ Specify where the macro will be stored:
- In the Normal template so that it's available to all documents
- In the current document so that it's available only in this document
- In the template the document is based on so that the macro is available to all documents based on that template

Record Your Actions

(1) Execute the series of actions you want to record as a macro, using your keyboard to select text and move the insertion point. (Note that, with the exception of clicking a command, most mouse actions aren't recorded.)

(2) If you want to execute any actions in Word without recording them as part of the macro, click Pause Recording. Click Resume Recorder to resume recording your actions.

(3) When you've recorded all the actions that compose the macro, click Stop Recording.

(4) Point to Macro on the Tools menu, and choose Macros from the submenu to display the Macros dialog box.

(5) Select the macro you just recorded.

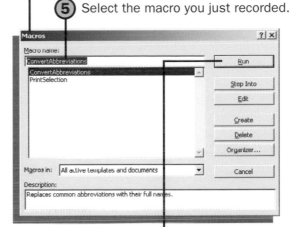

(6) Click Run. If the macro performs correctly, assign it to a menu, a keyboard shortcut, or a toolbar. If it doesn't perform as expected, rerecord it using the same name.

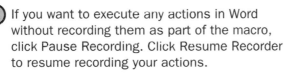

The Recorder mouse pointer reminds you that you're recording all actions.

Any commands you execute and all settings in dialog boxes are recorded.

> **TIP:** The word "macro" can fill people with terror—they think macros are only for techies. Not true! All you do is record the actions you already know how to do. If you make a mistake, you can start all over again. If you don't believe us, try the *Try This* at the right.

> **TRY THIS:** In a document, select a short piece of text. Start recording a macro named "PrintSelection." Choose Print from the File menu, click the Selection option under Page Range in the Print dialog box, and click OK. Now stop the recording. You just created a macro! When you add your macro to the File menu or to the Standard toolbar, you can print whatever you select in any document without having to open the Print dialog box. Easy, isn't it?

Transferring Styles, AutoText, and Macros

If you have a template that contains styles, custom toolbars, macros, or AutoText, and you'd like to use those elements in another template, you can copy them quickly and easily using Word's Organizer.

! TIP: You can select several items at one time in the list you're copying from by holding down the Ctrl key as you click each item.

Transfer Items

1 Open a document (or start a new document) based on the template into which you want to copy items from another template.

7 Click a different tab in the dialog box, and copy any other items you want.

4 Click Close File. (Note that the Close File button becomes the Open File button after you close the template.) Click the Open File button, and open the template you're going to copy from.

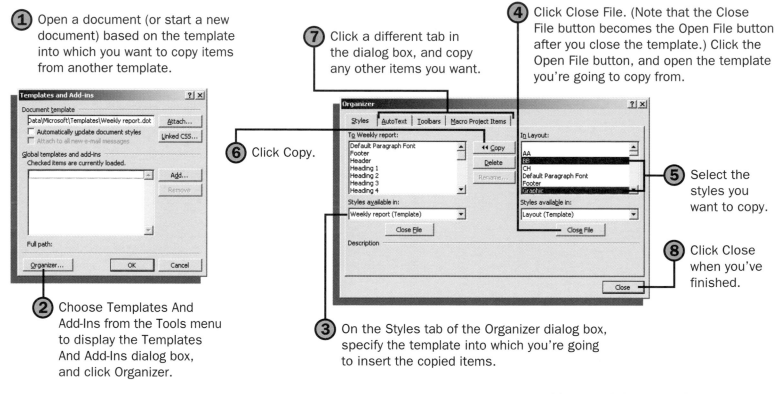

6 Click Copy.

5 Select the styles you want to copy.

8 Click Close when you've finished.

2 Choose Templates And Add-Ins from the Tools menu to display the Templates And Add-Ins dialog box, and click Organizer.

3 On the Styles tab of the Organizer dialog box, specify the template into which you're going to insert the copied items.

✋ CAUTION: When you switch tabs, verify that you have the correct source and destination templates listed. Switching tabs can cause these templates to change in the dialog box.

! TIP: To transfer your AutoCorrect entries, locate and open the Support.dot template, and use the macros to back up and then restore the AutoCorrect entries. If the Support.dot template isn't installed on your computer, you can install it from the Office CD.

Repairing a Document ⊕ NEW FEATURE

This has probably *never* happened to you, and you might be shocked to hear it, but the terrible truth is that sometimes things actually go wrong on computers! However, if a document has somehow been damaged, Word normally tries to repair it. In the unlikely event that Word can't fix the document, you can try to recover it yourself.

Fix the Document

③ Choose Open from the File menu, and locate the document.

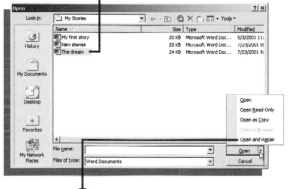

② Click the down arrow next to the Open button, and choose Open And Repair from the menu.

④ If there are still problems in the document, select any portions of the document that are undamaged, and copy them (press Ctrl+C). Open a new document based on the same template as that of the damaged document, paste the copied text (press Ctrl+V), and save it with a new name.

> ⚠ **TIP:** If you opened the document over a network, try closing and then reopening it. The error might have been a temporary anomaly caused by too much noise or traffic on the network.

③ Review the document to see whether Word has been able to correct it.

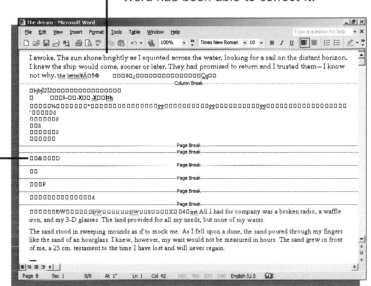

Garbled text usually means that there has been an error in the file and that some data has been lost.

⑤ If there are still problems with the content of this new document, choose Save As from the File menu, save the document with a different name, click Rich Text Format in the Save As Type list, and click Save. Open the document and examine it.

⑥ If there are still problems, open Notepad from the Start menu, paste the text, and save it as a text document. You'll lose all the formatting and any non-text elements such as pictures and graphs, but your text should be salvageable. Examine the document and delete any garbled text. Save the text document, and then open it in Word and make sure it's no longer corrupted. Format the text, and add any missing text or other elements.

Controlling the Office Assistant

Some people love their Office Assistant—that little animated character who hangs around on your Desktop waiting to give you advice and answer your questions. Others can't *stand* it, and still others don't even know it exists. Depending on how you feel about the Assistant, you can change the way it works, choose your favorite among different Assistants, or banish it forever if it drives you crazy.

> **! TIP:** To remove the Assistant temporarily, right-click it, and choose Hide from the shortcut menu. If you do this several times, Word will ask you if you want to turn off the Office Assistant permanently. Bye-bye!

Design Your Assistant

(1) If the Office Assistant isn't displayed, choose Show The Office Assistant from the Help menu to display the Assistant.

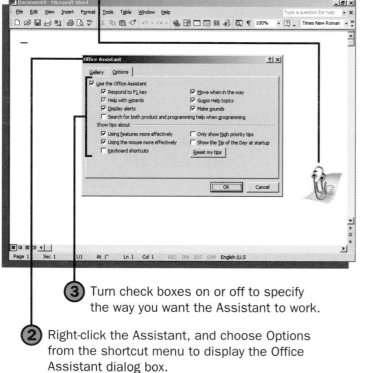

(4) Click the Gallery tab.

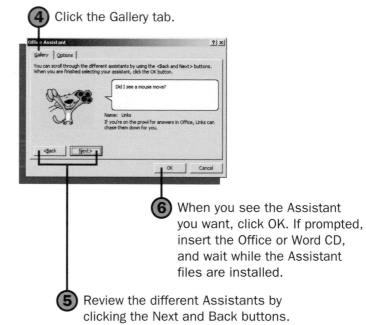

(6) When you see the Assistant you want, click OK. If prompted, insert the Office or Word CD, and wait while the Assistant files are installed.

(5) Review the different Assistants by clicking the Next and Back buttons.

(3) Turn check boxes on or off to specify the way you want the Assistant to work.

(2) Right-click the Assistant, and choose Options from the shortcut menu to display the Office Assistant dialog box.

Index

Send feedback about this index
to mspindex@microsoft.com

B

background colors, 126, 162, 225
backgrounds
  blue with white text, 225
  diagrams or pictures, 99, 126
  e-mail, 66
  themes, 162
  troubleshooting, 163
  Web pages, 165
back-to-back printing, 35, 156
bar codes, 53
Basic Search task pane, 11
basing styles on existing ones, 42, 43
binding, page setup and, 35, 220
Black & White picture option, 126
blank documents, 8–9, 165
blank Web pages, 165
blue background with white text, 225
blue squiggles, 18, 217
bold text, 30, 31, 36, 142
booklets, 156
bookmarks, 92–93, 160
borders
  art borders, 139
  on drop caps, 148
  line borders, 138
  margin notes, 153
  on pages, 138–39
  on paragraphs, 140
  on pictures or drawings, 127,
    131, 132
  in styles, 26
  on tables, 110
  on text boxes, 154
  on text-wrapped shapes, 147
Borders And Shading dialog box, 132,
  138, 139, 140
bound documents, 35, 220

breaking
  documents into sections, 88
  pages, 212–13
  text wrap around shapes, 88, 147
brightness, 126
Browser, 7
browsers, Web, 164
browsing documents by items, 80, 219
bulleted lists. *See* lists
Bullets And Numbering dialog box, 77, 162
buttons. *See* tools and toolbars

C

callouts, 143
cameras, 125
capitalized text, 85, 185, 197
captions, 103, 104, 187, 219
Cascading Style Sheets, 70
categories
  of AutoText entries, 183
  of clip art, 124
  of fields, 187
cautions. *See* troubleshooting
cell markers, 109, 110
cells, 110
  dividing and merging, 115
  margins, 137
  merging, 110
  resizing, 114
  sideways text in, 154
  text alignment in, 113
centering pictures, 128
centering tables, 116
centimeters, 49
certificates, digital, 227
changes. *See* editing; tracking changes
chapters in documents, 88

characters
  drop caps, 148
  hidden formatting characters, 7, 8
  for Office Assistant, 240
  selecting text, 16
  small caps, 36
  space, 7, 8, 213
  spacing between (kerning), 141
  special (*see* special characters and symbols)
character styles, 26–27, 28
  creating new styles, 42–43
  emphasizing text, 31
  inline headings, 142
  line numbers, 105
charts and diagrams, 99, 102, 132, 143
chat areas for Word assistance, 21
checking spelling and grammar. *See* grammar
    checking; spelling
check marks, 22, 205
chevrons (») toolbar button, 229
clearing text or formatting, 15, 29, 87, 218
clip art, 124, 132, 139
Clipboards, 14–15, 17, 87
cloning styles, 42
closing
  documents, 9
  Print Preview, 19
  task panes, 8, 13
cm (centimeters), 49
collapsing Document Map, 76
collapsing outlines, 78
collated print jobs, 19
colons in indexes, 92
color photographs, 126
colors
  borders and shading, 132, 139, 140
  diagrams, pictures or drawings, 99, 126,
    131, 133
  e-mail, 66

double-sided printing, 94, 156
downloading
    fonts into documents, 215
    stored files on Internet, 167
    translation services, 189
draft output, 215
dragging
    buttons to new positions, 230
    commands on menus, 231, 233
    items to grid, 144
    mouse to draw shapes, 130
    picture borders, 127
    pictures on pages, 128
    to select text, 12
    table boundaries, 114
    text to new location, 17
    toolbars, 229
Draw button, 144, 145
drawing
    diagrams, 99
    formatting drawings, 133
    grouping shapes, 133
    pictures, 130–31, 201
    tables, 115, 130
Drawing Canvas, 4
    AutoShapes on, 149
    combining text and graphics, 143
    drawing pictures, 130, 131
    grid positioning, 144
    replacing with text boxes, 154
    text wrap, 146
Drawing Grid dialog box, 144, 145
drawing objects, printing, 215
Drawing Pad, 130, 201
drawing tablets, 198, 201
Drawing toolbar, 7, 22
    AutoShapes, 99, 149
    displaying, 144, 149
    formatting with, 133, 151
drop caps, 148
duplex printing, 94, 156

headers in e-mail, 68
headings
    browsing by, 80
    inline or run-in, 142
    linking to, 160
    numbering, 77
    side heads, 137
    styles, 74, 75
height of cells, 114
help, 20, 37
    context-sensitive, 20
    getting help with Word, 20–21
    keyboard shortcuts, 36
    Microsoft Office Assistance Center, 21
    newsgroups and chat rooms, 21
    Office Assistant, 46, 240
    question-mark Help button, 37
    ScreenTips, 6, 32
    starting letters, 46
    "What's This?" help, 20
hidden characters, 7, 8, 215
hidden content in e-mail, 70
hidden items on toolbars, 229
hiding
    Document Map, 76
    formatting characters, 7, 8
    Office Assistant, 20, 240
    red and green squiggles, 206
    ScreenTips, 228
    toolbars, 22
highlighting text, 179
horizontal lines, adding to documents, 162
HTML e-mail, 64, 70
HTML-format Web pages, 164
hyperlinks. *See* links
hyphens and hyphenation, 192, 211,
    213, 219

icons
    inserting files as, 158
    for styles, 26
IF fields, 55
ignoring suggestions, 18, 217
images. *See* drawing; pictures
inches, 49
inch marks ("), 219
incompatible Web formatting, 164
inconsistent formatting, 27, 217
incorporating review comments, 175, 177
indenting, 6, 32, 116
Index And Tables dialog box, 91, 92,
    93, 104
Indexes
    compiling, 93
    in Help, 20
    in Word, 92–93
Indexing Service, 11
in (inches), 49
Ink button, 199
inline discussions, 170
inline headings, 142
inline pictures, 128
inserting
    correct spellings, 184–85, 193
    dates or times, 83
    discussions about documents, 170
    fields, 55, 187
    files, 69, 158
    footnotes, 97
    frequently used text, 182–83
    handwritten text, 198–99
    hyperlinks, 158, 160, 161
    information automatically, 55, 187
    number of pages, 83
    page numbers, 83

pasted items, 15
pictures or drawings, 51, 124, 125, 201
summaries of documents, 202
tables, 108, 137
insertion points, 6, 218
inside margins, 34, 35
installing
    Handwriting tools, 199
    Speech feature, 192
    translation services, 189
    Word components, 222
Internet, 167, 168, 189. *See also* Web pages;
    Web sites
intranets, 168, 170
italic text, 30, 31, 36

jumps. *See* links

keeping words or lines together, 212, 213
kerning, 141
keyboards, on-screen, 197
keyboard shortcuts, 42, 234. *See also* shortcuts
keywords, 20, 124

labels
    on pictures, 143
    printing, 53
    smart tags, 186
landscape orientation, 23, 34, 89
Language Bar, 194, 196
Language dialog box, 207, 208, 211

S

Save As dialog box, 164, 167, 168, 239
saving files, 9
  address lists, 61
  changes to styles, 43
  in different formats, 223, 239
  documents, 9, 25, 33, 47, 223
  with fonts embedded, 215
  to Internet, 167
  for previous versions of Word, 223
  signatures, 67
  templates, 39, 40
  versions of documents, 214
  as Web pages, 164
scaling. *See also* resizing
  drawings, 131
  print jobs, 19
scanners, 125, 190
screen fonts, 215
ScreenTips, 7
  adding to hyperlinks, 160, 161
  displaying, 6, 32, 228
  voice commands and, 196
scroll bars, 7
scrolling through documents, 219
searching. *See* finding
section breaks, 88
sections, 79, 80, 88, 89, 90
security features, 159, 226–27
See also entries in indexes, 92
Select Browse Object button, 219
selecting browse objects, 80, 84, 219
selecting columns in tables, 108
selecting data sources, 56
selecting objects, 133, 146
selecting text, 12, 16
  for formatting, 27, 28, 29
  for moving or copying, 14
  multiple items, 15, 134

outline sections, 79
specifically formatted text, 217, 218
to translate, 188
with voice commands, 196
selection rectangle, 146
sender information, 46
Send Fax Wizard, 72
sending
  documents, 68, 172–73, 177
  e-mail, 64, 65, 68
  faxes, 71, 72
  file attachments, 69
sentences, 8, 16, 140, 206
servers, discussion, 170
setting up pages. *See* pages and page setup
shading
  document backgrounds, 162
  drop caps, 148
  fields, 47
  margin notes, 153
  paragraphs, 140
  in styles, 27
  tables, 109, 110
  text boxes, 154
shadows, 131, 132, 133, 151, 163
shapes. *See* AutoShapes
SharePoint Portal Service, 168
SharePoint Team Services, 4, 170
SharePoint Team Web site, 24, 168, 169, 172
sharing documents or templates, 168, 169, 180
shortcut menus, 47, 197, 217, 231
shortcuts
  browsing documents, 80
  Ctrl key and hyperlinks, 161
  displaying key commands, 228
  displaying toolbars, 22
  dividing table cells, 115
  expanding or collapsing outlines, 78
  highlighting text, 179
  keyboard shortcuts, 234

moving in tables, 108
moving margin notes, 153
moving or copying text, 17
moving sections, 79
saving, 9
searching for documents, 11
selecting text, 16
superscripts and subscripts, 98
updating fields and links, 219
Versions icon, 214
"What's This?" help, 20
short menus, 228
showing. *See* displaying
side-by-side layouts, 137
side heads, 137
side margins, 35
sideways text, 154
signatures, 66–67, 226, 227
Sign In With Microsoft Passport
  dialog box, 167
simulating mail merges, 55
single documents in windows, 224
size. *See* file sizes; paper; resizing
Size box, 110, 114
sizing handles, 127, 151
skipping text in spelling and grammar
  checking, 207
slow voice recognition, 195
small caps, 36
smart tags, 4, 14, 70, 181, 186
snapping items to grid, 144, 145
sorting mailings and data, 54, 60, 61, 62
sound clips in documents, 158
source, paper, 49
sources, data, 54
source templates, 238
space characters, 7, 8, 213
spacing
  around text-wrapped shapes, 146–47
  between cells, 137

U

underlined text, 31, 36. *See also* smart tags
undoing actions, 12, 33, 77, 86, 127
uninstalling Word components, 222
Unprotect Document dialog box, 178
unsigned macros, 226
unusual words, adding to dictionary, 195
updating
  dates and times, 41
  field data, 187, 215, 219
  links, 215, 219
  mailing lists, 62
  styles, 43, 44
  tables of contents, 91
uppercase letters, 85, 185, 197
user information or profiles, 52, 58, 193

V

versions of documents, 176, 214, 215
versions of Word, saving and, 223
verso pages, 35, 83
vertical blocks of text, selecting, 16
vertical lines, 136
vertical text, 110, 154
video clips in documents, 158
viewing. *See* displaying
viruses, 173, 226
voice recognition and commands, 192–95,
  196, 235

W

warnings. *See* troubleshooting
watermarks, 50–51
Web browsers, 164

Web Layout view, 76, 91, 97, 162, 163, 175
Web pages. *See also* Web sites
  adding hyperlinks, 165
  creating from templates, 165
  creating with Web Page Wizard, 166
  hyperlinks to, 161
  linked tables of contents, 91
  saving documents as, 164
Web Page Wizard, 166
Web sites. *See also* Web pages
  creating, 166
  discussing documents on line, 170
  editing templates from, 38
  frames, 166
  Microsoft Office Assistance Center, 21
  MSN Web sites, 167
  shared documents, 169
  SharePoint Team Web site, 24, 168, 169, 172
  templates on, 24, 25
  Web translation services, 188
Web toolbar, 22
weight of lines, 133, 140
"What's This?" help, 20
white text on blue background, 225
wide paper orientation, 23, 34, 89
widows and orphans, 212–13
widths
  of cells, 114
  of characters, 141
  of columns, 136
  of lines, 133, 140
wildcards, 85
windows, 9
  changing appearance, 225
  moving toolbars, 229
  opening new documents in, 9
  resizing task pane windows, 28
  single or multiple documents in, 221, 224
  splitting into two views, 202

Windows Clipboard, 14–15, 17, 87
wizards, 24, 25, 26. *See also names
  of specific wizards*
Word. *See* Microsoft Word
WordArt, 22, 150, 151
Word Count toolbar, 22
words
  borders and shading, 140
  finding alternatives, 210
  hyphenating, 211
  pronouncing, 194
  searching for, 85
  selecting, 16, 196
  spacing between, 141
workgroup templates, 25, 180
worksheets, inserting data from, 100–102
wrapping lines in WordArt, 150
wrapping task panes to windows, 28
wrapping text
  around diagrams, 99
  around pictures or drawings, 7, 128,
    132, 201
  around pull quotes, 149
  around shapes, 146–47
  around WordArt, 151
  handwritten text, 199
  to next line, 8, 150
writing
  by hand (*see* Handwriting tools)
  macros, 236–37
Writing Pad, 198

X

X marks, 205
XP Setup program, Microsoft Office, 199

Y

Yen symbol (¥), 184

Z

About the Authors

Jerry Joyce has had a long-standing relationship with Microsoft: he was the technical editor on numerous books published by Microsoft Press, and he has written manuals, help files, and specifications for various Microsoft products. As a programmer, he has tried to make using a computer as simple as using any household appliance, but he has yet to succeed. Jerry's alter ego is that of a marine biologist; he has conducted research from the Arctic to the Antarctic and has published extensively on marine-mammal and fisheries issues. As an antidote to staring at his computer screen, he enjoys traveling, birding, boating, and wandering about beaches, wetlands, and mountains.

Marianne Moon has worked in the publishing world for many years as proofreader, editor, and writer—sometimes all three simultaneously. She has been editing and proofreading Microsoft Press books since 1984 and has written and edited documentation for Microsoft products such as Microsoft Works, Flight Simulator, Space Simulator, Golf, Publisher, the Microsoft Mouse, and Greetings Workshop. In another life, she was chief cook and bottlewasher for her own catering service and wrote cooking columns for several newspapers. When she's not chained to her computer, she likes gardening, cooking, traveling, writing poetry, and knitting sweaters for tiny dogs.

Marianne and **Jerry** own and operate **Moon Joyce Resources**, a small consulting company. They are coauthors of *Microsoft Word 97 At a Glance, Microsoft Windows 95 At a Glance, Microsoft Windows NT Workstation 4.0 At a Glance, Microsoft Windows 98 At a Glance, Microsoft Word 2000 At a Glance, Microsoft Windows 2000 Professional At a Glance, Microsoft Windows Millennium Edition At a Glance, Troubleshooting Microsoft Windows 2000 Professional*, and *Microsoft Windows XP Plain & Simple*. They've had a 20-year working relationship and have been married for 10 years. If you have questions or comments about any of their books, you can reach them at <u>moonjoyceresourc@hotmail.com</u>.

The manuscript for this book was prepared and submitted to Microsoft Press in electronic form. Text files were prepared using Microsoft Word 2002. Pages were composed using Adobe PageMaker 6.52 for Windows, with text set in Times and display type in ITC Franklin Gothic. Composed pages were delivered to the printer as electronic prepress files.

Cover Graphic Designer

Tim Girvin Design

Interior Graphic Designers

Joel Panchot, James D. Kramer

Interior Graphic Artist

Kristin Ziesemer

Typographer

Kristin Ziesemer

Proofreader/Copy Editor

Alice Copp Smith

Indexer

Jan Wright (Wright Information Indexing Services)

Get a **Free**
e-mail newsletter, updates,
special offers, links to related books,
and more when you
register on line!

Register your Microsoft Press® title on our Web site and you'll get a FREE subscription to our e-mail newsletter, *Microsoft Press Book Connections.* You'll find out about newly released and upcoming books and learning tools, online events, software downloads, special offers and coupons for Microsoft Press customers, and information about major Microsoft® product releases. You can also read useful additional information about all the titles we publish, such as detailed book descriptions, tables of contents and indexes, sample chapters, links to related books and book series, author biographies, and reviews by other customers.

Registration is easy. Just visit this Web page and fill in your information:
http://www.microsoft.com/mspress/register

Microsoft®

- -

Proof of Purchase

Microsoft® Word Version 2002 Plain & Simple
0-7356-1450-4

CUSTOMER NAME

Microsoft Press, PO Box 97017, Redmond, WA 98073-9830